Republic at Risk
Self-Interest in American Politics

Republic at Risk
Self-Interest in American Politics

Walter J. Stone

University of Colorado, Boulder

Brooks/Cole Publishing Company
Pacific Grove, California

Brooks/Cole Publishing Company
A Division of Wadsworth, Inc.
© 1990 by Wadsworth, Inc., Belmont, California 94002. All rights reserved. No part of this book may be reproduced, stored in a retrieval system, or transcribed, in any form or by an means—electronic, mechanical, photocopying, recording, or otherwise—without the prior written permission of the publisher, Brooks/Cole Publishing Company, Pacific Grove, California 93950, a division of Wadsworth, Inc.

Printed in the United States of America
10   9   8   7   6   5   4   3   2   1

Library of Congress Cataloging-in-Publication Data
Stone, Walter J.
     Republic at risk: self-interest in American politics / Walter J.
  Stone.
          p.   cm.
     Includes index.
     ISBN 0-534-11610-8
     1. Pressure groups—United States.   2. Representative government and representation—United States.   3. Political participation—United States.   4. Elections—United States.   I. Title.
  JK1118.S76   1989
  324'.0973—dc20   89-9691
                                                                                    CIP

Sponsoring Editor: *Cynthia C. Stormer*
Editorial Assistant: *Mary Ann Zuzow*
Consulting Editor: *Roger Davidson*
Production Editor: *Marjorie Sanders*
Manuscript Editor: *Barbara Salazar*
Permissions Editor: *Carline Haga*
Interior and Cover Design: *Lisa Thompson*
Cover Illustration: *Ron Grauer*
Art Coordinator: *Lisa Torri*
Interior Illustration: *Maggie Stevens-Huft*
Typesetting: *Kachina Typesetting*
Cover Printing: *Phoenix Color Corp.*
Printing and Binding: *The Maple-Vail Book Manufacturing Group, Manchester, PA*

For Ann and for Ken, Jennifer, and B. J.

Preface

In one way or another, often without realizing it, I have been working on this book since I began to teach a course in American government in 1976. I brought to that task a youthful dissatisfaction with the usual way such a course is taught. Unlike many youthful dissatisfactions, however, this one became more intense with experience. This book is based directly on my experience in teaching the course at Grinnell College and the University of Colorado. I have found the approach to be equally successful with small seminars of highly motivated liberal arts students and with huge lecture sections of 500 undergraduates, many of whom are required to be there to meet the distributional expectations of their major or college.

Simply put, the approach is conceptual rather than descriptive, focused rather than comprehensive. A theoretically focused approach to the introductory course is neither original nor very startling. Colleagues in such related disciplines as economics and sociology routinely approach their beginning courses in this fashion. We in political science need not acquaint our students with a complex vocabulary or methodology before the central issues can be understood. We have only one shot at most students, so why not give our best? My experience is that students react very favorably when they are asked to think about some of the pivotal questions that motivate our discipline.

I think the theoretical issues of political science are inherently interesting, even to beginning students. By "inherently interesting," however, I do not mean that we can assume our students will naturally take to work in the discipline. Rather, it is possible to convey our enthusiasm about these questions, provided we are willing to address them. This is not to deny the problems associated with the abstract and complex nature of many of our questions, nor is it to ignore the fact that most of those questions have no settled

vii

answers. Indeed, the lack of consensus on many issues in political science can be turned into an asset as students are invited to take part in the debates by considering competing theories and interpretations of the available evidence.

Probably the biggest stumbling block to a theoretical approach is the lack of agreement in the discipline about what the most productive theoretical point of entry may be. There are several excellent books that adopt a Marxist perspective, but the ideological implications of such an approach are difficult for many students to accept. Other books are organized around a "systems" approach, or an analysis of "democracy." My experience with them is that they do a better job of being comprehensive than of being theoretically coherent.

I have adopted a uniquely American political theory as the basis for this book. The "republic" posited by James Madison serves nicely because it is a rigorously argued political theory and because it explains and justifies a system of government that has been put into practice. Once the theory is understood, it can be put "at risk" in analysis of theories and evidence generated by political science research. As we examine the theory, we are inevitably led to scrutinize some critical questions about our political process. In this way, we can come to see that more than a theory is at risk.

One consequence of a theoretical approach to the introductory course is the coverage it makes possible. In teaching the course, I have gradually come to focus on the problem of representative government as it is realized in national institutions whose members are chosen by popular election. There is much to say about the problem when it is defined in this way, but much is also left unsaid. A perusal of the contents reveals a fairly standard set of topics, from political participation to the presidency, from parties and interest groups to the Congress. Not covered are such equally standard topics as federalism, the courts, and the bureaucracy. I have kept the book brief enough so that it can be supplemented by collections of readings or by other books to round out the coverage in a manner responsive to the instructor's interests. I will be interested to learn how useful the framework developed here is in addressing topics I do not cover. Of course, the book can be supplemented in other ways as well—by works that challenge the argument I make, by works that add to the descriptive detail I tend not to emphasize, or by other primary texts.

When I teach the course, I am not especially troubled by incomplete coverage. First of all, the same could be said of any course, since the mass of detail that *might* be included is immense. Presumably one needs criteria for selecting some details and omitting others, and the question that motivates the course provides one.

More important, what is it we want our students to know (and remember)? An understanding of one important political theory and of the way the theory may be evaluated in the light of competing conceptions and a body of evidence is both a reasonable and an ambitious goal for the introductory course. If we adopt it, our students may remember enough to come back for more.

Acknowledgments

Writing a book of this sort has necessarily taken me well beyond the relatively safe boundaries of my normal scholarly habitat. I have been fortunate in receiving a great deal of help from others who have warned me of the pitfalls in unfamiliar terrain. If I have at times neglected to heed their advice, the failing is mine, not theirs.

I am grateful to graduate and undergraduate students who have helped with the research: Eric Bryant, David Davis, Jay McCann, and Amy Okubo.

I have benefited from the comments and suggestions of many friends and colleagues, among them Terry Andres, Anne and Doug Costain, Larry Dodd, Megan Edmunds, Leon Halpert, Calvin Jillson, John Kingdon, David Mapel, Dan O'Connor, Glenn Parker, Ronald Rapoport, Sven Steinmo, Donald Stone, Robert Stover, and Ira Strauber. Just as I did not always know when I was working on this book, some of these people did not know when they were assisting me. That does not diminish my gratitude or my affection.

I owe a special debt of thanks to Dennis Eckart, whose involvement in this project was crucial to whatever merit and success it can claim. I hope he will recognize the results of his efforts.

I thank Leo Wiegman, an editor whose patient good humor and mounting enthusiasm as the writing progressed offset the misgivings of an author occasionally beset by quarrels within. I also benefited from the insightful suggestions and criticisms of Roger Davidson, Doug Mackey and the reviewers: Richard Bush, Southern Illinois University at Edwardsville; and Jerome J. Hanus, School of Government and Public Administration, American University.

The Honorable David Skaggs deserves thanks for allowing me to reprint one of his constituent newsletters in Chapter 6, and Physicians for Social Responsiblity graciously permitted me to reproduce one of their membership appeal letters in Chapter 5.

Many students have read earlier drafts of this book, and I have learned from their comments, both positive and negative. They and their colleagues in the classroom are hidden collaborators by virtue of the interest, puzzlement, and occasional dismay with which they greeted my attempts to make sense of American politics. Their encouragement has been most responsible for my willingness to try these arguments on a broader audience.

Finally, I am grateful beyond measure to my family for their love and support throughout this endeavor and in everything else I attempt. My wife, Ann, and our children constantly remind me there are far more important lessons to be learned than those of self-interest.

Walter J. Stone

Contents

PART III

The Problem with the Solution   151

Republic at Risk
Self-Interest in American Politics

Self-Interest as the Problem and the Solution

Self-interest is the problem; it is also the only possible solution. The problem with what? The solution to what? This is a book about American government and politics, and both the problem and the solution are concerned with how best to conduct our politics. The title of Part I states an apparent paradox: the thing that causes the predicament—self-interest—also gets us out of it. That is the claim examined in Part I, whereas Parts II and III challenge that position in the light of what we know about the way American government and politics actually work.

Where does this claim about self-interest being both the problem and the solution come from? I have taken James Madison's defense of the American Constitution found in two of the *Federalist Papers* he authored and restated its bare essentials. Madison's argument is a theory of American government and politics which explains and justifies the central elements of American national government found in the Constitution. To give credit where credit is due, I have named this theory after James Madison. But to separate the theory from the rest of Madison's writing, I have chosen a name that he never used to characterize his ideas. The name I employ is "Madison's Republic." This theory about self-interest in American politics is not to be confused with Plato's *Republic*. Plato's book is one of the greatest works in political theory, so I don't mind paraphrasing his title. Madison's Republic is my interpretation of Madison's argument about self-interest. Not all scholars will agree that my interpretation is completely faithful to Madison's ideas about politics. But I have found it to be a very useful way to think about American politics.

When Madison identifies self-interest as both the problem and the solution, he is saying that people behave in selfish ways in their political life, and that that behavior creates problems for the com-

1

munity or nation. Madison is also saying that this selfish way of behaving can be the basis of the "solution," or the society that works despite the failures of the individuals who make it up. No one tries to further the common good—that would be distinctly virtuous, unselfish behavior. Everyone is after his or her own interest. But in the well-constructed political system, self-interest can be channeled and organized to produce an enduring and just social order.

This idea that self-interest can be harnessed to produce the public good forms the central theme of this book. In reading Chapter 1, you should take care to understand how Madison develops his argument. Madison's Republic is a good example of a coherent political theory, and understanding it as a theory is an important goal of Part I. It is also important to know what political scientists do with a theory. They test it. They challenge it. They revise it. Is self-interest the problem Madison thought it was? Can it be organized to achieve the solution he defended? The theme of self-interest encourages critical analysis because one cannot state the theory without asking whether it adequately comprehends reality. Has it left anything important out? Does it square with the evidence? Does it seek to shape the political world in a way consistent with appropriate values?

The theory embodied in Madison's Republic originated at a point in time, with an individual who lived in a particular historical period. The *Federalist Papers* were written as newspaper articles to persuade people to support the recently proposed Constitution. Madison's writings have often been analyzed from a historical perspective. What specific problems were Madison and the other Founding Fathers trying to solve? What sources did they draw upon as they thought and wrote about these problems? What were their underlying motives in writing the Constitution?[1] These questions are of enduring interest, but they are not the ones that motivate this book. The fact that the theory was conceived by a smart young political activist named James Madison more than two hundred years ago is of only passing interest. Moreover, the theory need not be an accurate description of what the Framers were thinking as they drafted the Constitution. It is enough if the Republic is a plausible, coherent defense of the American system of national government.

The reason the Republic can serve as the basis for the analysis

---

[1]Many examples of insightful historical analysis of the founding period are available. Among influential works are John P. Roche, "The Founding Fathers: A Reform Caucus in Action," *American Political Science Review*, December 1961, pp. 799–816; and Charles A. Beard, *An Economic Interpretation of the Constitution* (New York: Macmillan, 1941). An excellent recent analysis is Calvin Jillson, *Constitution Making: Conflict and Consensus in the Federal Convention of 1787* (New York: Agathon, 1988).

in this book—apart from its excellence as a political theory—is that the Constitution it was written to justify two centuries ago still exists with relatively few changes. The rules for the nation's political life described by the Constitution affect all citizens' day-to-day lives. Evaluating those rules, deciding whether they should change or continue, is an important activity for the thoughtful citizen. These decisions require critical analysis of the theory in the light of contemporary experience with its results, not an examination of the theory's historical origins or validity.

As you read Chapter 1, therefore, try to treat the theory described there not as a historical document but as an argument in favor of the framework within which the American Republic should function. The Republic we experience as taxpayers, voters, readers of political news, and the rest bears a relationship with the Republic that is spelled out in Chapter 1. An examination of that relationship is worth the effort, because as we comprehend the links between theory and practice, we find the ability to control our shared destiny.

Big Answers, Bigger Questions

Madison's Theory of the Republic

Throughout the years since World War II, the threat of nuclear war has hung over American society. In the 1950s, schools conducted air-raid drills, during which the children scrambled under their desks and covered their eyes, an exercise that presumably prepared them to protect themselves in the event of a nuclear attack. Bomb shelters were the craze in the early 1960s, and many Americans felt they had tottered on the brink of nuclear war during the Cuban missile crisis. The Vietnam and Watergate episodes were not reassuring, although they did succeed in distracting the nation from its preoccupation with nuclear destruction. In the 1980s, however, the issue emerged once again to dominate much of the political landscape. Second-graders discussed it, church groups met to plan prayer or study groups, and articles about it appeared in magazines. Scientists discussed the possibility of "nuclear winter" and students protested against the Reagan administration's policies. Catholic bishops wrote a highly publicized letter about nuclear war, and a television movie vividly portrayed a nuclear attack on an American city.

Fear of nuclear war has been with us since Hiroshima, and of course no one wants nuclear weapons to be used ever again. But it was not just fear that made the issue such a difficult one. People fundamentally disagreed about how best to avoid a nuclear exchange between the superpowers. Some argued that the best way to protect the peace was with a strong military, high-technology weaponry, and tough talk. These tactics would establish a firm position from which to negotiate with the Soviet Union. Others felt the best way was to stop the arms race, halt research and development of fancy new weapons, and reduce the amounts spent on the military. These tactics would signal to the Soviet Union that the United States was serious about peace, and that similar gestures on its part could reduce international tension.

5

What made the issue especially difficult was that each side in the controversy was convinced the surest way to have a nuclear war was to follow the advice of the other. Yet people on both sides honestly believed that theirs was the best way to reduce international tension. This disagreement expressed itself in many ways, some of which sound political and some not so political. Are television ads showing the "hotline" telephone and asking you to consider whose hand should pick it up after the next presidential election political? Are debates on the floor of Congress over which missile to build (if any) political? Is a meeting of the local chapter of Physicians for Social Responsibility political? Was the bishops' letter political? Are the nightmares of a second-grader after watching the TV movie *The Day After* political?

All of these things are political. They all relate to a public debate over what the community should do about an important issue. They relate, in Harold Lasswell's famous definition of politics, to "who gets what."[1] People are fighting about literally hundreds of issues all the time. On any issue, some people win and some lose. Some get tax breaks, others get electrocuted. Some get a free college education, others get assaulted in the halls of their high schools. Some have high-status jobs, others have no jobs at all.

Recognizing that some get more than others, people write letters to the newspaper, they protest when the government ships nuclear weapons through their community, they organize themselves into groups, or they contribute a few dollars to their favorite candidate. They might even help make a TV movie. And they vote. They do such things because they want to have an effect on who gets what. Maybe they just want their share.

But then there are many people who don't read letters to the editor about political issues (much less write them). They don't protest against the shipment of nuclear weapons, and they don't protest against the protesters. They don't have much of an idea about who is running for office or what they stand for. They don't join groups or even vote.

Actually, most of us are *both* kinds of people. Sometimes we care and sometimes we don't. We may vote in a presidential election in the fall but not even know a school-board election is going on the next spring. This book is about politics. It is about why some people win and others lose; why some people get involved and others do not. Understanding *why* who gets what is the job of political theory. If a political theory is at all valid, it should help us understand who wins and who loses, and why.

The political theory that serves as the foundation for the anal-

[1]Harold Lasswell, *Politics: Who Gets What, When, How* (New York: Meridian, 1958).

ysis in this book is Madison's Republic. Most of the theory of the
Republic is found in two articles Madison wrote, *Federalist Papers*
10 and 51. They are reprinted in the Appendix and you should read
them now. As you do so, try to imagine yourself in a society in need
of a new set of rules. A constitution, after all, is just a set of rules that
describe how the public life of a society will be regulated. The
Republic is a theory that justifies a set of rules: the United States
Constitution. Ask yourself these questions: Could Madison's Republic work? What assumptions does Madison make about the way
people behave in public life? Do you agree with those assumptions?
Could you live with the rules his theory is trying to justify? These
are important questions because Madison's Republic justifies a constitution that defines the rules that govern contemporary American
society. That's important because these rules help determine how
much of "what" each citizen gets.[2]

The Problem of Self-Interest in Politics

If you had to build a bridge, one of the first questions you would ask
is: "Out of what?" The kind of bridge you would build would depend
on whether it was to be made of stone or of steel. When James
Madison set out to construct a government, he also had to ask
himself: "Out of what?" This question led him to consider what
people are like, especially what they are like in politics. At the
beginning of *Federalist* 10, he stated the major problem his theory
set out to solve. That paper concludes with the solution, and *Federalist* 51 develops the solution more fully.

In answering the question "What are people like?" Madison
makes some simple assumptions about human nature. He assumes
that people usually act in predictable ways. Like other theorists
before him, Madison argues that when people get involved in public
affairs, they are motivated by decidedly negative features of their
nature: their "passion," "partiality," and "self-love." To be sure, he
admits people are capable of reason, but their passionate side pro-

---

[2]Many interesting commentaries on the *Federalist Papers* have been published. Not
all of them agree with the interpretation in this book. See, as good examples of the
various interpretations of Madison's work, Martin Diamond, "Democracy and the
Federalist: A Reconsideration of the Framers' Intent," *American Political Science
Review*, March 1959, pp. 52–68; Maynard Smith, "Reason, Passion, and Political
Freedom in the *Federalist*," *Journal of Politics*, August 1960, pp. 525–544; Robert
Dahl, *A Preface to Democratic Theory* (Chicago: University of Chicago Press, 1956);
George W. Cary, "Separation of Powers and the Madisonian Model: A Reply to the
Critics," *American Political Science Review*, March 1978, pp. 151–164; David F. Ep-
stein, *The Political Theory of the Federalist* (Chicago: University of Chicago Press,
1984); Hannah F. Pitkin, *The Concept of Representation* (Berkeley: University of
California Press, 1967), chap. 9, is especially helpful. For an interpretation quite at
odds with mine, see Garry Wills, *Explaining America* (New York: Doubleday, 1981).

vides a stronger impulse in political activity, usually dominating opinion and overwhelming any consideration of the public good. In a word, people act according to their *self-interest*. Consequently, if you want to understand the way people will act—not as parents or as Little League coaches but as political beings—look to the self-interested side of their nature. Don't count on altruism or unselfish concern for others and the common good. Do count on the fact that men and women will pursue their own interests, even if in doing so they threaten others or destroy the common good. Count on the worst from people in politics and you will seldom be disappointed.

Self-interest, then, is a big part of Madison's problem. The problem is complicated by the way self-interest normally expresses itself in politics. Madison argues that self-interested people naturally band together to form "factions" to get their way against those in society who disagree with them. Recall his definition of faction:

> By faction I understand a number of citizens, whether amounting to a majority or a minority of the whole, who are united and actuated by some common impulse of passion, or of interest, adverse to the rights of other citizens, or to the permanent and aggregate interests of the community.

Thus a **faction** is a group of self-interested, passionate citizens who have banded together to try to get their way. Self-interest makes factions the central problem for Madison. People form factions to increase their influence (many people joined together are more powerful than only one or a few). They must do so because others with conflicting interests are also banding together into factions. These conflicting interests arise because people respond to their passions, not their reason, and because they are looking out for themselves rather than for what is best for all. Factions, no less than individual citizens, are self-interested. The problem of self-interest in political life, therefore, is really the problem of faction.

Madison is clear about the **sources of factional conflict:** they include different religions, geographical locations, attachments to political leaders, and the like. The most important differences are due to economics; to "the various and unequal distribution of property." So when you see a political fight over national security policy, or over an import quota on automobiles, or over stricter environmental standards for the steel industry, Madison is inviting you to look beneath the surface at the factions that form and the self-interest that actually motivates them, whatever members or leaders of the factions may say about the public good, common decency, or the American way. And, perhaps most important, he is telling you that this factional conflict, if not controlled by government, is dangerous. It could rip society apart, because factions are more concerned about their own interests than about the "permanent and aggregate interests of the community."

The fact that factional squabbling threatens the stability of society is the first part of Madison's problem with self-interest. He feared that human nature, at least in its political expressions, leads to short-sighted and unreasonable behavior. Controlling factions (or breaking the "violence of faction," as he put it) became an important function of the government Madison was trying to set up. Government must control people; it must protect them from their own worst impulses. Put positively, government exists to provide social stability and order.

The Problem Extended: Tyranny

Creating a political system that avoids the chaos of unregulated conflict among factions does not require much imagination. A police state of one sort or another would suffice. But Madison is not satisfied merely to achieve stability. He also wants to control factions without imposing an unacceptable tyranny. Most of the governments Madison saw in human history that had successfully provided stability did so by being tyrannical, by abandoning his other goal of protecting liberty.

The reason that stability *and* liberty are so difficult to achieve takes us back to our discussion of self-interest. What if Madison had settled upon the fairly obvious solution of concentrating enough power in a central government (say, a monarchy) to ensure stability? This solution to the threat of instability leads to tyranny because whoever has the power will use it to pursue his or her self-interest. Why? Because that's human nature in politics. We cannot expect people in public life to behave otherwise. Even rulers (especially rulers?) will be self-interested. Therefore, if Madison's constitution were to give power to a single ruler (or a single faction—it would amount to the same thing), he would expect that power to be used for the benefit of the ruler and *against* the interests of those without power. Remember, reason will be swamped by passion, and the public good will be lost in the face of an overwhelming drive to realize one's interest. Presidents, prime ministers, kings and queens are all motivated by self-interest, and governments that concentrate too much power in their hands, no matter how long those governments last or how stable the society is, destroy liberty.

Even democracies, as Madison takes pains to point out in *Federalist* 10, fail on this score, because even if they succeed in promoting order, they destroy liberty by concentrating power in the hands of a majority faction. Madison used the term **democracy** in a rather more limited way than we do today. He meant a system in which every citizen was a legislator, and each had one vote. Such a system relies on majority rule to settle differences. Majority rule concentrates power in a single faction—the majority. A majority is just another faction "united by some common impulse of passion" against the rights of others. Majority rule may be all right for picking fifth-grade hall monitors or even union leaders, but Madison rejects it as the organizing principle of his constitution because it always leads to tyranny.

For Madison, then, the definition of **tyranny** is simple: any system that does not permit its citizens to pursue their own conception of their self-interest. Systems that permit interests to differ and get a hearing from the government protect liberty. As he says in another of the *Federalist Papers* (Number 47), tyranny is: "The accumulation of all powers, legislative, executive, and judiciary, in the same hands, whether of one, a few, or many. . . ."

So that's the problem. Human nature is a fixed quality of the "raw material." In politics, at least, human nature may fairly be characterized as self-interested. People naturally form factions to further their interests. Those factions will not be squeamish about threatening social stability and the common good if they see a possibility for short-run gain. The successful government provides stability, but because the people who control the government pursue their own interests, the government cannot be trusted. As Madison says in *Federalist* 51, he does not see any good prospects for a government of angels. He is stuck with creating a government of humans over humans. Self-interest means chaos. Power can control chaos. But when self-interested people have power, the result is tyranny. Chaos or tyranny? It seems like an impossible choice.

Self-Interest as the Solution

One thing is very clear to Madison: there is no way to change human nature. Therefore, he has to use self-interest, not try to finesse it, or give "every citizen the same opinions, the same passions, and the same interests." To think such an idea possible would be silly. To make the attempt in real life would be to create a tyranny, a cure worse than the disease. We've already seen that democracy cannot work because it is based on majority rule. Statesmanship, self-sacrifice, or heroic leadership can't make this government work because all of these things are less likely to occur than self-interested, impulsive behavior in government. When good things such as statesmanship emerge, we may be grateful. But Madison warns against depending on statesmanship and great leaders. His solution is much more hardheaded than that.

In a variation of the theme "If you can't lick 'em, join 'em," Madison's solution to the problem of self-interest is self-interest. He is like the engineer who must build a bridge of stone. The same qualities that make stone difficult to work with permit one to build a strong structure with it. The correct design turns the difficulties into strengths. Madison thought he could build a successful government—one that was strong enough to promote stability but that did not result in tyranny—out of the raw material of self-interested people. That's the genius of Madison's Republic. Self-interest is the problem; it is also the only possible solution.

Republican government, according to Madison, successfully employs self-interest to avoid the pitfalls of self-interest. A republic is "a government in which the scheme of representation takes place." **Representation** is a system in which a relatively small group of citizens is delegated to act by and for the nation's citizenry. Representatives are empowered to act—to make laws and other forms of public policy—because they are elected. People living in a "constituency" (a state or a congressional district, for example) hold an election, and the winner "represents" those back home to the national government.

How is this any kind of solution to the problem of self-interest? The argument here gets a little complicated and involves the conclusion to *Federalist* 10 and most of *Federalist* 51. So it will take a while to develop fully.

One common defense of representation is that the representatives are somehow better at governing than the people they represent. Madison refers to this argument when he says that a system of representation may "refine and enlarge the public views by passing them through the medium of a chosen body of citizens, whose wisdom may best discern the true interest of their country." This sounds contradictory if you believe Madison's own argument that self-interest applies to leaders and followers alike. Indeed, he points out that representatives could just as easily be "men of factious tempers, of local prejudices, or of sinister designs . . . [who] betray the interests of the people." Once again, there's the point: statesmanship is fine, and there's no denying it can happen. Just don't bank on it.

Self-interest is the key, and representation works because it depends on self-interest. Madison concludes *Federalist* 10 by arguing that the saving virtue of representation lies in its ability to "extend the sphere" of the nation-state to include a large population and a large geographical area, because constituencies can send delegates to the national government in their place. Representation makes popular government possible without requiring everyone actually to be part of the government. This turns out to be an important advantage. Madison argues that a large nation includes many factions in its population. Thus it is much more difficult for a majority to form and seize control of government in a large nation than in a small one. When factions are many and diverse (as a result of many different religious traditions, different kinds of economic activity, different degrees of wealth, and so on), most often no majority will even exist. The many factions, each clamoring for its own interest, check the interests of competing factions. Self-interest checks self-interest and thus prevents government from imposing a tyranny. A single faction pursuing a "wicked project" (a demagogic leader, a religious sect bent on promoting its own view of the good and the beautiful, the abolition of debts, and paper money are examples Madison offers) would very likely be opposed by other factions who would see it as contrary to their interests.

Why Does It Work? Self-Interest, Representation, and Conflict

When Madison says that the key to the Republic is its size, we may at first be disappointed by the apparent naiveté of the solution. Before you get fooled by the simplicity of the solution, let's look beneath the surface a bit to see how it works. By the end of *Federalist* 10, Madison has turned things around. Factions are no longer the problem. In fact, factions never were the problem. It is only factions uncontrolled by government that present a difficulty. Factions must be permitted to pursue their interests if there is to be liberty. By pursuing their interests, factions control one another, thus preventing tyranny. Factions unregulated by government destroy the fabric of society. But in the well-constituted state, factions are forced to compete with one another in an institutional context that controls them. Therefore, *conflict is a necessary and desirable component of the Republic.*

If factions keep each other in check within governmental institutions, what about the representatives who are the links between factions in society and government? They are no wiser than anyone else, no more likely to discern the public good, and no less self-interested than any other citizen. Why should they represent their constituencies' interests and not their own? They shouldn't and they won't. But the beauty of it is that in seeking their own interests, they represent the interests of their constituencies. Representation works for two reasons: First, the constituency's interest is probably the same as the representative's. After all, the constituency elected the representative. And voters in constituencies are self-interested. So they elect someone who shares their interests and who will effectively pursue those interests in government.

Second, representatives represent their constituencies' interests because they want to get reelected. They have an interest in retaining their positions of power in government. They cannot stay in power without their constituents' approval. Constituencies will force representatives to conform to their interests, or they will send them back to the farm. So no one in the Republic, not the citizen and not the governmental leader, is assumed to act for other than the basest of motives. Selfish concerns—"What's in it for me?"; "How will this help advance my political career?"—are the lifeblood of the Republic. Representation, the defining characteristic of the Republic, works because of human nature, not in spite of it. It does not depend on some hope for statesmanship, wisdom, or self-sacrifice by politicians. It depends on the pursuit of self-interest by leaders and followers alike.

So far, then, we have the following argument: Self-interest leads to representation. Representation is based on the self-interest of *both* the represented and the representative. Representation ensures that all significant factions will be brought into government.[3] The inevitable conflict among them in government is desirable because it serves to check tyranny. Government will be unable to use its power for tyrannical ends because the diverse interests in government prevent the use of public policy for "wicked projects."

What will government do? Many of the *Federalist Papers* we are not examining go to great lengths to justify a national government strong enough to do such things as raise an army and regulate interstate commerce. To the eighteenth-century mind, those were impressive powers, and they raised fears of tyranny. But in Madison's Republic, the government could be given significant powers because conflict would frustrate arbitrary governmental action. Conflict would prevent government from pursuing the peculiar interests of a single faction, whether a minority or a majority. It would force delay, encourage debate, and promote the cooling of passions. One could hope, then, that deliberation and reason might be given a chance. Compromise might result, in which case competing interests would be accommodated and tyranny would be avoided. Or perhaps government would be unable to act. For Madison, inaction was preferable to the use of governmental powers to deny liberty to the people.

The Solution Extended: Ambition vs. Ambition

So far, the institutional structure of the Republic is very simple. A national legislature appears to be all that is necessary to achieve

---

[3]In Madison's definition, a faction is made up of people who agree with one another, who are "actuated by a common impulse of passion." In the case of a legislative constituency, perfect agreement is obviously never present. Neither is it present in a contemporary interest group, although we will find it convenient to use Madison's theory of factions in analyzing interest groups. In general, there will always be some slippage between a theoretical concept such as "faction" and its real-world counterpart. In the case of legislative constituencies, there is usually enough agreement to warrant speaking of the "constituency's interest." Thus we can very profitably apply Madison's argument to the problem of legislative representation.

the solution of representative government. Yet we know the Constitution is more complex than that, and the justification for a more complicated governmental structure is found in *Federalist* 51. The theoretical principles behind the famous "checks and balances" are identical to those found in *Federalist* 10: *Self-interest leads to representation, which leads to conflict in government.* This statement is the theoretical core of the Republic.

A fundamental question that any political theory must answer is: What should be done with government power? Madison's answer is simple: Disperse it. That much is evident in *Federalist* 10. Representation disperses power by bringing many factional interests into government and by permitting the inevitable conflict to check power. The system of checks and balances further disperses power among the various branches of government, ensuring even more conflict than would exist in a simple legislature made up of representatives of diverse constituencies.

Take a look at Figure 1-1 and Table 1-1. They depict some of the more important features of the three branches of the American national government. Note that the institutions, especially those based primarily on the principle of representation (House, Senate, and president), have important structural differences. Most significant, they have different constituencies and thus different ambitions. Other structural differences, such as different terms and sizes of membership, also promote disparate interests within each institution, and thus encourage conflict among institutions.

Consider these statements in *Federalist* 51:

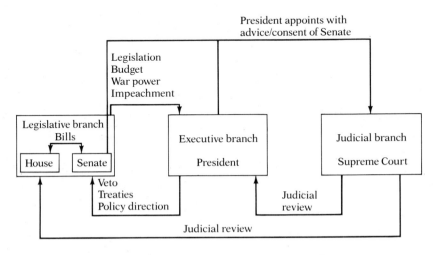

Figure 1-1 Ambition vs. Ambition: The Separation of Powers

Table 1-1 Structural Characteristics of the Three Branches of the Federal Government

| | Congress | | Executive (president) | Judiciary (Supreme Court) |
	House of Representatives	Senate		
Constituency[a]	Congressional district	State	National	—
Type of office	Electoral	Electoral	Electoral	Appointive
Apportionment	Proportional	Federal	Proportional + federal	—
Term	2 years	6 years	4 years	Life
Membership	435	100	1	9

[a]The Constitution as originally written does not specify the nature of House constituencies. Single-member districts developed through historical practice and formal legislation. Originally the formal constituency of the individual senator was the state legislature. The Seventeenth Amendment requires that senators be elected by the citizens of their states.

> Ambition must be made to counteract ambition. The interest of the man must be connected with the constitutional rights of the place.
>
> . . . the constant aim is to divide and arrange the several offices in such a manner as that each may be a check on the other; that the private interest of every individual may be a sentinel over the public rights.

If you agree that the "private interest of every individual may be a sentinel over the public rights," Madison has you hooked. This statement is the conclusion to the argument: Self-interest ("the private interest") can be harnessed to produce the public good ("may be a sentinel over the public rights"). Each individual in society single-mindedly pursues his or her own selfish interest, but the public good results. This happy result occurs without any intention on anyone's part to produce the public good. Remember, this is a government not of angels but of "men over men."

Let's see how the public good can result from each individual's private interest by examining the institutional arrangement depicted in Figure 1-1. The idea of **bicameralism** means that the legislature has two houses—a House of Representatives and a Senate. All legislation, before it can go to the president for his signature, must pass both houses in identical form. But the chambers of Congress are very differently constituted, all the better to promote diverse ambitions, conflict, and hence insurance against tyranny. As Table 1-1 indicates, the House and Senate differ in constituency, length of term, apportionment, and size of membership; they even differ in constitutional eligibility for office. Self-interested, ambitious members of each house represent their constituencies so they can stay in power. "The constitutional rights of the place"—in other words, the right to make laws—are directly linked to the "interest of the man"—the ambition to retain power by satisfying one's constituency.

The differences among legislators create conflict within each chamber. Senators from New York fight with senators from Alabama because their respective constituencies (and hence interests) are so different. But because each chamber is so differently constituted, there will be "checks and balances" across institutions as well. The state of California, for example, has some forty-five legislators in the House of Representatives but only two in the Senate. California's much less populous neighbor Nevada also has two senators, since every state, regardless of population, is accorded this number. But representation in the House is determined by population, so there California has twenty-two times as many representatives as Nevada. The nine largest states in population constitute a numerical majority in the House of Representatives. If all the representatives from those states decided to band together, they could control all legislation coming from the House. Talk about wicked projects! But the senators who represent those same nine largest states make up only 18 percent of the vote in the Senate. Indeed, if the twenty-six smallest states in the nation decided to band together in the Senate, they could dominate that chamber, yet they have only about 16 percent of the population of the United States. As they have much less than a majority in the House, it is difficult for one bloc to dominate both House and Senate at the same time.

Institutional differences can add up to some interesting fights between the House and the Senate. The conflict between House and Senate because of institutional differences gets repeated again when the president confronts the Congress. The differences in term, constituency, and membership size mean that ambition confronts (and checks) ambition. Once again, notice how important conflict is to the Republic. Leaders tied to different constituencies, representing those constituencies out of self-interest (exercising their "constitutional rights of the place"), fight with one another. The fight guarantees that power will not be used in a tyrannical way.

Madison's Republic Summarized

Self-interest, representation, and conflict in government: these are the essential ingredients of the Republic. They are also major themes of this book. By now you should have a clear idea of how they are linked in Madison's theory. The three concepts are explicitly connected in a causal chain:

Self-interest leads to representation because leaders in government represent out of their own interest in retaining power. To stay in government they must represent the selfish interests of those who elect and reelect them.

Representation in turn leads to conflict in government because it is through representation that the many interests in society are brought into government. Once those interests are represented in government, conflict is inevitable because the different interests want different things from government. They pursue different "wicked projects." Conflict in government is desirable because that is what prevents governmental power from being used in a tyrannical way. Note that this causal chain, from self-interest through representation to conflict, works only because of the institutions described by the Republic. Without them, indeed, self-interest leads to chaos or tyranny or both.

You should take time now to reread the two *Federalist Papers* in the Appendix. See if you can reconstruct the argument better now from your own reading.

This book is a critical analysis of Madison's Republic. It is an invitation to take apart the theory and see how well it works. We live in a society governed by institutions that are justified by the Republic. So we must turn to some critical questions that the theory raises.

The Nature of Politics and the Public Good

To understand Madison's concept of the public good, we must first examine his ideas about the nature of politics. A reading of *Federalist* 10 and 51 suggests that Madison thinks of political life as akin to all-out war, a conflict among deadly enemies intent on maximizing gain and destroying the opposition. Political leaders are nefarious characters motivated solely by personal ambition and the pursuit of power. Everybody is constantly on guard to prevent others from taking advantage of him. Life in such a world is hectic, perhaps only a slight improvement on the philosopher Thomas Hobbes's characterization of life in the state of nature: "nasty, poor, solitary, brutish, and short."

Obviously, Madison's Republic could not work unless some areas of consensus existed in the political system. For example, the electoral connection linking the self-interest of followers to the self-interest of leaders depends on everyone's agreement that elections are an appropriate way to select leaders. Without such agreement, losers might attempt to seize power by staging a coup d'état rather than sit by and watch the victors run the government. Those in power might try to destroy the political base of the losers by forbidding them to assemble or publish their ideas—freedoms guaranteed by the Bill of Rights in the Constitution. Without an assumption that such areas of consensus exist, Madison's exercise in defending the newly proposed Constitution would make no sense, because he could not hope that most people would abide by it if it were adopted.

Madison's focus on conflict reveals a limited conception of politics as including only those areas in public life where there is likely to be a clash of competing interests. Certainly, conflict cannot be expected to dominate all of social life. Consensus will exist around such matters as the rules governing political life, the sanctity of the nation's borders, and areas of life excluded from public concern. Family life and issues of personal or religious morality, for example, are excluded from "politics."

If the idea of politics is limited, the notion of the public good will inevitably be limited. If personal moral development is beyond politics, then the public good cannot include such moral development. Whether and how much you develop morally is a matter of your private concern as an individual. The sole function of the Republic is to provide stability and to protect against tyranny. Stability and freedom from tyranny, then, amount to the public good. The theory of the public good in the Republic goes no further. Typically, however, those who compete in the political arena have a more specific vision of the public good in mind.

Consider an environmental group opposed to a new water project that would flood a wilderness area. The group would probably equate protection of the area with the public good, or the public interest. Many environmental groups even call themselves "public-interest groups," in part because they (along with lots of other "public-interest groups") honestly believe they are pursuing the public interest against those who would endanger or destroy the public good. The problem, from the perspective of Madison's theory, is that groups opposing the environmental group—in this example groups seeking to complete the water project—very likely believe they too are pursuing the public interest. They might argue that the water project would permit the irrigation of rich but arid land, which would increase food production. What could be more consistent with the public interest, they ask, than increased food production?

What to do? We have in this example (which illustrates what happens in regard to hundreds of issues) competing groups convinced that what they want is in the public interest. Madison's answer is clear: Label them "factions" and don't trust them. Don't give them power, don't take sides. Construct your political system so that *all* sides are represented, and let them fight it out in the political arena. Their equation of their factional interest with the public interest may be a matter of political strategy, or it may reflect the fallibility of human nature. It may even be true. But since no one can be certain what the public interest is when significant differences among factions exist, the public good is served by arranging things in such a way that all factions are involved but that no single interest can seize power.[4]

You may agree with this limited concept of the public good, but at least you should recognize it comes at a cost. It is an extremely cautious theory that may inhibit the government from achieving fundamental justice. Some people have argued, for example, that the excruciatingly slow progress on matters of racial equality in the United States can be tied to Madison's reluctance to have the government take sides in conflicts among factions. A well-organized faction can block governmental action for social justice which is favored by an overwhelming majority. And that is just one kind of cost. Other, more subtle costs are incurred when one limits one's idea of the public good to social order and avoidance of tyranny. One does not adopt a theory such as the Republic without real-world, human consequences. That's why it is so important to understand the theory behind the rules of the political game we all play.

The Madisonian Republic as Theory

As theories go, Madison's Republic is impressive. It ties together such broad concepts as self-interest, representation, and conflict into a cogent defense of the unique form of government in the United States. But it is only a theory. As with any theory, it is fair to ask: to what extent is it correct? A major purpose of this book is to

---

[4]This example also illustrates the nature of self-interest as applied to factions. For Madison, the conflict between those who wish to protect the environment and those who support the water project is what is important. The difference of opinion may result from "selfish" self-interest, as when those who support the water project stand to gain economically. The conflict may also result because those who support the water project genuinely seek to increase food production and reduce world hunger. This, too, is a form of self-interest, although it is not narrowly selfish. Madison clearly was concerned about both kinds of self-interest when he pointed to economic as well as religious sources of faction. Economic differences might motivate narrowly selfish behavior, but religious differences most often would not. In both cases, however, there is the likelihood that factions will act against other factions and against the interests of the whole.

analyze the system to determine just how good the theory is. Before we embark on that ambitious undertaking, it is worth reflecting for a moment on what constitutes a good theory.

The purpose of **descriptive theory** is to describe and explain reality. This exercise almost always requires reality to be simplified so that it can be understood. In a way, a map of a city is a "theory" of that city. It simplifies the city by describing where the streets are located in relation to one another and the distances between points of interest. When one puts the map down and begins to drive around, one sees that the city is a good deal more complex than the representations on the map. But as a theory—probably a better term is "model"—of the city, the map can be an extremely useful, even indispensable guide. Of course it is useful only so long as it accurately describes the features of the city it seeks to model, and so long as it includes the features of interest to the user. Obviously a map that confuses street names and contains other errors of fact is worse than useless. Likewise, if we are interested in the various architectural styles found in Boston, an ordinary street map does not model the appropriate features.

One test of a theory, then, is to ask how well it describes the features of the reality it seeks to simplify. Does it have its facts straight? To find out, we must have evidence that is relevant to statements in the theory. If a map places Maple Street between Broadway and Vine, an appropriate "test" would be to go to the neighborhood of Broadway and Vine and see where Maple Street is. In the same way, political scientists who wish to test a theory such as the Republic collect evidence about statements found in the theory. Many times political scientists do not set out consciously to test ideas directly found in Madison's theory, but they have questions that are closely related to Madison's ideas.

Explanation is a goal of descriptive theory which requires more complexity than just getting the facts straight. A descriptive statement in Madison's theory is "Factions are present in political life." The theory goes well beyond merely stating that fact about politics, to explain not only why there are factions but also what some of the consequences of factions are. Factions, according to Madison's Republic, are the result of the self-interested nature of human beings. Factions can be brought into government to control the arbitrary use of power.

Testing a theory's explanation is a much more complex task than testing a simple descriptive statement. We might carry out careful observations, for example, and conclude that Madison was correct in saying that factions exist in political life. That conclusion would not necessarily compel us to agree that they result from human nature, or that factional conflict controls the exercise of governmental power. To find evidence in support of those state-ments would require extensive inquiry. Nonetheless, the ideas and questions suggested by the Republic are so important that it is worth the effort to find as much evidence as we can, even if it is not always complete.

In saying that a theory is an attempt to describe and explain reality, we admit that the theory may be wrong—that it does not describe the real world, or that the explanations it offers are not good ones. A very large portion of this book is devoted to assessing the accuracy of the explanations and descriptions found in the Republic. In a real sense, we put the theory at risk. For example, Chapter 2 asks whether it is true that people behave in self-interested ways in politics. If people are not self-interested, the theory may be in genuine trouble, because the Republic depends on the linkage of self-interest with representation and conflict. Without conflict and representation, tyranny is a distinct possibility. Any theory that attempts to understand some segment of reality, then, is put at risk when it confronts the evidence. It is important to subject a theory to this kind of risk in order to determine how good the theory is.

Assume for a moment that the theory is perfectly accurate in its descriptions and explanations of reality. Is that all there is to a good political theory? The answer is a resounding no, especially if the theory is one that is going to be put into practice. To see why, we must consider the frankly *political* dimension of a theory such as the Republic.

The Republic as Politics

You can't adopt a theory such as the Republic without adopting its values. In contrast to description, values make up **normative theory**—that is, what the theory argues *should be* rather than what *is*. The original fight over whether to adopt the Constitution was mostly about what should be, whether the values embedded in the Republic were ones that people wanted to live with. Consider the fight that would take place if a significant part of the American public wanted to change the Constitution today. Certainly part of the dispute would be over whether we ought to change something as universally revered as our Constitution. But a good part would (rightly) be over whether we should adopt a new set of values to govern our political life. So in accepting the Republic, we are inevi-tably subscribing to a set of norms or values about how we *ought* to behave, not just a set of descriptive statements about how we *do* behave.

Political scientists have a word for a package of values that prescribes how we should live our public life. It's called an ideology. So the Republic is not just a theory; it is also an ideology. One value in the ideology is right up front for all to see. The Republic is unabashedly clear about what to do with political authority. Disperse it; check it; frustrate it; don't trust it. So we have a political system built on the idea that political authority is a dangerous thing. That idea has many consequences we won't go into right now, but at least the basic value is apparent. Let's take a value that is a little more subtle to see how the Republic as politics affects our daily lives. The value is individualism.

Have you ever wondered why Americans are so attached to their automobiles? We polish them, we discuss them in loving detail, we spend millions of dollars to advertise them, and we have magazines and clubs to celebrate them. We even think of them as extensions of our personalities. There is really no problem here, except that our attachment to automobiles probably hinders our ability to consider public policies that might be beneficial to all.

Almost everyone has been stuck on a freeway waiting for traffic to clear. In fact, this may be part of the daily routine of people who live in or around a large city. Yet most of our urban areas have woefully inadequate mass transit systems. Mass transit is expensive (who gets what; remember?), and a really good mass transit system would cost millions of dollars. It's not that we can't afford it, though. Many countries have good mass transit systems, and they don't rely on the automobile nearly as much as we do.

The reluctance to build mass transit systems worthy of the name results in part from the powerful strain of individualism in American culture. We Americans want to go exactly where we want when we want. The automobile gives us that individual freedom, and we cherish it. As a result, our freeways are too crowded, and often we can't go anywhere on them. We get home (or to the ball game, or to class) late and frazzled, but at least we did it our way.

This is not to say that Madison is responsible for our inadequate system of mass transit. But the Republic celebrates individualism, thereby reinforcing it as an important value in our public life. As a result, we do not fully consider the policy options we might if we worked from the assumptions of a different ideology.

How does the Republic celebrate individualism? For one thing, it treats factions as essential to the maintenance of liberty. The Republic does not (indeed, cannot) take sides when factions are in conflict. To give power to one side over the other is the "very definition of tyranny." On the contrary, the Republic preserves liberty, or the freedom to pursue one's *individual* interests. To abolish factions in order to break their "violence" would be to adopt a cure worse than the disease. *Self*-interest. Individualism is at the very core of the Republic.

As descriptive theory, *Federalist* 10 says that people are self-interested. But the statements Madison made about self-interest are more than pure description. Maybe by adopting the Republic we encourage selfish behavior and discourage cooperative behavior.[5] Maybe if the Republic celebrated individualism a little less and community a little more, we would have better mass transit systems.

Other theories might have different consequences. An alternative was suggested by a near-contemporary of Madison's, Jean-Jacques Rousseau. Writing *The Social Contract* about thirty years before Madison wrote his *Federalist Papers,* Rousseau celebrated community (at no small cost to individualism). He argued that people are strongly influenced by their social environment. He would have said that what Madison considered "natural" behavior is really behavior encouraged by society. If you create a more cooperative environment, people will be a good deal more likely to cooperate. When self-interested behavior is expected, even encouraged, selfish behavior is what you will get.

This is not to say that one should automatically reject such a value as individualism. But neither should the thoughtful citizen routinely accept individualism or any other value embedded in a powerful ideology such as the Republic. The values and normative statements in the Republic must also be put at risk in a truly critical analysis. By accepting the Republic as the proper way to conduct our political business, we are choosing certain values and rejecting others. These choices are themselves intensely political. With better information, we can be clearer about what the choices are and more thoughtful in making them. Understanding the values that support the Republic may free us to consider a broader range of policy options. We may decide to encourage more community and less individualism. We may even get serious about mass transit. Or we may think of new and better ways to avoid nuclear war.

Whatever the results of our analysis, it is fair to say that James Madison offers a good place to start. He suggests some big answers to bigger questions. His Republic is a political theory that provides a coherent understanding of politics, as well as a set of values designed to guide political choices. The task is all the more important because of the compelling nature of his theory. So let's get on with it.

---

[5]David Schuman, *A Preface to Politics* (Lexington, Mass.: D. C. Heath, 1977).

Key Concepts

bicameralism

democracy

descriptive theory

faction

normative theory

representation

republican government

sources of factional conflict

tyranny

The Problem
with the Problem

Chapters 2 through 5 focus on citizens in American politics. These
chapters are concerned with the implications of Madison's conception of self-interest. Chapter 2 introduces an important distinction
between two kinds of self-interest, one that Madison understood and
one that he didn't understand. That distinction is developed in the
context of a discussion of political participation. Chapter 3 is concerned with the most common form of participation, voting.
Participation by citizens is important because it is supposed to be
the basis of republican government. Citizens participate out of
self-interest; politicians must respond to citizens out of their
self-interest. Alas, the argument in Part II is that things are more
complicated than that. The problem with the problem is that Madison's understanding of self-interest as it operates in politics is incomplete.

Various theories have been developed to address the more complicated concept of self-interest. Much as I have done in describing
Madison's Republic, I simplify from more extensive works two
alternative theories of American politics. Neither of these alternative theories can be attributed to one individual, and neither has a
"manifesto" as readily available as *Federalist* 10 and 51. The first of
these theories is pluralism. Pluralism is introduced briefly at the
end of Chapter 3 and receives sustained attention in Chapter 5.
Pluralism is presented here as an updated version of Madison's
Republic. Many pluralist writers quite frankly look to Madison's
ideas as their starting point, so thinking of pluralism in this way
does no violence to their position. Pluralists accept the major conclusions of the Republic, especially the critically important judgment that power must be dispersed and checked. Moreover, pluralists do not see any substantial need to reform the Constitution
justified by the Republic. Interestingly, however, pluralists agree

with the position in Chapters 2 and 3 that Madison oversimplifies the nature of political self-interest.

The second theory introduced in Part II is party theory (Chapter 4). Party theory is truly an alternative to the Republic. It is critical of the Republic both in its description of politics and in the normative conclusions it draws. In failing to comprehend self-interest, party theorists contend, Madison built his Republic on sand. Its conclusions are wrong because it starts in the wrong place. Therefore, party theorists argue for fundamental reform of American national government. Their argument is not only that the demands of the late twentieth century require an appropriately current theory of governance but that because Madison misunderstood political self-interest, his Republic fails to achieve its own goals. In dispersing governmental power, it actually promotes tyranny rather than liberty. In building a government that checks itself through representation, the Republic undermines citizen participation and representative government.

The debate between pluralism and party theory illustrates some fundamental issues of contemporary political science. The debate should heighten awareness about the stakes involved in political analysis and shed light on some important unanswered questions. Although their understanding of the implications of self-interest is very different, both pluralism and party theory assume that people are self-interested in their political behavior. The search for a way to produce the public good out of self-interest motivates both theories.

The chapters of Part II analyze the citizen in politics. Citizen participation, voting choice, and citizens involved in politics through the political parties and through interest groups will occupy our attention. An understanding of representative government compels this focus on the citizen because governmental institutions are supposed to respond to citizen interests. Whether and how institutions respond depends a great deal on how those interests are organized and presented to government.

Citizen Participation in Politics

An Interest in Self-Interest?

Citizen participation is a good place to start our analysis of the Republic. Madison expected self-interested participation by citizens to be the foundation of the system. Political participation can be defined for now as any attempt to influence what government does.

Voting is the most common form of citizen participation in politics. Millions of people turn out to vote in American national elections. But usually, even more millions *don't* turn out to vote. In 1988 49.1 percent of those eligible to vote did so. And that was a presidential election year, when interest was high. Turnout in the 1986 midterm elections was only 37 percent. In other words, fully 63 percent of the eligible electorate didn't vote.

This is self-interest? Something is wrong somewhere. Although Madison's Republic is silent about exactly how high turnout should be, low rates of voting do not seem to be consistent with a theory of human nature which posits a high degree of political self-interest. Of course, there are lots of reasons why people don't vote, and a lack of self-interest is only part of the story.[1] But when almost two-thirds of the electorate don't vote in national legislative (House and Senate) elections, one can be forgiven for wondering whether there is more to the story of citizen participation than meets the eye. We need to take a close look at the concept of self-interest and what it means for political participation. It's not so much that Madison had it wrong by centering his theory on self-interest. But when we ask why so many citizens don't vote, we become aware of an important gap in his theory.

---

[1] One recent study estimates that national voter turnout could be increased by 9 percent if the effects of mobility could be removed. People who change residences encounter difficulties in reregistering to vote which substantially increase the chances that they won't vote. See Peverill Squire, Raymond E. Wolfinger, and David P. Glass, "Residential Mobility and Voter Turnout," *American Political Science Review* 81 (March 1987): 45–66, for a good discussion of the factors related to voter turnout.

Instrumental vs. Cost-Benefit Concepts of Self-Interest

A large part of my critique of Madison's Republic rests upon a distinction between two kinds of self-interest. The first type is goal-oriented and is referred to as **instrumental self-interest.** Action is instrumentally self-interested when it is designed to help produce some outcome that is consistent with the individual's goals. In elections, the instrumentally self-interested citizen acts to uphold her interests when (for example) she votes for the candidate most likely to produce public policy favorable to her. This instrumental concept of self-interest is really what Madison had in mind when he wrote about political behavior. It is important to the Republic because instrumentally self-interested participation in elections produces representation. (Chapter 3 spells out this instrumental conception of how elections work in more detail.)

I call the second type of self-interest **cost-benefit self-interest.** This concept recognizes that individuals have many goals that they would like to achieve. But because their resources are limited, people often do not act to achieve those goals. Ask a friend whether he'd like a new BMW and he's likely to say, "Sure, but what's it going to cost me?" Your friend, in other words, may have some abstract interest in getting a BMW, but he has no interest in paying for it. The cost outweighs the benefit. As the admittedly clumsy name implies, a cost-benefit concept of self-interest asserts that individuals weigh the costs of achieving their goals when they contemplate action in pursuit of those goals. If the costs are greater than the anticipated benefit, the individual does not pursue the benefit. In addition, if the benefit is available at a lower cost (if vendor *A*, say, sells it more cheaply than vendor *B*), the self-interested person purchases the benefit at the lower cost. In general, self-interested individuals seek to minimize costs and maximize benefits.

Notice that the cost-benefit concept of self-interest is more complete than the instrumental concept. The instrumental concept emphasizes only the goals of the individual. The cost-benefit notion includes a recognition that achieving a goal almost always involves some cost. Therefore, individuals are selective about which goals they pursue and which they forgo. I use the term "self-interest" here in the broader sense to include a weighing of costs and benefits. When necessary for clarity, I modify the term by specifying "instrumental" or "cost-benefit" self-interest, as appropriate.

Madison's concept of self-interest does not take into account the costs to the individual of political action in pursuit of policy or other political goals. A major purpose of this chapter is to show that this omission creates serious problems for Madison's theory of the citizen. We begin by examining the implications of the recognition that political participation is costly, and then we move to a comparison of the costs and benefits of participation, with special attention to voting.

The Costs of Political Participation

All forms of political participation, from voting to running for office, involve some costs. The out-of-pocket costs associated with going to the polls to vote are normally small—perhaps bus fare, or the gas it takes to drive a car a few blocks. The out-of-pocket costs of running for public office may run into the thousands, hundreds of thousands, or even millions of dollars.

Generally speaking, the costs associated with political participation include the expenditure of anything of value, such as time, effort, and, of course, money. This notion of costs is closely related to the economists' concept of **opportunity costs.** Opportunity costs are incurred when an individual gives up resources that might be used to do something else. Thus if a citizen decides to go door-to-door to persuade residents in a neighborhood to vote for her candidate, she is spending time in political participation which she might have used to study for her exams, work at her job, or enjoy the company of her family or friends. The dollar costs associated with canvassing a neighborhood are probably small, but the total opportunity costs can be substantial. Of course, some forms of participation, such as mounting a campaign for the United States Senate, are extremely costly in dollars, time, and effort. The point here is simply that all forms of political participation cost something, and some cost more than others.

Four Propositions About the Costs of Participation

Four propositions follow more or less directly from the recognition that political participation is costly. These propositions shed light on why some people participate in the political process while others do not. They also permit speculation on some of the implications of nonparticipation for the political system.

1. *The more costly the form of participation, the lower the rate of participation.* General Motors sells more Chevrolets than Cadillacs. Chevrolets are cheaper than Cadillacs, and as a result more people can afford the less expensive car. The same is true of political participation. Figure 2-1 shows some forms of participation ordered roughly according to their costs. The Chevrolet of participation, voting in presidential elections, is the cheapest as well as the most common form. More expensive forms of participation, such as try-

ing to persuade others to vote for a candidate, attending a political meeting, contributing money to a candidate, and working for a party or candidate, are much less common.[2] Working for a candidate or political party is hardly the Cadillac of political participation, yet only about 4 percent of the eligible electorate in 1984 chose to participate in this way. Of course, the percentage of the population that participates in very expensive ways, such as running for the U.S. Senate, is minuscule. Perhaps running for the Senate is the Rolls Royce of political participation.

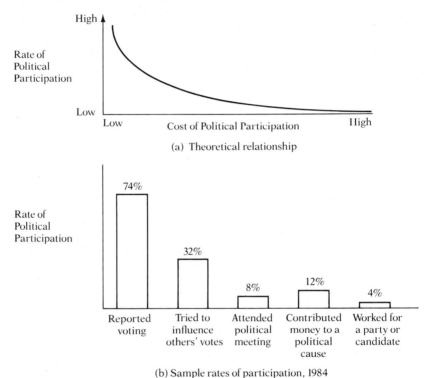

(a) Theoretical relationship

(b) Sample rates of participation, 1984

Figure 2-1 Cost and Rate of Political Participation. SOURCE (part b): Center for Political Studies, University of Michigan, American National Election Study, 1984 (Ann Arbor: Interuniversity Consortium for Political and Social Research, 1986).

_____

[2]Unfortunately, respondents in surveys consistently overreport having voted. The actual turnout in 1984 was about 53 percent rather than the 74 percent shown in Figure 2-1. Also note that I have ordered the types of participation only roughly according to cost. The survey did not measure how much money was contributed, and it would be difficult to compare the dollar cost associated with a contribution with the time cost of attending a meeting or working for a candidate. In any case, according to the order in Figure 2-1, the rate of contributing money is unexpectedly high.

2. *The rate of participation can be manipulated through public policy that increases or decreases its costs.* Rates of participation tend to be higher in states where it is easy to get to the polls than in states where voting is made more difficult.[3] The national turnout would almost certainly increase if elections were held on a national holiday or on a Sunday. Or instead of voting on a single day, why not vote over the course of a week? If such a change were made, fewer people would have to take time off from work and the ability to bear the costs of voting would increase, especially for those who worked for hourly wages. Public policy affects other kinds of participation as well. Currently, for example, the law limits the amount of money an individual can give to a campaign other than his own. Most states have laws that hinder candidates who wish to run for public office under a party label other than that of one of the major parties. These laws raise the costs of third-party candidacies, thereby decreasing the chances that such candidacies will occur. For better or for ill—and there are arguments on both sides—laws that manipulate the costs of participation affect the rate of participation.[4]

3. *Those with more political resources are better able to bear the costs of participation; therefore, they participate at higher rates than those with fewer resources.* **Political resources** are assets that can be used to facilitate participation. Figure 2-2 shows that in recent presidential election years the reported rate of voting has differed regularly and substantially between people with some college education and those who have only an elementary education. Education is a politically relevant resource that permits a better understanding of one's political environment and the way it affects one's interests. The more highly educated are also more likely to have the time that permits them to bear the opportunity costs associated with political participation. Level of education has been found to be a powerful explanation of why some citizens vote and others do not.[5]

That those with resources are more likely to participate leads to a **resource bias** when actual participants are compared with those who are eligible to participate. In other words, not only is the number of participants *smaller* than the pool of people eligible to participate, but participants also *differ* from nonparticipants. Participants are "richer" in such political resources as education, time,

---

[3]Benjamin Ginsberg, *The Consequences of Consent* (Reading, Mass: Addison-Wesley, 1982), p. 36.
[4]For a good overview of the effect of policy on participation rates, see M. Margaret Conway, *Political Participation in the United States* (Washington, D.C.: Congressional Quarterly Press, 1985), especially chap. 5.
[5]Raymond E. Wolfinger and Steven J. Rosenston, *Who Votes?* (New Haven: Yale University Press, 1980).

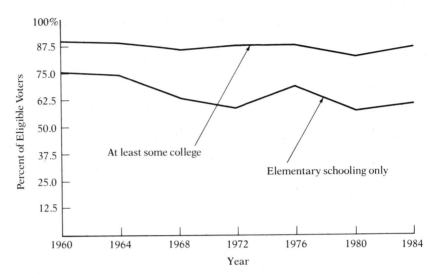

Figure 2-2 Reported Voter Turnout Among Citizens of High and Low Education Levels, 1960–1984. SOURCE: Adapted from M. Margaret Conway, *Political Participation in the United States* (Washington, D.C.: Congressional Quarterly Press, 1985), p. 132.

money, and social status than those who do not participate. As a result, the number of resource-rich people in the participant pool is larger than one would expect on the basis of their proportion of the larger population.

This resource bias is important, particularly since political resources are linked to political interests. Consider the following example. Assume that the people who contribute money to candidates do so for instrumental reasons (they want to influence policy outcomes in the direction of their interests). They will support candidates with whom they agree and oppose candidates they find objectionable. Now recall Madison's argument that political leaders respond to the interests of their followers because if they don't they will be unable to retain their positions of power. If the people who contribute to candidates tend to have higher incomes than those who do not contribute, and if level of income is related to political interest, wealthier people will have disproportionate influence in the electoral process. In general, the consequence of the resource bias is that citizens with substantial political resources have greater influence over public affairs than those with fewer resources.

4. *The greater the cost of a form of participation, the greater the resource bias.* The theoretical relationship stated in this proposition is illustrated by Figure 2-3, and data on several ways citizens participate in the electoral process are presented in Table 2-1. In 1984, 42

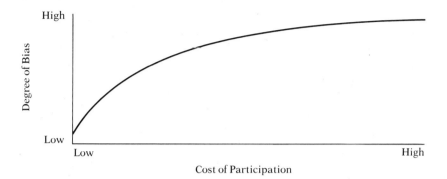

Figure 2-3 The Theoretical Relationship Between the Cost of Participation and Resource Bias

percent of all eligible voters had some college education, and 28 percent had personal incomes of $20,000 or more. These education and income levels set the standard against which the degree of bias can be assessed. For example, the proportion of nonvoters with at least some college education is substantially smaller than the proportion of such people among eligible voters as a whole (22 and 42 percent, respectively). This difference results in a negative bias (−48 percent), which means that the well educated are underrepresented among nonvoters by almost 50 percent. People with some college, in contrast, are overrepresented among voters, an indication of a bias in favor of those with the resource of education. As the theoretical relationship depicted in Figure 2-3 suggests, the degree of bias in

Table 2-1 Education and Income Levels by Type of Participation, 1984

Type of Participation	Some college education (%)	Bias[a]	Personal income of $20,000 or more (%)	Bias[a]
Eligible voters	42	—	28	—
Nonvoters	22	−48	16	−43
Voters	49	+17	33	+18
Influenced others	54	+29	37	+32
Attended meeting	61	+45	41	+43
Contributed money	68	+62	54	+93
Worked for Party or candidate	61	+45	50	+79

[a]Bias shows the percent of under- or overrepresentation of education and income among participants compared with eligible voters.
SOURCE: Center for Political Studies, University of Michigan, *American National Election Study, 1984* (Ann Arbor: Interuniversity Consortium for Political and Social Research, 1986).

favor of both education and income increases with more expensive forms of participation, such as attending meetings, contributing money, and working for a political campaign. All of the forms of participation shown in Table 2-1 are relatively inexpensive in comparison with such activities as running for public office. As a result, the degree of bias associated with the kinds of participation mentioned in the table is relatively small, even though it does plainly increase with cost. In 1966 (when the percentage of the eligible electorate with some college education was about half what it was in 1984) fully 93 percent of the members of the House of Representatives and 96 percent of U.S. senators had at least some college education.[6]

The fact that the resource bias increases with the cost of participation is important because expensive forms of participation, such as working for a candidate, contributing money, and running for office, have a greater impact on political outcomes than less expensive ways of participating. Thus the average contributor of $500 to a political campaign probably has more influence than the average voter, and the bias in the political system may be compounded. If contributors of $500 (to say nothing of people who run for the Senate) are more influential than ordinary voters, and if they are richer in political resources as well, the tilt in the political process toward the resource-rich is even greater than we would expect on the basis of the differences between voters and nonvoters alone.

Of course, one might expect the electorate as a whole to wield the greatest influence because it is to the electorate that political leaders are ultimately accountable. Politicians may not be able to attend only to constituents with enough resources to participate in extraordinary ways. The electoral connection is supposed to force political leaders, whatever their personal inclinations, to respond to the policy preferences of voters. Contributors to campaigns may help candidates appeal to voters, but the bias associated with contributing money (or any other form of participation beyond voting) may be swamped by the self-interest of leaders in satisfying voters as a way to retain political power.

Or it may not be swamped. The real test is whether people vote according to their instrumental self-interest. If they do, leaders must respond to those interests in order to stay in office. Therefore,

[6]Malcom E. Jewell and Samuel C. Patterson, *The Legislative Process in the United States*, 3rd ed. (New York: Random House, 1977), p. 71. For evidence from other political systems relating to proposition 4, see Robert D. Putnam, *The Comparative Study of Political Elites* (Englewood Cliffs, N.J.: Prentice-Hall, 1977), pp. 33–36. Putnam refers to the pattern described in this proposition as the "law of increasing disproportion."

we proceed by examining a bit further the question of why people bother to vote.

Voting and Nonvoting: Comparing Costs and Benefits

Largely because the associated costs are low, voting is the most common form of citizen participation. Madison's Republic assumes that people vote because they have a self-interest in doing so. That is, voters participate in order to help produce outcomes consistent with their interests. This explanation sounds good, but it does not take into account the costs of voting. Because Madison did not consider the cost-benefit side of self-interest, his ideas about voting as an expression of self-interest need rethinking.

Consider the concept of self-interest as it is usually applied to the consumer. An individual who is hungry for a hamburger, say, spends the least in dollars, time, and energy to purchase a hamburger (the benefit) that will satisfy her hunger. She includes in her cost-benefit calculations the dollar cost of the hamburger and the time costs associated with making the purchase, such as driving or walking time, time spent waiting in line, and so forth. If she is not hungry enough to justify these expenses (the costs outweigh the benefits), she will not buy a hamburger. If she is hungry enough (the benefit is greater than the costs), she makes the purchase. In other words, if the benefits outweigh the costs, the consumer in our example has a self-interest in purchasing a hamburger; if the costs are greater than the benefit, the consumer's interest is to forgo the hamburger.

This cost-benefit concept of self-interest can usefully be applied to voting. The citizen, no less than the consumer, calculates the costs and benefits and decides to vote on the basis of his comparison of benefits and costs. In the Republic, what are the benefits of voting? Presumably the benefit is linked to the voter's perception of the policy and other benefits associated with the election victory of the candidate he favors. Assume the voter cares a great deal about who wins a presidential election and would pay a large sum of money (say, $10,000) to see his favored candidate in the White House. We have already seen that the costs of voting are small. They include slight out-of-pocket costs, such as the gasoline or bus fare to get to the polls, and perhaps forgone wages if the citizen must take time off from work. He must also bear the costs associated with the time spent in transit and waiting in line at the polls. These opportunity costs will surely be much less than the $10,000 worth of benefit associated with winning the election. Therefore, the self-interested citizen in this example will doubtless vote, right?

Wrong. To see why, we need to compare our examples of the consumer and the citizen a little more carefully.

Private Goods, Collective Goods,
Free Riders, and the Paradox of Collective Action

Consider the nature of the benefit in the hamburger example. In the lingo of the economist, the hamburger is a **private good.** A private good, once produced, can be restricted to the person who pays for it. If you don't put your money on the counter, you don't get the hamburger; if you do, a hamburger is quickly forthcoming. In the exchange of resources for a private good, there is a direct relationship between bearing the costs and receiving the benefit.

Think, in contrast, of the benefit associated with an election outcome. An election outcome is a **collective good.** A collective good, once it is produced, cannot be denied to any member of the public, whether or not the individual helped pay for it. The outcome of a presidential election benefits everyone in the nation, whether or not they voted, contributed money, or canvassed on behalf of a candidate. Note that the "benefit" can be positive or negative. Thus the citizen who values the outcome very highly (at $10,000) gets the outcome (his favored candidate will win or lose) even if he refuses to bear the costs associated with voting. With collective goods, then, the direct relationship between costs and benefits is severed. The citizen receives the benefits of the election outcome whether or not he helps pay for its production by voting. Therefore, the strictly self-interested citizen who minimizes costs and maximizes benefits—even one who attaches a very high value to an election outcome—will not bear costs associated with producing the outcome. He is a **free rider;** that is, he enjoys (or suffers) the collective outcome without helping to pay for it.

Notice that the conclusion here applies to a collective good, to which the relationship between bearing costs and receiving benefits does not apply. That is, once produced, the outcome is available to all—not only to those who helped pay for it. Thus our self-interested citizen who cares a great deal about the election would be willing to pay the $10,000 *if that payment would guarantee the desired outcome.* Since he cannot purchase an election outcome for $10,000, he is a free rider who does not pay even the minimal costs of voting.

Certainly one possible objection to this argument is that if an individual does not pay the costs (does not participate), she is also affecting the chances that the collective good will be produced. In the example of an election, a citizen who decides not to vote has decreased the chances that her favored candidate will win. Isn't it then in her self-interest to vote? While it is true that the nonparticipation of a single citizen who otherwise would vote for a candidate reduces the chances of that candidate's victory, the loss of a single vote in a very large electorate amounts to such a small reduction in the candidate's chances as to be insignificant. The citizen might ask herself before the election, "What are the chances that this election will be a tie?" If the chances of a tie are reasonably large, then she should vote, because her vote might break the tie and determine the outcome. But in a national electorate of 80 to 90 million souls, the chance that a single vote will break a tie is minuscule. The winner of a presidential election is going to win quite independently of what any individual citizen does or fails to do. The citizen in our example benefits from the outcome (she gets or fails to get her favored candidate) whether or not she votes. Her vote cannot affect the outcome. Therefore, she would act against her self-interest to bear *any* costs to affect an outcome that she cannot, in any case, affect. She would be better off using her time to study for her exams or socialize or mow the lawn, because if she does any of these things instead of voting, she still benefits from the election. She can get the benefit without cost. If she is truly self-interested in the cost-benefit sense, she will be a free rider.[7]

This argument that the self-interested citizen will be a free rider rather than help pay for collective goods is critical to the relationship between the citizen and the political system. It leads to the **paradox of collective action,** which is a fundamental problem any theory of politics must somehow confront. The paradox is that even though the individual has an interest in the collective good (the favored candidate's victory), he or she has no interest in helping to produce the collective good (by voting, in this example). More abstractly, the paradox of collective action says that self-interested individuals will not contribute to the production of collective goods in a large public, no matter how great their instrumental self-interest in having the collective good produced.[8] In the case of voting, the paradox suggests that the self-interested citizen stays home and receives the benefits of the election outcome without contributing any effort toward helping his favored candidate because that candidate will win or lose whether or not he bears the costs of voting. In short, *it is not in the individual's self-interest to pursue his instrumental self-interest in electoral politics.*

The point of introducing the paradox of collective action is not to argue that it perfectly describes reality. In fact, the paradox

---

[7]See Anthony Downs, *An Economic Theory of Democracy* (New York: Harper & Row, 1957), especially chap. 14. For an attempt to test some of these ideas, see William H. Riker and Peter C. Ordeshook, "A Theory of the Calculus of Voting," *American Political Science Review* 63 (1968): 25–43. Downs's discussion is very readable; Riker and Ordeshook's article is much more technical, but it does present some interesting data that are readily understood.
[8]Mancur Olson, *The Logic of Collective Action* (New York: Schocken, 1971).

makes a prediction that on its face is pretty silly. It says that no one in a large electorate will bear the costs of voting. In such a world, democracy would collapse for lack of interest.[9] But a body of citizens composed entirely of self-interested free riders obviously does not describe the American electorate. While eligible voters do not participate at anything close to 100 percent, millions of Americans nonetheless turn out to vote in presidential and other national elections.

So the paradox of collective action applied to voter turnout makes a prediction—no one will vote—which does not square with reality. Nonetheless, it is an absolutely essential insight into the way citizens relate to politics. And it is completely unanticipated in Madison's Republic. Madison did not recognize the distinction between the instrumental and cost-benefit concepts of self-interest, and as a result he failed to see that many people would not be willing to bear the costs of political action, even when they had a compelling interest in the outcome. Thus the paradox is an important part of our critical examination of the Republic. But in order to pursue the argument, we must examine the reasons for the paradox's false prediction. Why are so many citizens willing to bear costs to vote when a free-rider strategy makes more economic sense?

Voting as Symbolic or Instrumental Action?

The short explanation of why people vote is that a cost-benefit concept of self-interest does not explain everything. Moreover, the costs of voting are very low, particularly the out-of-pocket costs. Therefore, the degree to which citizens violate a cost-benefit concept of self-interest by not being free riders is slight. Of course, most voters do not sit down and calculate the costs and benefits associated with voting. Rather, most citizens respond to a sense of duty when they go to the polls to vote. Americans typically are well trained (or "socialized") at school and at home to believe that it is the duty of every citizen to cast a ballot. Citizens who have this sense of duty are far more likely to vote than those who do not. Such attitudes as a basic trust in the government and a sense of efficacy (a feeling that the government is responsive and accountable) are also closely associated with voter turnout. People who do not feel an

---

[9]The existence of democracy is a collective good. Therefore, the free-rider problem applies. If democracy survives, individual citizens benefit whether or not they contribute to its survival. If democracy is to fail because of nonvoting, the individual's vote will not, alas, prevent its collapse.

obligation to vote or who are cynical about the government are much less likely to vote.[10]

This conclusion that people vote primarily because they feel they have a duty to do so is important. Strictly speaking, it suggests that in order to respond to an obligation to vote, citizens need not have thought seriously about the candidates, weighed the benefits of one candidate against the other, or calculated how their self-interest would best be served by the policies espoused by the political parties. Going to the polls, then, is not primarily the result of instrumental self-interest, as Madison supposed. Rather, it is an expression of the citizen's faith in the system and a response to his or her citizenship training. Those who have learned their lessons well vote because they know it is their duty to do so; those who have not been well socialized are much less likely to vote. This sense of duty apparently works tolerably well in presidential elections, in which a majority turns out to vote. In midterm congressional elections, however, the turnout is usually substantially below 50 percent, and in many city and school-board elections the turnout is extremely low.

The suggestion that citizens who vote typically do so because they feel a duty or obligation to vote amounts to a rejection of Madison's theory that people vote out of self-interest. To say that people vote out of a sense of duty is to call into question the instrumental explanation, that the citizen weighs the advantages associated with the various candidates and votes because he sees one candidate as better fulfilling his self-interest than the other. Chapter 3 analyzes voting choice in detail, but it is enough now to see that a simple instrumental explanation is in trouble.

If people go to the polls in response to a sense of duty rather than because of their self-interest, what does this phenomenon mean for the Republic? It seriously undermines Madison's expectation that self-interest would produce representation through elections. If duty motivates people to vote (at relatively low cost), is it reasonable to expect duty to motivate people to become informed about alternatives available in an election? Such information (about candidates, where they stand on issues, what they have done and failed to do in office, etc.) is necessary to a self-interested vote in the Republic. But the costs of becoming informed are high. Therefore, it is unlikely that duty is a strong enough motivator to produce

---

[10]See Lester Milbrath and M. L. Goel, *Political Participation* (Washington, D.C.: University Press of America, 1982); Conway, *Political Participation*, chap. 3; Sidney Verba and Norman H. Nie, *Participation in America* (New York: Harper & Row, 1972), chap. 8.

much of a drive for information. In other words, the citizen can satisfy his sense of duty to vote by casting an uninformed vote just as well as he can by casting an informed vote. And an uninformed vote is much cheaper (or cost-effective). Why should the citizen bear the significant opportunity costs associated with becoming informed about politics when his vote will not affect the outcome, and when he will share in the benefits whether or not he becomes informed?[11]

All of this suggests that voting is not first and foremost an instrumental activity. It is not primarily an effort by the individual citizen to produce outcomes consistent with his interests; it is not goal-oriented behavior. Rather, voting is an expression of the individual's faith in democracy as a symbol. It reflects his commitment to democratic ideals and his belief that the system is legitimate. Thus voting is better understood as a **symbolic action** rather than as an instrumental action. Citizens feel a duty to support the political system because they believe it is working the way it should and because it is based on moral principles they support. Thus voting becomes a mark of commitment to the goals of the political system, such as liberty, justice, and equality. The admonishment that people who do not even bother to vote should not complain is based on this idea.

In fact, the level of voter participation is often used as an indication of how healthy the political system is. Declining rates of voting in American national elections since 1960 are closely associated with declining trust in the institutions of national government and with increased cynicism about politics.[12] Moreover, the fact that participation is as high as it is probably reflects a significant commitment by public institutions to promote the legitimacy of the political system. The schools, for example, play an important role in teaching the values of citizenship and encouraging a sense of duty to participate. Public leaders also encourage popular participation through their speeches and other public pronouncements. Expanding the right to vote can foster the acceptance of public policies

---

[11]Consider the citizen who is one of many potential voters in a congressional election. In such elections, the average citizen is not very well informed. Only about half of American citizens know the name of their representative in Washington, and fewer know the name of the challenger. A very small percentage in the typical district knows anything about what the representative has actually done in Washington. But run the following mind experiment. Instead of making the citizen one of thousands of voters in her district, give her the right to determine, by herself, the next representative from her district. Assume she must choose the Democratic or Republican nominee. How likely is it under these hypothetical conditions that she will remain uninformed? Since she and she alone has the responsibility to select the winner, isn't it very likely she will expend considerable resources in making the choice?

[12]For a good account, see Richard A. Brody, "The Puzzle of Political Participation in America," in *The New American Political System,* ed. Anthony King (Washington, D.C.: American Enterprise Institute, 1978), pp. 287–324.

actually detrimental to the interests of those given the right to participate. The lowering of the voting age to eighteen, for example, may have contributed to young people's acceptance of the draft and a questionable war in Southeast Asia.[13]

In sum, we have two different reasons for such political action as voting. First, there is the instrumental reason, which Madison expected to impel people to be active politically. Instrumental action is motivated by an interest in achieving some goal. But this conception of self-interest is not complete until the benefits political action are supposed to promote are compared with the costs of the participation. Once these costs are taken into account, and once we recognize that many of the benefits political action seeks to promote are collective goods, the expectation of instrumentally self-interested behavior in politics becomes questionable. The second explanation for political participation is a symbolic one. This explanation emphasizes the personal, subjective rewards associated with affirming one's duty or one's support of shared political values.

A word of caution is appropriate at this point. To argue that for the typical citizen voting is more a symbolic act than a pursuit of instrumental self-interest is not to argue that elections have no effect on the distribution of benefits in the political system. It matters a great deal which party or candidate wins a presidential election. Presidential candidates and parties differ in the goals they expect the political system to pursue, in the kinds of people they would appoint to important government positions, and in the kinds of legislation they would propose to and accept from the Congress. Candidates also vary greatly in the skills and other personal characteristics they would bring to the presidency. But to say that elections matter is not to say that the individual voter can influence the outcome. The importance of the collective outcome (the election result) need not have any bearing on the importance of an individual participant in determining that outcome. Many individuals, acting together, determine an important political outcome. No single individual's participation, however, has a significant effect. Since the individual does not "matter" in this sense, he or she has no reason to act apart from the symbolic gratification associated with the action.

If most people vote for symbolic rather than instrumental reasons, what are the implications for the resource-bias propositions advanced earlier? If duty motivates people to do something that a

---

[13]Ginsberg makes this argument in *Consequences of Consent*. He suggests further that the state subsidizes voting by paying for polling places, printing ballots, enforcing election laws, and the like because it has a stake in a large turnout. When people vote, Ginsberg argues, they are more likely to feel positive about the system and they are less likely to engage in disruptive political action.

cost-benefit analysis suggests they won't do, why should the costs of voting create a bias in favor of citizens with political resources? The answer is simple: People with the most resources are also those most likely to have a sense of duty and other attitudes associated with voting. Though it is hardly a perfect explanation of voter turnout (political scientists are still a long way from a perfect explanation of anything), Figure 2-4 summarizes the relationship between resources and attitudes most closely associated with voter participation. The higher the social status of an individual, the more political resources that individual is likely to have. Therefore, those with higher-status occupations and more education are also likely to have higher incomes, more time to devote to political participation, and more skill in the pursuit of political goals. The more of these sorts of political resources the individual has, the more likely he or she is to vote. The model represented in Figure 2-4 also suggests that not only are those with more resources better able to afford the costs of participation, they are also more likely to have the sense of duty and commitment to political values which motivate people to participate. Thus the middle-class student from a professional family living in a suburban school district is more likely to be socialized to value voting in elections than the working-class student who attends a relatively deprived inner-city school.

Participation Beyond Voting

The analysis of the free-rider problem and of the paradox of collective action has been applied so far only to voter participation. The four propositions about cost recognized that there are other,

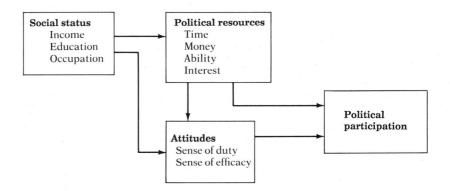

Figure 2-4 A Model of Political Participation. SOURCE: Adapted from the discussion in Sidney Verba and Norman H. Nie, *Participation in America* (New York: Harper & Row, 1972), chap. 8.

more costly forms of participation beyond voting. How does the paradox relate to them?

Consider again the citizen who wishes to contribute money to a candidate. If she is responding to a mail request for a small contribution—say, $15—and she considers the costs and benefits of making a contribution, she is likely to decide not to send any money. As the election outcome is a collective good, it is extremely unlikely that one more contribution of $15 will produce victory for the favored candidate. If the candidate has enough money to run a competitive campaign, one less contribution will not be missed; if the candidate does not have enough money to run an effective campaign, one more contribution of $15 won't put it over the top. The self-interested citizen in this case will be a free rider and enjoy the benefits of the election outcome without sending any money.

Since contributing money to a candidate is a more costly form of political participation than voting, we are not surprised that fewer people do it (there are more free riders). Moreover, we are not surprised to learn that the resource bias associated with contributing money is sharper than that associated with voting (see Table 2-1). Because of the relatively high costs of contributing money, fewer people can afford to go against their self-interest in being a free rider by writing a check to help their favored candidate. Those who do so probably have a strong sense of duty and perhaps a strong commitment to the candidate, but they act for reasons other than a selfish concern with maximizing benefits at minimal cost.

Consider a citizen who wishes to contribute a large sum of money to a candidate—say, $1,000 to a congressional candidate.[14] Is it possible that writing a check for $1,000 is in the self-interest of the contributor, while writing one for $15 is not? In a close election (particularly if the electorate is relatively small, as in a congressional race or a presidential primary) a large contribution could make a difference in the outcome. Certainly it is easier to believe that an extra $1,000 will significantly help a candidate mount a viable campaign than will an extra $15. Thus a person who cares deeply about the outcome of an election might affect that outcome with a larger contribution, and (provided he can afford it) act in his self-interest by forgoing the free-rider option and writing the check.

More probably, however, contributing a large sum of money purchases more than a better chance at producing a collective good. Such a contribution may buy a private benefit, such as an invitation to a black-tie dinner at the White House or access to the member of Congress when the contributor has a problem or wants to express

---

[14]Current campaign finance legislation limits the amount of money an individual can give to a single candidate to $1,000.

his interest in a piece of legislation. Indeed, *the most costly forms of participation are almost always associated with a private good that compensates for the outlay of resources demanded of the participant.* Doubtless many candidates for higher office run because they wish to affect the course of public affairs (collective good), but they also are motivated to secure the prestige, power, and perquisites attached to a political career (private goods).

Several points can be made by way of differentiating costly forms of participation from those that require little in the way of resources. First, because voting is very inexpensive, the economic self-interest the citizen has in being a free rider can be overcome relatively easily by a sense of obligation or a commitment to the values of the political system. More expensive forms of participation, such as contributing large amounts of money, are less likely to provide enough gratification to compensate the citizen for the additional cost. Although many people who contribute large amounts of money or run for office probably have a strong commitment to the political system, they almost certainly get some private good as well. They are also much more likely to affect the distribution of collective goods (such as the election outcome) than are those who can afford only to vote.

We are now back to the resource bias. Contributors of money in campaigns have more resources than the average voter, and hence are better able to afford expensive forms of participation. It takes political resources to wield effective political influence. This is a variant on the old saying "It takes money to make money." Not only are people with resources more likely to participate, but the more costly the form of participation, the greater the resource bias. We may reasonably conclude that those who seek the private benefit of access to officeholders which results from a costly form of participation are likely to be very well off in political resources. They are also likely to be much more influential than citizens who participate in less costly ways, such as voting. If, for instance, campaign contributors flock to a particular candidate and ignore his potential opponent in a race for a party's nomination, the candidate with backers to help pay the bills can run, while the candidate with no financial backing cannot. The voters have no opportunity to vote for the opponent who failed to attract support from people with money to spend on political campaigns.[15]

---

[15]For an intriguing theory of how very active participants (such as contributors of money and potential candidates) influence the choices offered to voters, see Gary C. Jacobson and Samuel Kernell, *Strategy and Choice in Congressional Elections* (New Haven: Yale University Press, 1981).

The argument so far is crucial to my critique of the Republic. The greater the cost of a form of participation, the greater the resource bias is likely to be. Thus influence is unevenly distributed in the political system in favor of those with wealth, an exclusive education, and other related political resources.

Self-Interest vs. Self-Interest: A Problem for the Republic

We saw in Chapter 1 that Madison built his argument for the Republic on the proposition that the citizen is self-interested. This attribute of human nature, while carrying the threat of the "violence of faction," also promotes representative government: self-interested citizens will force self-interested leaders to provide representation. The resulting conflict in government will be the mechanism to check governmental power. In this way, "the private interest of every individual may be a sentinel over the public rights."

The problem with the Madisonian solution is that representation and the desirable things that result from it (conflict and a government that controls itself) are collective goods. As a result, the theory of representation must survive the paradox of collective action. That is, despite individual citizens' instrumental interest in being represented, they have no interest in bearing the costs of promoting representation. Representation will occur or fail to occur independent of an individual citizen's actions. The "private interest" of the citizen is in being a free rider. If the private interest of every individual is to be a free rider, is it reasonable to believe that self-interest can be "a sentinel over the public rights?"

If collective goods could be produced without cost, individuals who cared about representation would have no incentive to be free riders. But representation is not free. The costs of representation are closely associated with the costs of participation. Large numbers of individuals must be willing to vote and to maintain some degree of vigilance over governmental leaders. The act of voting is low in cost (but there are costs), while the information necessary to vote in a way that will maximize the chances of increasing representation is much more costly. The self-interested voter—no matter how greatly he or she desires representation—will not bear those costs.

Because the costs of going to the polls are low, many people can afford to act against their selfish interest in maximizing benefits at minimal cost. Those who can afford to do so are those with more political resources. The resource bias that results from the cost of participation also has disturbing implications for Madison's

Republic. It indicates that some interests will be underrepresented among participants. By Madison's own argument, such under-representation gives self-interested leaders little incentive to represent the interests of constituents poor in resources. Moreover, the fact that many citizens participate out of a sense of duty and not out of instrumental self-interest may weaken the ability of the electoral connection to check the stronger biases that result from relatively expensive forms of participation, such as contributing large sums of money or running for high political office.

Madison's Republic is jeopardized by its failure to recognize the central point of this chapter: *self-interested citizens have no interest in participating to produce political representation.* Madison's theory fails to take into account the complexity of self-interest. A theory of voting choice (the topic of Chapter 3) which ignores the implications of information costs and the paradox of collective action may fall considerably short of explaining how citizens vote as well as the incentives leaders have to respond to the public. Such a theory may posit unrealistic expectations about representation, conflict, and the degree to which government can control itself. The introduction of complications in the concept of self-interest at the base of the Republic inevitably will have consequences for the rest of the theory.

When the logic of citizen participation is examined in some detail, critical questions about Madison's theory are raised: What will make representatives represent citizens' interests? What will ensure conflict in government? How will a government "of men over men" control itself? The Republic's failure to comprehend the paradox of collective action does not necessarily blow its conclusions out of the water. Representative government may exist despite the fact that citizens individually have little reason to bear significant costs to promote it. The cost-benefit concept of self-interest, free riders, and the paradox of collective action cannot explain all political behavior. We shall see in Chapter 3 that they help us understand why people are not very well informed when they vote, but as we have seen in this chapter, they cannot explain why anyone would bother to vote at all. These concepts are an important part of the critique of Madison's Republic, but they are not the whole story. Certainly the American government works in ways more complex than Madison anticipated. Recognition of the complexity of self-interest and of the relationship between citizens and politics is an important first step toward a more sophisticated understanding of politics. It is also essential to a mature evaluation of the system, and of the many alternatives and suggestions for reform offered for the thoughtful citizen's consideration.

Key Concepts

collective good

cost-benefit self-interest

free rider

instrumental self-interest

opportunity costs

paradox of collective action

political resources

private good

resource bias

symbolic action

Who's in Charge Here? 3
Voting Choice in Elections

On November 4, 1986, the sun set on yet another election day. In this particular city and state, we were asked to vote on more than thirty offices and ballot issues. The races ranged from those for U.S. senator and state governor to those for county coroner and local judgeships. And we were asked to vote on several ballot questions that, if passed, would have the effect of law. Candidates actively solicited votes before election day, TV debates were held, leaflets were passed out, and campaign-related mail was frequently added to the usual take of junk mail and bills.

If nothing else, the number of candidates and issues on the 1986 ballot demonstrates an American infatuation with elections. And of course, biennial national elections, of which 1986 was an example, are not the only times Americans are summoned to pass judgment on one aspect or another of their governance. Local elections to select members of school boards and city councils, to accept or reject bond issues, and to settle innumerable questions from pet control to zoning regulations are frequently held throughout the year.

Who's in charge here? It would seem the people are in charge. Frequent elections seem to be the perfect way to ensure popular control over government, since in elections the people convene formally to exercise their choices in regard to who shall govern and, when issue questions appear on the ballot, how. Formally, at least, elections ensure that the currency of politics is the vote and that all citizens have an equal share. The government of a large and complex society is too far removed from the average citizen to permit strict democracy, in which every citizen would also be a legislator. But elections permit citizens to go about their ordinary business while maintaining final control over what government does.

The idea that elections put the people in charge sounds good,

49

but the argument in Chapter 2 raises serious questions about whether elections can really serve this purpose. Large percentages of citizens eligible to vote do not do so, even in highly publicized national elections. The paradox of collective action is that those who do vote have little reason to bear the significant information costs associated with finding out where candidates stand on the issues and how competent they may be as political leaders. Even a political scientist who is supposed to be well informed about politics may find himself voting in some races with very little information. After all, with more than thirty questions on the ballot and given the very small chance that a single vote would make any difference in the outcome, a voter has little reason to go out and collect very much information.

Our question in this chapter, then, is: How do citizens decide how to vote? The way voters decide has a bearing on who is in charge. In the Republic, voters act out of instrumental self-interest, and those self-interested actions put them in charge by producing representation. In this chapter the cost-benefit concept of self-interest is applied to the problem of voting choice in elections. Our goal is to understand how much control citizens are able to exert over government through their participation. We depart even further from the ideas in the Republic by suggesting alternative ways in which elections can be understood and by introducing additional concepts that help us to comprehend how elections actually work rather than how they are supposed to work in the Republic. As always, the point is to provide a critical perspective on the Republic so that alternatives to it can be evaluated in the light of contemporary experience.

Instrumental vs. Symbolic Models of Elections

The Instrumental Model of Elections

The **instrumental model of elections** works if citizens choose between competing candidates on the basis of their instrumental self-interest. For example, a citizen might examine his positive and negative evaluations of each of the major-party candidates running for president. He might then simply add up the positive and negative attributes he sees in the candidates and parties and vote for the candidate with the greatest net value.[1] If every voter were to do this, the winning candidate could be said to represent best the pref-

---

[1] Stanley Kelley, Jr., and Thad W. Mirer, "The Simple Act of Voting," *American Political Science Review* 68 (June 1974): 572–591.

erences of the voting public. If we assume that the winner's behavior in office is consistent with the promises he made and the expectations he raised during the campaign, significant popular control over the office could result from the election. Whatever the mechanisms at work (and there are many possibilities), the instrumental model's answer to "Who's in charge?" is: the people. Two broad expectations in regard to the way elections put the people in charge of government are associated with the instrumental model of elections:

Elections communicate popular preferences. Often one hears the claim that an election result is an **electoral mandate,** or popular endorsement of a program espoused by the winning candidate or political party. The idea behind this claim is simple. Candidates for office speak out on a broad range of issues in debates and make their positions known in their advertising and in the speeches they make before the electorate. Presidential candidates are backed by their party's "platform," which is a set of positions adopted by the party convention on a wide variety of national issues. Particularly when the two candidates differ on the issues raised during the campaign, it seems logical to infer that the winner is preferred by the electorate in part because he or she has taken more popular positions on the issues. By voting, the electorate communicates its preference not only for the individual candidate but also for the positions that candidate has taken on the issues. The outcome then amounts to an electoral mandate for the policies espoused by the winning candidate and directs him or her, once in office, to fulfill the promises made during the campaign. The people have spoken, and government responds accordingly.

Elections promote governmental accountability to the people. A second way elections can be instruments of popular control over government is by promoting **accountability.** An organization such as a university makes people be accountable by requiring them to report to other people who are in positions of greater authority in the organization. Faculty members are accountable to deans by virtue of the control the dean has over such resources as salary increases. Faculty members who do not follow the dean's policies may be punished in various ways, in serious cases by dismissal. Likewise, public officials are accountable to the people. Elections force officials to go back to their "bosses" and justify their behavior in office. If their behavior is satisfactory, the people may be expected to return them for another term. If their behavior has been unacceptable in any way, the people have the option of dismissing them in favor of the opposition.

The instrumental model of elections puts the people in charge by connecting their self-interest to that of leaders who want to retain power. The mandate idea focuses on the behavior of officials *following* the election. It assumes that officials have an interest in responding to the wishes of their constituency, and that the choice made by that constituency in the last election carries with it an interpretable message about those preferences. Of course, it assumes that voters choose candidates in part on the basis of issue preferences, and in particular that they are aware of the differences between competing candidates in the policies they promise to put in force if they are elected.

The idea of accountability focuses on what has happened *before* the election rather than on the period following the election. It assumes that voters will have some idea of how well officeholders have carried out their duties. More important, it assumes that voters will know whether they have been helped or hurt by what officeholders have done.

Ultimately, the two ideas about how elections serve to put the people in control are very closely related. For example, if elected officials do not respond to the mandate given to them in an election, might they not be held accountable for their failure in the next election? We will find it convenient, however, to distinguish between the two ideas in our thinking about the instrumental model of elections and the way voters decide whom to support. The main reason is that accountability demands less of citizen voters than does the communication of their preferences. At its very simplest, accountability requires only that the citizen know whether she is doing well or poorly, and who the incumbent candidate is. If she is doing well (however she defines "well"), she votes for the incumbent; if things are not going well, she votes for the challenger.[2]

The Symbolic Model of Elections

The **symbolic model of elections** asserts that elections do not necessarily serve as instruments whereby the people control the government. Nor can they be understood as linking self-interest to self-interest in the manner anticipated by the Republic. Rather, as Murray Edelman put it, elections "give people a chance to express discontents and enthusiasms, to enjoy a sense of involvement." They are best understood as rituals or symbols that "draw attention to common social ties and to the importance and apparent reasonable-

---

[2]This is an admittedly minimal standard for accountability in elections. It suggests, for example, that if the voter is out of work on election day or ill or just having a bad day, he may vote against the incumbent. If this is the way voters decide, incumbents have powerful incentives to make sure that as many voters as possible are employed, healthy, and having a good day. Some people would say that this is not a bad way to describe how many officeholders behave.

ness of accepting the public policies that are adopted."[3] Rather than promoting control by the people over government, in short, elections promote control of the people by government.[4] Elections do not communicate meaningful preferences, nor can they be said to produce accountability of leaders to the public. They only *seem* to enhance these things. According to the symbolic model, the appearance of popular control is critical to the success of elections as symbols, but that appearance does not withstand close scrutiny.

The idea that elections are primarily ceremonial rituals has a ring of truth to it. Certainly the flag-waving, the balloons, the speeches evoking images of past heroes and future glories have a strong flavor of the symbolic. Elections are unique symbols both of conflict within society (debates, rhetoric against the opposition) and of that which unifies society (a common commitment among losers and winners alike to the rules of the game, concession and victory speeches that affirm a commitment to "working together").

In contrast to the instrumental model, the symbolic model of elections places only minimal expectations on the citizen. Citizens need do no more than believe that elections matter, that their participation is important, and that they have a duty to participate. We saw in Chapter 2 that the duty to vote is a very important explanation of why people participate in elections.

The instrumental and symbolic models of elections need not conflict with each other, although such theorists as Edelman posit a fundamental difference between them when they assert that elections only *appear* to put the people in charge. But those who see some degree of validity in the instrumental model would not deny the symbolic aspect of elections. After all, elections do offer an opportunity to celebrate the democratic character of the political process. And if the instrumental model of elections is correct, such a celebration may be entirely appropriate. Nonetheless, the symbolic model of elections offers a critical perspective on the role of elections in the Republic. Most of the analysis in this chapter focuses on the instrumental ideal because it is so central to the Republic, and because many critics of contemporary American politics are so concerned with enhancing some version of the instrumental ideal. However, the symbolic model alerts us to the possibility that elections serve functions other than and even contrary to those anticipated by the Republic.

---

[3]Murray Edelman, *The Symbolic Uses of Politics* (Urbana: University of Illinois Press, 1964), p. 3.

[4]For some interesting evidence to support the notion that participation in elections brings about more favorable attitudes toward the government, see Benjamin Ginsberg, *The Consequences of Consent: Elections, Citizen Control, and Popular Acquiescence* (Reading, Mass.: Addison-Wesley, 1982).

In attempting to understand how citizens make their choices in elections, we must come to grips with some essentials. In particular, if the instrumental model of elections is to be vindicated, it must get past some rather harsh realities about how citizens relate to elections. I present these ideas in the form of two propositions:

1. *Politics is remote from the concerns of most citizens most of the time.* That is to say, politics does not have much **salience** to the average citizen. Politics is not central to the citizen's perception of his well-being; people generally do not care very much about what goes on in the world of politics, nor do they expend much energy in becoming informed or in pursuing their own interest. This is a proposition quite at odds with Madison's argument about human nature, factions, and self-interest in politics.

The reasons behind this departure from the Republic are easy to see. They relate directly to the paradox of collective action (discussed in Chapter 2). To have an interest in politics would be to pursue goals consistent with one's self-interest, to join a faction "actuated by a common impulse of interest or of passion," in Madison's words. Yet the paradox of collective action tells us that citizens, though they may have an interest in political outcomes, will not help produce those outcomes if they can be free riders. In the case of an election, the outcome is usually a collective good that the citizen cannot reasonably expect to affect.[5]

The most immediate implication of the low salience of politics is that most people are not very well informed. Information is costly, and citizens are generally unwilling to make a special effort to collect it because politics is remote. Countless surveys report that large percentages of Americans do not know basic facts about the political system, candidates running in elections, or common terminology used by the media to describe political debate.[6] Consider Table 3-1. In national surveys conducted following the 1982 and 1984 elections, respondents were asked to indicate which party controlled the House and Senate both before and after each

---

[5]Most of the things that really excite the average citizen's passions and interest are in the private, not the public, realm. For example, most people devote a lot more energy to their careers and families than they do to public affairs. Success in a career or in raising a family is a private good. More or less, you get what you pay for, and there are no free riders. So these things are more salient than politics.

[6]For many examples of the low levels of information among the public on a variety of questions related to public affairs, see Robert Weissberg, *Public Opinion and Popular Government* (Englewood Cliffs, N.J.: Prentice-Hall, 1976), pp. 32–43.

Table 3-1 Percentage of American Electorate with High Level of Information, 1982 and 1984, by Voting Activity, Level of Political Interest, and Education Level

Year	Eligible voters	Non-voters	Voters	Level of political interest			Level of education		
				Low	Medium	High	Grade school	High school grad	Some college
1982	20	8	29	9	22	32	8	14	32
1984	26	11	31	10	22	44	13	18	38

NOTE: Respondents were considered to have a high level of information if they answered correctly at least three of four quesions about which party controlled each house of Congress before and after the election.
SOURCE: Center for Political Studies, University of Michigan, *American National Election Study, 1982* and *American National Election Study, 1984* (Ann Arbor: Interuniversity Consortium for Political and Social Research, 1984, 1986).

election.[7] This information is potentially important for the citizen to have, because without it the voter might have difficulty determining whom to blame (or credit) for the results of congressional actions.

Several important points can be made in regard to Table 3-1. First, only a minority of the electorate—both of those eligible to vote and of those who actually voted—was well informed about which party controlled the two chambers of Congress. Note also that voters are considerably better informed than nonvoters. This finding is consistent with the argument in Chapter 2 that voters have more resources than nonvoters (hence they are better able to bear information costs) and that voters are more interested in politics than nonvoters. In short, politics varies in salience, and it is more salient to those who participate than it is to those who do not. Indeed, Table 3-1 shows that people ranked high in political interest are considerably more likely to be well informed than those who are not interested in politics. And it is no surprise to see that people with more education are better informed than people with less education.

But recognize that low levels of information are not the result of stupidity or of a perverse refusal to understand politics. Rather, people will not go out of their way to collect political information. Even among those who are highly interested or who have a college education, only a minority are well informed. Those who acquire political information normally pick it up quite casually.[8]

Finally, note that overall levels of information were slightly higher in 1984 than in 1982. This finding does not indicate that information levels are increasing. Rather, it is almost certainly due to the fact that 1984 was a presidential election year, whereas 1982 was a midterm election. When a presidential election is under way, much more free information about politics is available in the media. Indeed, it is difficult to avoid information in TV and radio ads, network news, and the like. Less information is easily available in the absence of a presidential race, and as a result, the public is less well informed and less likely to vote. This difference in information levels between presidential and congressional elections has im-

---

[7]Before and after both the 1982 and 1984 elections, Republicans held a majority in the Senate and Democrats had a majority in the House. Confusion arises in the minds of inattentive citizens because of this situation of divided control, and because the Republicans also held the White House.

[8]After all, people rated high on political information because they know which party controlled Congress have not passed a very rigorous test of their political information. For a more complete analysis of political information and its effects, see W. Russell Neuman, *The Paradox of Mass Politics: Knowledge and Opinion in the American Electorate* (Cambridge: Harvard University Press, 1986).

plications for the way people vote in the two kinds of elections. The important thing to see at this point is that Madison's argument about self-interest must be modified to recognize that most people do not think of politics as intensely interesting. They often do not participate, and when they do, they may well lack basic information about the political process.

2. *Politics is a fundamentally ambiguous realm of activity.* The **ambiguity of politics** results in part from its complexity. The American constitutional and institutional structure is complicated. As proposals make their way through the legislative labyrinth, many individuals and groups get into the act, so that the task of tracing the origins or effects of proposed legislation can be very difficult. Complexity and ambiguity result also from the difficulty of solving contemporary issues of public policy. What is the best way to manage the national economy? What are the likely effects of proposed changes in the tax system? Will a reduction in certain weapons systems increase the chance for peace? These and dozens of similar questions confound the experts. What is the ordinary citizen to think?

In addition to the inherent complexity of modern political issues, ambiguity results from the very enterprise of politics. Consider the kinds of questions the thoughtful voter must ask about the candidates before she makes her choice. How competent, honest, responsible, and moral is each candidate likely to be if he or she is elected to the office in question? Such questions are almost impossible to answer. Even the candidates themselves may have great difficulty answering them if they are completely honest with themselves. In the case of an incumbent running for reelection, the best guide would probably be found in his or her past behavior. But even that criterion presents immense ambiguity. Take the question of how guilty a sitting president is when a scandal rocks his administration. When serious questions were raised about officials in the Reagan administration who sold arms to Iran and diverted the proceeds to the *contra* rebels in Nicaragua, it was very difficult to know just how responsible the president was for whatever misconduct occurred. In the case of the Watergate scandal under Richard Nixon, after extended debate in the media, the courts, and the Congress, and even following Nixon's resignation from office, many citizens were not at all sure just how guilty he actually was.[9] In choosing between candidates, voters are asked to pass judgment on motives and abilities. Can anyone doubt that these judgments must be made on the basis of incomplete and tentative information?

---

[9]George C. Edwards III, *The Public Presidency* (New York: St. Martin's Press, 1983).

How do people react to the ambiguity of politics? This is the important question, and the answer is not simple. One part of the answer is that much of the ambiguity of politics is ignored. Because politics is remote, people have little tolerance for its ambiguities and complexities. They tend to make snap judgments about a politician's guilt or innocence, competence or incompetence. To do otherwise would be to introduce intolerably high information costs. Because of the complexity and ambiguity of politics, moreover, some evidence can almost always be found on both sides of a question. People who decide that a president is not competent can point to failures in the administration, mixups in policy, and unwise appointments to lower offices. Those who decide that the same president is doing a good job can point to an upswing in employment or to reduced inflation or to a prolonged period of international tranquility. Both will be "right" in that the record provides examples supportive of both positions. But both are also reading that record selectively. There is much wisdom in the maxim that one should not argue about politics.

The ambiguity of politics cuts deeper than a tendency to make snap judgments. Social psychologists have recognized for a long time that human beings unconsciously strive to maintain "cognitive balance" in their perceptions of the world. That is, perceptions are often slanted to be consistent with beliefs that are already held about an object *even when the perceptions are manifestly contrary to reality.*[10]

This principle works in a variety of ways, but a simple example from a recent presidential election will illustrate the phenomenon. In 1984 Walter Mondale ran as the Democratic party's nominee and Ronald Reagan ran for a second term as the Republican nominee. As in all presidential elections, the candidates took positions on a variety of issues. They did so in their speeches, in their answers to questions in press conferences, and in published position papers. They also associated themselves with their political parties, both of which were known to have taken long-standing positions on some of the issues debated in 1984. To be sure, sometimes candidates tend to be ambiguous on the issues. But candidates' positions on issues are less ambiguous than the question of their competence or trustworthiness as potential officeholders. Nonetheless, consider how citizens perceived the candidates' positions on the issues.

---

[10]For a very readable description of the theory of "cognitive dissonance"—or "balance," as it is often called—see Elliot Aranson, *The Social Animal* (San Francisco: W. H. Freeman, 1972), chap. 4. For an application of the theory to political attitudes and behavior, see Bernard C. Hennessy, *Public Opinion*, 5th ed. (Pacific Grove, Calif.: Brooks/Cole, 1985), pp. 320–321.

Cognitive balance theory suggests that individuals who like a candidate for whatever reason will tend subconsciously to bring their perceptions of candidates' positions on the issues into line with their own preferences.[11] This sort of psychological adjustment of perceived reality may be referred to as **rationalization.** Table 3-2 shows evidence of rationalization among citizens in the 1984 election. The issue in question is whether the U.S. national government should attempt to guarantee jobs and a reasonable standard of living to every citizen. In a national survey, respondents were asked to give their own opinions on this issue *and* to indicate where they thought Ronald Reagan and Walter Mondale stood on the question. Notice that respondents who liked Ronald Reagan exhibited a marked tendency to see his position on the issue as agreeing with their own opinion. Among respondents who thought that the national government should guarantee jobs, over half saw Reagan as taking the same position. Of those who took the opposite position and thought the government should let people get ahead on their own, 92 percent thought Reagan agreed with them on this issue. The effect was not so strong among respondents who liked Walter Mondale, but it still existed. Those who favored government guarantees

Table 3-2 Respondents' Positions and Perceptions of Candidates' Positions on the "Government Guarantee of Jobs" Issue, 1984

		Respondents who liked Ronald Reagan			Respondents who liked Walter Mondale		
		Perceptions of Reagan's position on government guarantee of jobs			Perceptions of Mondale's position on government guarantee of jobs		
		Reagan Favors	Reagan Opposes		Mondale Favors	Mondale Opposes	
Respondents' own position on government guarantee of jobs issue	Favors (%)	55	45	100%	86	14	100%
	Opposes (%)	8	92	100%	55	45	100%

NOTE: Respondents were asked the following question: "Some people feel the government in Washington should see to it that every person has a job and a good standard of living. Others think the government should just let each person get ahead on his own. Where would you place yourself on this issue, or haven't you thought much about this?" They were then asked to say where they thought Reagan and Mondale stood on the issue. Those without an opinion on the issue of government guarantee of jobs or who could not place the candidates on the issue were excluded from the analysis.
SOURCE: Center for Political Studies, University of Michigan; *American National Election Study, 1984* (Ann Arbor: Interuniversity Consortium for Political and Social Research, 1986), pp. 210–211.

[11]Or the process may be reversed. Individuals may bring their own opinions on the issues into line with their perceptions of the candidate's positions.

of jobs were noticeably more likely than those who opposed govern-ment guarantees to see Mondale as also favoring that position. The cognitive balance theory predicts such results. People rationalize their perceptions of the candidates' stands on the issues (or alter their own opinions) in order to promote balance among their attrac-tion to the candidate, their own issue preferences, and their per-ceptions of the candidates' positions.

Table 3-2 shows that a significant portion of the electorate misperceived the candidates' positions. This sort of rationalization probably results from **selective perception,** or a tendency to see the world in ways that reinforce what one already believes. Even the stands that candidates take on issues contribute to the ambiguity of politics, making it easier for each person to interpret them as supporting his or her particular point of view. The ability of ambiguity to encourage selective perception is not good news for the instrumental model of elections, nor is it consistent with the Republic. It complicates the way self-interest works in politics be-cause it means that voters may *think* they are voting in their self-interest (that is, voting for a candidate who favors the same policy they favor) when in fact they are voting against their self-interest. In the case of the issue analyzed in Table 3-2, most impartial observers would agree that Ronald Reagan strongly preferred not to use the resources of the national government to guarantee a job to every citizen, while Walter Mondale was much more inclined to do so. Yet a significant proportion of the survey respondents misperceived both candidates' positions as being in agreement with their own preferences on the issue.

In fairness to the American public, we do not want to overstate the case. If people tend to see in their favorite candidate what they want to see, the tendency is hardly an iron law. Forty-five percent of those who liked Ronald Reagan and who wanted the government to guarantee jobs recognized that President Reagan disagreed with them. Likewise, a majority of those on both sides of the issue saw Mondale as favoring government guarantees. This tendency to mis-perceive candidates' positions coupled with a generally correct pic-ture of where the candidates stand is a pattern that holds on a wide variety of issues.

The implications of the two propositions—that politics is re-mote and ambiguous—will take some time to develop fully. Indeed, they extend well beyond the boundaries of this chapter. However, their importance for an explanation of voting choice cannot be overstated. We cannot assume the citizen is deeply interested in politics, nor should we expect voters to expend much energy to gather information. If the instrumental model of elections is to work, the citizen needs a **cost-effective way to vote.** That is, the way the voter chooses between competing candidates must not require much effort, but it must nonetheless result in a vote that approximates her self-interest.

A Cost-Effective Way to Vote?

Ideology

Many people think of ideology as a nasty element in politics. "Ideologues" are often considered to be unthinking "extremists," wild-eyed radicals who pursue their schemes without regard for the rights and wishes of others. Such people engage in unconventional and violent forms of political participation such as kidnappings and acts of terrorism.

But when political scientists refer to ideology, they have in mind a much more benign (and common) approach to political life. Indeed, ideology might provide the citizen with a cost-effective way to cast a self-interested vote. To see how it can do so, we must set aside the limited, popular view of ideology as linked to extremist political ideas of one sort or another and adopt the broader understanding of ideology as political scientists use the term.

An **ideology** is a package of ideas, a way of organizing one's thinking about political issues and leaders.[12] It is anchored by one or more core values or beliefs that serve to structure the other ideas encompassed by the ideology. A substantial portion of the ideological conflict in American politics is captured by the differences between liberals and conservatives. A core value that distinguishes between them and influences their positions on a variety of political issues is whether government should actively promote individual equality (Figure 3-1). Liberals are often concerned about economic and social equality and feel the government should promote it. Unless the government uses its power to help the disadvantaged, people with economic or political resources will use their assets to enhance their relative advantage. As a result of their position on this core value, then, liberals generally argue for a progressive tax structure, and they are more likely to want to raise taxes as a way to redistribute wealth. They also support civil rights policies that enforce equality between the races and the sexes (such as affirmative action and busing programs); they are in favor of various kinds of welfare policies, from educational programs to expanded health and unemployment benefits; and they are quite willing to regulate

---

[12]This definition relies heavily on Philip Converse's classic analysis in "The Nature of Belief Systems in the Mass Public," in *Ideology and Discontent*, David E. Apter (New York: Free Press, 1964), pp. 206–261.

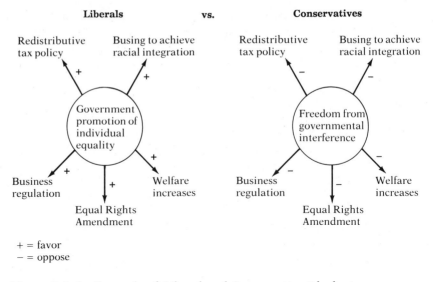

Figure 3-1 An Example of Liberal and Conservative Ideologies

business activities to protect the worker and the consumer from potential threats to safety or from various kinds of exploitation.

Conservatives disagree with liberals on all of the issues depicted in Figure 3-1 because they disagree about the core value. They identify government as a potential threat to individual freedom and are loath to add significantly to its power. In contrast to government-sponsored equality, they value freedom from intrusion by the government in private lives, including the economic activities of citizens and the marketplace. It is not so much that they oppose equality (any more than liberals oppose freedom) as that they value freedom more than an equality brought about by government policy. The issue is a central one for liberals and conservatives because conservatives view many government attempts to promote equality as infringements on freedom, whereas liberals believe that true freedom is not possible without equality.[13]

How is ideology a potentially cost-effective way for the citizen to vote? Consider the plight of the citizen who wishes to vote in a

---

[13]This description of the differences between liberals and conservatives is overly simple and incomplete. It does not include, for example, differences on foreign policy issues, nor does it address conflict over civil liberties or questions of "public morality." The broader the scope of an ideology, the more sloppy it becomes as a shared perspective on political conflict. For instance, most liberals support affirmative action programs, are "pro-choice" on the abortion issue, and favor significant cuts in the defense budget. But that particular combination of issue positions is not logically required by a single core value, and could change.

Senate election for the candidate who best represents his interests. One way of proceeding would be to find out where each candidate stands on all the policy issues under debate or likely to be faced by the Senate in the next six years. This task obviously is unlikely to be carried out by the typical voter. But what if our voter has an ideology? If, for example, he is a liberal, he need only find out which of the two candidates is more liberal. That information is quite readily available. Democratic candidates are usually more liberal than Republican candidates. The mass media often use the terms "liberal" and "conservative" to describe candidates, so even cursory attention to the press would probably yield the necessary information. An ideological voter need not know where each candidate stands on a variety of issues in order to cast a self-interested ballot. Indeed, a citizen with an ideology can vote *as if* he were well informed without knowing where the candidates stand on all the current issues, what other issues may arise before the next election, or what the candidates have done while holding office in the past. The ideological voter who is told that candidate *A* is more liberal than candidate *B* has enough information to vote in a cost-effective manner because he can predict reasonably accurately (though not perfectly) where each candidate stands on a variety of issues. Given the costs of gathering more complete information, that's not a bad way to proceed.

But there is a problem with ideology as a cost-effective way for people to vote: most people do not think about politics in ideological terms. To be sure, it is possible to ask people to place themselves on an ideological scale from "extremely liberal" to "extremely conservative," as was done in a 1984 survey of the American electorate (see Figure 3-2). Notice that the largest percentage of respondents indicate they don't know where they belong on the scale. The second largest percentage is composed of those who place themselves in the "moderate" category. In fact, fewer than half of the respondents were willing (or able) to place themselves on the liberal or conservative side of the scale. More detailed studies indicate that most voters do not think in ideological ways about politics. Issue positions do not generally hang together in ways consistent with a central ideological value.[14]

This is not to say that ideology is irrelevant to voting choice among those in the electorate who think ideologically. But there are

---

[14]The studies are numerous and controversial. See Converse, "Nature of Belief Systems," and Philip E. Converse, "Public Opinion and Voting Behavior," in *Handbook of Political Science*, ed. Fred Greenstein and Nelson Polsby, vol. 4 (Reading, Mass.: Addison-Wesley, 1975), pp. 75–169, for work that supports this conclusion. For a summary of the controversies and an extension of Converse's work, see Neumann, *Paradox of Mass Politics*.

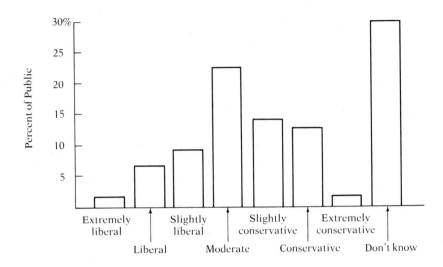

Figure 3-2 Ideological Positions of American Public on Liberal–
Conservative Scale, 1984 (percent). NOTE: Respondents were asked: "We
hear a lot of talk these days about liberals and conservatives. Here is a
seven-point scale on which the political views that people might hold
are arranged from extremely liberal to extremely conservative. Where
would you place yourself on this scale, or haven't you thought much
about this?" The "Don't know" category includes respondents who said
they hadn't thought much about the matter as well as those who said
they didn't know.
SOURCE: Center for Political Studies, University of Michigan, *American
National Election Study, 1984* (Ann Arbor: Interuniversity Consortium for
Political and Social Research, 1986), pp. 186–187.

several reasons why ideology is not a cost-effective decision rule for
the electorate at large. First, thinking about the central values
involved in an ideological position and linking those values to various issue positions are themselves difficult and time-consuming
tasks. People who are used to thinking abstractly are most likely to
adopt and employ an ideological framework. In 1984, 72 percent of
college graduates adopted some ideological label other than "moderate," whereas only 27 percent of respondents with grade school
educations did so.[15]

Just as important, however, American elections are not normally conducted in highly ideological ways. Candidates usually do not
clearly associate themselves with extreme ideological views, nor do
the political parties trumpet their ideological differences (although

[15]Computed from Center for Political Studies, University of Michigan, *American
National Election Study, 1984* (Ann Arbor: Interuniversity Consortium for Political
and Social Research, 1986).

the differences can be seen if one looks for them). The exceptions prove the rule. When candidates take reasonably clear ideological stands, the electorate responds by increasing its level of ideological thinking, by linking various issues together in more tightly organized ideological patterns, and by voting more along ideological lines.[16]

So ideology cannot provide the cost-effective means of voting we are looking for. It certainly has the potential to do so for those who make the effort, and we could suppose that more people would think ideologically if parties and candidates presented themselves in overtly ideological ways. Ideology is present, and it is relevant to voters' choices, but it is not widespread enough to be the whole story.

Party Identification

Party identification takes us much closer than does ideology to an adequate explanation of voting choice, although it too remains unsatisfactory in some important respects. The concept of **party identification** is best thought of as a standing decision the individual makes about the two political parties in American electoral politics. The decision is not irrevocable by any means, nor does it always determine the voter's choice. But it is the single most profound influence on the typical citizen's vote, so it is important to understand how it works.

One way of thinking about the standing decision is to think of the citizen as saying to himself, "Unless I hear otherwise, the Democratic [Republican] party is for me." Of course, the citizen actually says nothing of the kind. But the statement is a useful fiction because it acknowledges that politics is not very salient to the citizen. "Unless I hear otherwise" means "I am willing to vote without information. If I am to hear otherwise, it will be because someone else has told me. I will not actively seek information." This stand is possible because, aside from the names of the candidates, party is the one piece of information provided on the ballot in national and almost all state elections. The voter can go to the polls without remembering the names of the candidates, without hearing any speeches by the candidates, without reading any position papers or seeing any ads, and without talking with anyone about the campaign. So long as the voter has made the standing decision—so long

---

[16]Norman H. Nie, Sidney Verba, and John R. Petrocik, *The Changing American Voter*, enl. ed. (Cambridge: Harvard University Press, 1979). For some intriguing evidence on Senate elections, see Alan I. Abramowitz, "Choices and Echoes in the 1978 U.S. Senate Elections: A Research Note," *American Journal of Political Science* 25 (1981): 112–118.

as she identifies with one of the parties—she can cast a vote that is consistent with her decision.

"Unless I hear otherwise" also means that the standing decision may not be appropriate for a given race. The voter may cast a vote contrary to his party identification if he encounters information that overrides it. He may learn as the result of talk at his workplace that his party's nominee supports an issue position he does not like—busing schoolchildren to achieve racial balance in local schools, for example, or abortion on demand. Or the party's nominee may have been involved in a scandal, or may simply be widely perceived as incompetent. If the voter encounters information of this sort, he may defect from his standing decision. Most often, such information does not cause the voter to change the standing decision altogether. Rather, the voter who identifies with the Democratic party may simply vote Republican in that particular year for that particular office.

Party identification has other properties that help us to understand voting choice. But before we go into detail, consider the data in Table 3-3. The first row of the table shows the party identi-

Table 3-3 Party Identification and Candidate Choice, 1984 (percent)

	Democrats	Independents	Republicans	Don't know
Party identification	48%	11%	39%	2%
Vote for president				
Reagan	22%	78%	95%	
Mondale	78	22	5	
Total	100%	100%	100%	
Vote for House of Representatives				
Republican	19%	38%	73%	
Democratic	81	62	27	
Total	100%	100%	100%	

NOTE: To establish party identification, respondents were first asked, "Generally speaking, do you usually think of yourself as a Republican, a Democrat, an independent, or what?" Those who indicated they were Republican or Democrat were then asked, "Would you call yourself a strong Republican [Democrat] or a not very strong Republican [Democrat]?" Those who said they were independent were asked, "Do you think of yourself as closer to the Republican party or to the Democratic party?" The 48% of respondents who identified themselves as Democrats or as leaning toward the Democratic party break down as follows: strong Democrats, 17%; weak Democrats, 20%; independent Democrats, 11%. The 39% who identified themselves as Republicans or as leaning toward the Republican party break down as follows: strong Republicans, 12%, weak Republicans, 15%; independent Republicans, 12%.

SOURCE: Center for Political Studies, University of Michigan, *American National Election Study, 1984* (Ann Arbor: Interuniversity Consortium for Political and Social Research, 1986).

fications of the American electorate in 1984. If we include in-

dependents who "lean" toward a party as identifying with that
party, 48 percent of the public identify with the Democratic party
and 39 percent identify with the Republicans. Notice that, in contrast to responses to the ideology question (Figure 3-2), only 2
percent say they don't know, and just 11 percent remain strict
independents, failing to express a general partisan predisposition.
This finding results from the fact that the parties are so visible in
American electoral politics. Most people have no trouble thinking
about their political preferences in a partisan framework, whereas
an ideological predisposition is much more abstract and removed
from their thinking.

When we examine the relationships between party identification and voting choice in the 1984 presidential and House elections,
we find a marked tendency for partisans to vote for the party with
which they identified, although some Democrats and some Republicans voted in opposition to their partisanship. In the presidential
vote, Democrats were more than four times more likely than Republicans to defect. This finding does not necessarily indicate that
Republicans are more loyal than Democrats. Rather, Reagan was
doubtless a more attractive candidate than Mondale. The fact that
independents voted overwhelmingly for the incumbent president is
just one indicator. Indeed, one can see that Republicans were *less*
loyal to their party in House elections than Democrats were. Again,
this finding is almost surely due to candidate factors: in the 435
House elections, more Democratic candidates than Republicans
were incumbents. As we shall see, incumbency is a significant
advantage in House elections, one that probably accounts for the
high Republican defection rate as well as the tendency of independents to vote Democratic.

Implications of Party Identification

Does party identification offer hope that the typical citizen will vote
in an instrumentally self-interested way, thus promoting electoral
accountability and communication? To answer this question, we
must look in more detail at the way party identification affects
voting choice and voters' perceptions of politics.

First, it must be said that party identification *is* cost-effective
for the citizen. It allows voters to avoid significant information
costs. It permits them to reduce the ambiguity of politics by making
a standing decision. If party identification were to result from a
careful comparison of the parties and what they stand for, it would
have the same potential as ideology for promoting instrumental
voting in elections. But that is a big if. We know that a careful
comparison of the parties is not likely, because politics does not

enjoy high salience among most citizens. Moreover, research shows that party identification most often results from learning acquired in the family.[17] Young children usually develop the rudiments of a party loyalty without being aware of what the parties stand for or what the issues and candidates are like.[18] Thus party identification may permit the voter to make a choice, even without information, but that choice may not be consistent with his or her instrumental self-interest.

Selective Perception

Selective perception, as we have seen, is an important means to reduce the ambiguity of politics. Particularly when reality presents a complex and indefinite front, selective perception protects cognitive balance. When a reasonably strong attitude such as party identification already exists, selective perception generally protects the existing attitude. In this way, party identification can serve as a "perceptual screen" or lens through which citizens view political events, candidates, and issues.[19] The characteristics that Democrats see in a political leader tend to differ from the characteristics Republicans see, or adherents of the two parties evaluate what they see differently in order subconsciously to maintain cognitive balance.

Figure 3-3 displays evidence of the effects of party identification on respondents' perceptions of the two presidential candidates in 1984. A general pattern is very clear. Republicans were much more likely than Democrats to rate Ronald Reagan positively on several characteristics. Indeed, the tendency to rate Reagan positively increases steadily with each step on the party identification scale. A similar (though less dramatic) effect is evident in respondents' ratings of Walter Mondale, the Democratic nominee. Democrats were a good deal more positive in their evaluation of their party's candidate than were those who identified with the GOP. These findings are entirely consistent with the concept of selective perception. Because candidates present ambiguous images (Does Reagan really provide strong leadership? Is he fair?), citizens tend to see in them the side that reinforces their loyalty to their party. Republicans saw the positive side of Reagan's character and by doing so subconsciously protected their cognitive balance by favoring their party's candidate. Democrats observed negative qualities in the

---

[17]M. Kent Jennings and Richard G. Niemi, *Generations and Politics* (Princeton: Princeton University Press, 1981).
[18]Fred I. Greenstein, *Children and Politics* (New Haven: Yale University Press, 1965).
[19]Angus Campbell, Philip E. Converse, Warren E. Miller, and Donald E. Stokes, *The American Voter* (New York: Wiley, 1960), chap. 6.

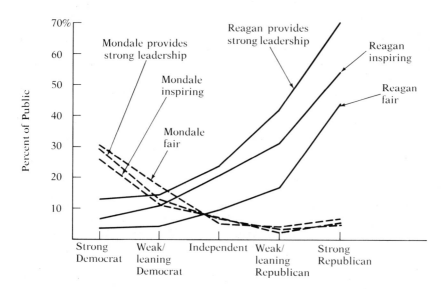

Figure 3-3 Effects of Party Identification on Ratings of Presidential
Candidates, 1984 (percent). NOTE: The question put to respondents was:
"I am going to read a list of words and phrases people may use to describe political figures. For each, please tell me whether the word or
phrase describes the candidate I name." Respondents were then asked
to respond to words as they applied to both Reagan and Mondale. The
respondents represented here said that the indicated traits fitted the
candidate named "very well."
SOURCE: Center for Political Studies, University of Michigan, *American
National Election Study, 1984* (Ann Arbor: Interuniversity Consortium for
Political and Social Research, 1986), pp. 169–179.

Republican party's candidate because they brought to the campaign a prior commitment to the opposing party.[20]

The process of selective perception does not render partisans
blind to the qualities of candidates, nor does it completely distort an
individual's judgment. Respondents of all partisan persuasions

---

[20]Of course, a different way of accounting for the data in Figure 3-3 is possible.
Rather than permitting their perceptions of the candidates to be influenced by their
party identification, those who see positive qualities in the Republican nominee may
adopt a party identification consistent with their positive evaluation of the party's
nominee. Such an explanation would mean that party identification is not a "standing decision." There is some truth (but only some) to the idea that party identification
is subject to change and modification, particularly over an extended period of time.
For example, if a party were to nominate a series of presidential candidates whom a
citizen found obnoxious, that person's party identification might gradually weaken
and even shift to the opposite party. On this point, see Morris P. Fiorina, *Retrospective
Voting in American National Elections* (New Haven: Yale University Press, 1981),
especially chap. 5.

generally agreed in rating President Reagan higher as a strong leader than they did as fair. The effect of partisanship is very strong; Reagan was rated much more highly on leadership by Republicans than by Democrats, but all were able to see that leadership was relatively high among Reagan's assets. Compare also the judgments of Reagan by members of his party with the judgments of Mondale by his fellow Democrats. There is no doubt that Reagan was dramatically more successful in appealing to Republicans than was Mondale in his appeal to Democrats.

The tendency of party identification to serve as a perceptual lens through which politics is viewed helps explain its importance to voting choice. Figure 3-4 depicts a model of voting choice which places party identification in the context of other factors that influence the vote.[21] Note first that a purely instrumental conception of elections would probably involve only "issue preferences" and "candidate evaluations" as influencing the voting decision. Figure 3-4 includes these factors, but they are themselves influenced by party identification. As we have seen, evaluation of candidates is powerfully influenced by party identification, and people's opinions

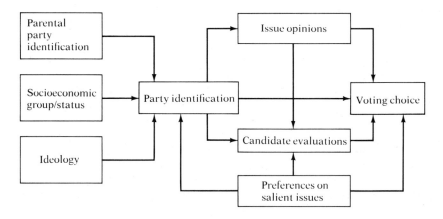

Figure 3-4 A Model of Voting Choice

---

[21]Several sources are relevant to this model. See Arthur S. Goldberg, "Discerning a Causal Pattern among Data on Voting Behavior," *American Political Science Review* 60 (1966): 913–922; and Mark A. Schulman and Gerald M. Pomper, "Variability in Electoral Behavior: Longitudinal Perspectives from Causal Modeling," *American Journal of Political Science* 19 (1975): 1–18, for attempts to estimate models similar to Figure 3-4. For an excellent general discussion of research on party identification, see Herbert B. Asher, "Voting Behavior Research in the 1980s: An Examination of Some Old and New Problem Areas," in *Political Science: The State of the Discipline*, ed. Ada W. Finifter (Washington, D.C.: American Political Science Association, 1983), pp. 339–388.

on policy issues that are not very salient to them are also influenced by party.[22]

Observe that "preferences on salient issues" are outside the purview of party identification. When a truly salient issue emerges in the course of a campaign, especially when candidates take clearly different positions on the issue, it can override the tendency toward selective perception and determine candidate evaluation and voting choice.[23] There are always some people who are powerfully motivated by an issue. In recent elections, for example, a small minority of voters have cared very deeply about abortion. These voters know where the candidates stand on the issue (they do not selectively perceive the candidates' positions) and they vote accordingly. Some issues may be salient to a large proportion of the electorate. The war in Vietnam and what to do about it, for example, was a salient issue to many voters in 1972. Those who wanted to end the war by withdrawing from the field of combat had in George McGovern a presidential candidate who represented their views.

A salient issue (or cluster of issues) can also influence party identification and bring about a change in partisanship. When such a change occurs on a massive scale, political scientists call it a realignment.[24] Many people have argued, for example, that the realignment of the 1930s resulted from the Great Depression, which created highly salient issues related to government's role in managing the economy and protecting individuals from economic and social hardship. The Democratic party supported governmental action on these fronts, while the Republican party was reluctant to expand the role of government. Many people reacted to these new issues and to the parties' positions on them by rethinking their partisanship or by turning out to vote for the party that best represented their views. The Republican party had been the majority party before the Depression, and the Democrats have enjoyed majority status since then. More recently the issue of racial integration has caused many white southerners to switch their allegiance

------

[22]Some highly technical questions surround the matter of how much influence party identification has on opinions on issues and candidates, and how much those opinions influence party identification. An excellent attempt to unravel the reciprocal effects involved is Charles H. Franklin and John E. Jackson, "The Dynamics of Party Identification," *American Political Science Review* 77 (December 1983): 957–973. See also Fiorina, *Retrospective Voting.* Without denying that party identification serves as a powerful force on citizens' perceptions of candidates and issues, these studies show that it is subject to change as a result of the individual's experience in elections.

[23]David E. Repass, "Issue Salience and Party Choice," *American Political Science Review* 65 (June 1971): 389–400.

[24]James L. Sundquist, *Dynamics of the Party System* (Washington, D.C.: Brookings Institution, 1973).

from the Democratic to the Republican party, especially in their presidential voting.[25]

Some of the factors in the formation of party identification are also included in Figure 3-4. The strongest is probably parental influence. A well-developed political ideology is usually reflected in party identification. And there is a connection (although not a very strong one) between socioeconomic factors (such as occupation, level of education and income, and race) and party loyalty.

Information Costs and the Effect of Party Identification

The impact of party identification on voting choice varies with the amount of information readily available during the campaign. The more free information available, the more likely voters are to hear things that cause them to vote against their party identification. The more information, the less likely it is that perception will be selective and the more knowledgeable about the candidates and issues the voter will be. An important example of varying amounts of information relates to candidates' behavior in presidential elections. When candidates' stands on the issues are easily recognized as different from each other, the **information costs** to the voter of differentiating between the candidates are relatively low. In contrast, when candidates take positions that are ambiguous or that are very close to each other, the costs to voters of figuring out which candidate's position is closer to their views are high.

Two examples from the not-too-distant past which illustrate the differences are the presidential elections of 1972 and 1976. In 1972 George McGovern was nominated by the Democratic party to run against the incumbent president, Richard Nixon. McGovern went to unusual lengths to distinguish his issue positions from those of the president, especially with respect to the war in Vietnam. He was a visible critic of the war and made it clear that he favored withdrawal of U.S. troops from the Southeast Asian conflict.[26] McGovern also addressed a number of other issues, including the penalties associated with marijuana use, amnesty for draft-age men who resisted conscription, and economic and welfare issues. In all of these cases, McGovern associated himself with liberal positions, thus differentiating his candidacy from that of Richard Nixon.

In 1976, neither the Democratic nominee, Jimmy Carter, nor

---

[25]Bruce A. Campbell, "Patterns of Change in the Partisan Loyalties of Native Southerners: 1952–1972," *Journal of Politics* 39 (August 1977): 730–761.

[26]On McGovern's candidacy, including the positions he took and the ways he modified those positions through the campaign, see Benjamin I. Page, *Choices and Echoes in Presidential Elections: Rational Man and Electoral Democracy* (Chicago: University of Chicago Press, 1978), pp. 132–142. Page's book is an excellent account of candidate strategies and their impact on voter decision making.

Gerald Ford, the Republican candidate, so clearly differentiated themselves on the issues raised during the campaign. Benjamin Page argues that incumbent presidents (including Ford in 1976) "issue the usual greetings for foreign dignitaries, general statements upon the signing or vetoing of bills, and occasional messages proposing legislation to Congress . . . but rarely discuss either present or future legislation in detail."[27] Carter, in contrast to McGovern four years earlier, did not define himself as sharply different from his opponent on the issues. Of course, the fact that both candidates were nominated by the major political parties conveys information about their likely stands on issues, as the parties' long-term records are reasonably consistent. Nonetheless, some differences in the responses of voters to the candidates in 1972 and 1976 should be evident.

Table 3-4 shows some of the ways in which the two elections differed in the clarity of voters' perceptions of the candidates. In 1972 an overwhelming majority of the electorate understood that George McGovern was more liberal than Richard Nixon on the Vietnam issue. Only 7 percent saw both candidates as taking the same stand on the issue, and an identical proportion mistakenly

Table 3-4 Perceptions of Presidential Candidates' Position on Issues, 1972 and 1976 (percent)

	1972			1976		
Issue	McGovern more liberal	Both same	McGovern more conservative	Carter more liberal	Both same	Carter more conservative
Vietnam	87%	7%	7%	—	—	—
Health insurance	—	—	—	60%	31%	10%
Inflation	40	26	34	—	—	—
Busing	—	—	—	37	30	33
Jobs guarantee	70	18	12	67	21	12
Rights of accused	53	33	14	32	44	24
Minority rights	65	23	12	47	37	16
Liberalism	84	7	9	76	12	13

NOTE: The issue and candidate placement questions were not defined to the respondents in terms of "liberal" and "conservative" positions. Rather, respondents were asked to place candidates on an issue scale defined by options associated with the particular issue. On the Vietnam issue, for example, respondents were asked to place McGovern and Nixon on a seven-point scale anchored at the extremes by "immediate withdrawal" and "complete military victory" as the policy options. For each issue I have associated the policy options identified on the seven-point scale with the generally recognized liberal and conservative positions. Respondents who could not place one or both of the candidates on the seven-point scale were excluded.

SOURCE: Center for Political Studies, University of Michigan, *American National Election Study, 1972* and *American National Election Study, 1976* (Ann Arbor: Interuniversity Consortium for Political and Social Research, 1974, 1978).

---

[27]Page, *Choices and Echoes*, pp. 168–169.

perceived McGovern as the more conservative of the two candidates. No other issue in 1972 achieved this level of clarity for the electorate, but there was a substantial consensus that McGovern was the more liberal candidate. The greatest amount of confusion was found on the question of government action against inflation: almost as many citizens saw McGovern as the more conservative candidate as saw him as more liberal than President Nixon. On the general liberal–conservative scale, there was substantial consensus that George McGovern was the more liberal candidate.

Responses on the 1976 election reveal more confusion on the part of the electorate for every issue included in the table, although respondents were nonetheless generally aware that Jimmy Carter was more liberal than Gerald Ford. The proportion of the electorate who could not distinguish between the two major-party nominees was consistently higher in 1976 than in 1972. There was also slightly more misperception of the candidates' positions on the issues. This comparison between 1972 and 1976 is consistent with more detailed research that shows that voters respond to the clarity (or lack of clarity) of the positions taken by presidential candidates in their perceptions of what the candidates stand for.[28]

In 1972, when information about the candidates was relatively cheap, one-quarter of the national electorate defected from their party identification to vote for the opposite party's nominee. In 1976, when the candidates did not differentiate themselves so clearly, the proportion of the electorate who deviated from their standing decision dropped to 15 percent. At the same time, of course, the percentage who voted in a manner consistent with their party identification increased.[29] The point should be clear: when candidates take clear positions, the impact of party identification is weaker than it is when the differences between the candidates are not so clear. This is true even in presidential elections, when in-

---

[28]"The voice of the people is but an echo. The output of an echo chamber bears an inevitable and invariable relation to the input": V. O. Key, Jr., *The Responsible Electorate: Rationality in Presidential Voting, 1936–1960* (Cambridge: Harvard University Press, 1966), p. 2. See also Gerald M. Pomper, "From Confusion to Clarity: Issues and American Voters, 1956–1968," *American Political Science Review* 66 (June 1972): 415–428.

[29]Center for Political Studies, *American National Election Study, 1972.* Over 85 percent of the defectors in 1972 were Democrats who voted for President Nixon. McGovern, in clarifying his issue positions, unwittingly took on the image of an extremist and lost millions of votes among Democrats who found his issue stands unpalatable. In almost a mirror image of the 1972 election, 1964 saw the Republican nominee, Barry Goldwater, clearly define himself as a conservative. As a result, he lost a large percentage of Republican identifiers in the electorate. That both Goldwater and McGovern lost their respective elections by a landslide was a fact not missed by future candidates who might have been tempted to clarify their issue preferences in a similar manner.

formation is relatively cheap and when the electorate is reasonably well informed about the stands the candidates take on the issues.[30]

Stability (and Instability) in National Elections

The fact that most voters have a party identification that can act as a filter for their perceptions of electoral politics has important consequences for the behavior of the electorate as a whole. It stabilizes American electoral politics by reinforcing the current two-party system. Presidential nominees of the Democratic and Republican parties receive a degree of legitimacy not available to people who run as independents or as candidates of minor parties. Major-party candidates are guaranteed millions of votes from party identifiers who grant them the benefit of the doubt.

Consider the 1980 election, in which three serious candidates ran for the presidency: Jimmy Carter as the Democratic nominee and incumbent, Ronald Reagan as the Republican nominee, and John Anderson as an independent candidate. Anderson had first sought the Republican nomination, but when it was clear that he would not be chosen, he mounted his independent general election campaign. His candidacy was an important one: he attracted just under 7 percent of the popular vote, which amounts to the support of millions of people. But there was never any doubt that once he lost the Republican party's nomination, he had no chance whatsoever of capturing the White House. He might have been successful in affecting the outcome of the election or in getting attention for some of his policy goals, but he had no chance of winning the election running as an independent.[31]

Now rerun the 1980 election as a mind experiment in which we change one simple fact. Let's give the Republican nomination to John Anderson. Let's also make Ronald Reagan a candidate, but in this version of the election, he runs as the independent candidate. Can there be any doubt that the victor of the 1980 election would *not* be Ronald Reagan? We can grant that the outcome in this hypothetical version is very much in doubt, as we cannot say whether John Anderson would have beaten Jimmy Carter, but there is no doubt

---

[30]Systematic and much more detailed analysis of presidential elections shows that the impact of issues and ideology on the vote is substantially greater in such elections as those of 1964 and 1972, when the candidates are clearly differentiated, than in elections in which the differences are not so obvious to the electorate. Even when the choice is clear, however, the impact of party identification on voting choice is greater than the independent effect of issue preferences. See Nie et al., *Changing American Voter*, p. 375.

[31]An excellent analysis of third parties in American presidential elections is offered by Steven J. Rosenstone, Roy L. Behr, and Edward H. Lazarus, *Third Parties in America* (Princeton: Princeton University Press, 1984).

that the winner would be one of the two major-party nominees. This is why the fight over the party nomination is so important. Each party has millions of supporters who identify with it—whose standing decision inclines them to support their party's nominee.

There is another way in which party identification stabilizes the electoral system. Since World War II, a majority of Americans who identify with a party have been Democrats. Moreover, as Figure 3-5 demonstrates, the percentage of Americans who identify themselves as Democrats has been quite stable (averaging 54 percent, including independents who lean toward the Democrats). Thus Democrats have an advantage over Republicans in national elections. If voters relied solely on party identification, the Democrats would win every national election. Notice that the percentage who voted Democratic in House elections through the period tracks rather closely the percentage of people who identified themselves as Democrats. One reason is that voters rely heavily on party identification when they cast their votes in House elections because information in these elections is relatively costly. As a result, the

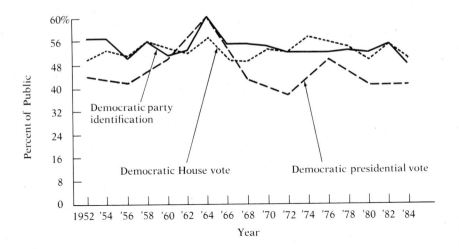

Figure 3-5 Democratic Party Identification and Democratic House and Presidential Votes, 1952–1984 (percent). SOURCES: Warren E. Miller et al., *American National Election Studies Data Sourcebook, 1952–1978* (Cambridge: Harvard University Press, 1980); Norman J. Ornstein, et al., *Vital Statistics on Congress, 1984–1985 Edition* (Washington, D.C.: American Enterprise Institute, 1984); Stephen J. Wayne, *The Road to the White House*, 3rd ed. (New York: St. Martin's Press, 1988); Center for Political Studies, University of Michigan, *American National Election Study, 1980; American National Election Study, 1982;* and *American National Election Study, 1984* (Ann Arbor: Interuniversity Consortium for Political and Social Research, 1982, 1984, 1986).

Democrats have a firm hold on the House of Representatives. In the period covered by Figure 3-5 they lost control of the House to the Republicans only once (in 1952). They regained control in the next election and have been the majority party in that chamber ever since. So long as they retain their advantage in party identification, they can be reasonably sure of continued control of the lower house.

The Democratic vote fluctuates more in presidential elections than in House races because voters are less dependent on party identification as a guide in presidential elections. As a result, party identification introduces less stability, and the vote division less closely approximates the division in party identification.[32] In 1964, for example, the Democratic candidate for president (Lyndon Johnson) won by a landslide (better than 61 percent of the vote). Just eight years later the tables were turned and the GOP candidate, Richard Nixon, won by almost as large a margin.[33]

The Incumbency Effect in House Elections

Madison believed that individuals in positions of power have an interest in retaining that power. This is the mechanism that links the interests of the people to governmental leaders and ensures representation in the Republic. But we have seen that voting in an instrumentally self-interested way is not automatic because it requires information that is costly. That citizens may not be well informed does not in any way discredit Madison's belief that representatives have a powerful interest in retaining their positions and that they will try to win reelection to satisfy this interest. The behavior of candidates in competition for the same office is important to the instrumental model of elections because the way voters choose depends on the choices they are offered. In the case of elections to the U.S. House of Representatives, there is a strong **in-**

---

[32]Throughout the period covered by Figure 3-5, the average aggregate deviation from the percentage of voters who identified with the Democratic party in House voting was 2.6 percent, whereas the average deviation in presidential voting was 7.6 percent.

[33]One question worth pondering is why the Republicans have been so successful in presidential elections (they won seven of ten between 1952 and 1988). It is an extraordinary record given their minority status, and it is a matter of considerable speculation. A short (and not very satisfactory) explanation is that they have nominated more attractive candidates than have the Democrats. Another explanation is that the Democrats have had trouble holding together their national coalition, which is extremely diverse. It is true that the Democratic party embraces northern liberals and southern conservatives, but it is not clear why Republicans should be any more successful than Democrats at assembling a national majority. They have been able to do so in part because they appeal to moderate and conservative Republicans on the basis of party identification and to conservative southern Democrats on the basis of issues and candidate appeal.

cumbency effect: voters have a marked tendency to choose incumbents more than one would expect on the basis of other factors, such as party identification and issue preferences.

The incumbency effect results from biases in the electoral process. Congressional incumbents can create and exploit an advantage over challengers who seek to replace them.[34] Because most voters do not go out of their way to become informed about House elections, they rely on the candidates to provide them with cues about how they should vote. If elections are to promote representation, the adversarial, competitive nature of campaigns must ensure a reasonably unbiased and complete flow of information from the contenders to the citizen.

But consider the evidence in Table 3-5: during the 1986 congressional election campaign, people were substantially more likely to have heard from the incumbent running in their district than from the challenger who was trying to unseat the representative. Incumbents have more resources at their disposal—more staff, more money, better access to the media—and as a result the flow of information to the citizen has a distinct bias to it. Gary Jacobson shows, for example, not only that people are more likely to have been contacted by the incumbent than by the challenger, but that as

Table 3-5 Percentage of Respondents Who Reported
Contact with Incumbent U.S. Representative
and with Challenger, 1986, by Type of Contact

Type of contact	Incumbent	Challenger
Met candidate personally	12%	3%
Saw candidate at public meeting	10	2
Contact with candidate's staff	9	1
Received mail from candidate	58	12
Read about candidate in newspaper	52	21
Heard about candidate on radio	26	8
Saw candidate on TV	50	19

NOTE: Respondents in districts without an incumbent seeking reelection or in districts where the incumbent was unopposed were excluded from the analysis.
SOURCE: Center for Political Studies, University of Michigan, *American National Election Study, 1986* (Ann Arbor: Interuniversity Consortium for Political and Social Research, 1988).

---

[34]The nature and reasons for the advantages enjoyed by incumbents are explored in greater depth in Chap. 6. Suffice it to say here that incumbents (who, after all, are lawmakers) benefit from resources they have given themselves and have not given to challengers trying to unseat them.

a result they are more likely to recognize the incumbent's name and to think highly of the representative.[35] Recognition of the name of a candidate and positive feelings toward him or her are important influences on voting choice, especially when information is scarce and expensive for the voter to get. That is a difficult advantage for a challenger to overcome.

Since candidates are not known for spreading negative information about themselves through the mail or their media advertising, we can rest assured that the effect of the bias documented in Table 3-5 works to the net advantage of incumbents. As most voters are essentially passive recipients of what the campaign has to offer, they are susceptible to biases in the flow of information. They are considerably more likely to receive information from the incumbent than from the challenger. The effect of this bias on voting choice was evident in the 1986 House elections. Among voters who received at least as much contact by challengers as by incumbents, the percentage who defected from their party identification to vote for the incumbent in 1986 was only slightly greater than the percentage who defected from the incumbent's party to vote for the challenger. Voting consistent with party identification was high among identifiers with both parties; but among voters who were contacted more by incumbents than by challengers (the great majority of voters, remember), defection in favor of incumbents was more than fifteen times greater than the defection rate in favor of challengers. Voters of the same party as the incumbent supported the incumbent almost without exception, while fewer than 40 percent of those who identified with the challenger's party voted for their party's candidate.[36]

This incumbency effect is important for an understanding of Congress, so we will return to it in Chapter 6, when we take up our analysis of that institution. For now, the incumbency advantage in House elections serves to illustrate some issues related to the question "Who's in charge?" Voters who rely on the standing decision of party identification as an important cue in making a choice are essentially passive. If campaigns provided an adequate flow of reasonably balanced information, one could hope that even a passive voter would approximate the expectations of the instrumental model of elections. But the incumbency effect in House elections belies this hope. It shows that the flow of information need not be balanced, especially if one category of candidate (incumbents) has significant advantages over the other (challengers).

---

[35]Gary C. Jacobson, *The Politics of Congressional Elections*, 2nd ed. (Boston: Little, Brown, 1987), pp. 108–134.
[36]Center for Political Studies, *American National Election Study, 1986.*

The Citizen and the Republic: Putting Things in Perspective

The argument in this and the preceding chapter has been critical of the understanding of the citizen offered by the Republic. The supposition that people are instrumentally self-interested in their political behavior is too simple. Such a concept of self-interest ignores the fact that political participation is costly. It ignores the fact that choosing between candidates and parties in a self-interested way is also costly. The reality is that most people vote rather casually. They vote without expending much effort, without being well informed. Politics is a complex, ambiguous world that voters must understand as well as they can without an unreasonable expenditure of resources. They rely on such shorthand cues as party identification; they perceive candidates in ways that reinforce their standing decision. They are subject to the flow of information from candidates, over which they individually have no control. If presidential candidates differentiate themselves clearly, voters see the differences and act accordingly. But if the candidates do not separate themselves clearly, voters are more likely to permit their perception of them to be "selective" in order to maintain their cognitive balance. If House incumbents have more resources than their challengers, voters will have experienced more contacts with the incumbents and will be more likely to vote for them.

Self-interest on the part of citizens cannot be taken for granted. Madison's Republic, based as it is on the argument that elections link the self-interest of followers to the self-interest of leaders, is in need of revision. Two perspectives on the Republic in the light of the understanding of the citizen in this and the preceding chapter are pluralism and party theory. Both theories are important to the rest of this book, and both will take a while to flesh out completely. Now is a good time to get started.

Pluralism and the Citizen: Elections Are Not Enough

The pluralist analysis of the Republic supports the larger goals stated in Madison's argument.[37] Pluralists accept the conclusion that power must be dispersed. As a consequence, they accept the essential ingredients of the U.S. Constitution, inasmuch as it is based on the principle of the dispersal of power. **Pluralists' understanding of the citizen,** however, does not accord with Madison's characterization of the citizen as self-interested. Indeed, pluralists

---

[37]Two works widely considered to be central to the pluralist view of American politics are David B. Truman, *The Governmental Process* (New York: Knopf, 1951), and Robert A. Dahl, *Who Governs?* (New Haven: Yale University Press, 1961).

look at the evidence and conclude that citizens are not instrumentally self-interested. Politics is remote from the concerns of most people. Citizens, to be blunt, are not very political.[38]

This recognition that the citizen is not self-interested creates a problem for pluralists. They accept the conclusions of the Republic without accepting the basis for those conclusions. Pluralists argue that representative government and dispersal of power can be achieved, but elections are not the primary method of linking citizens to government. They are one way, but only one. And the electoral process has distinct limitations as a way of producing representation, for all the reasons suggested by our analysis.

Pluralists admit that elections set limits on government and the people in it. Citizens, though largely indifferent to the details of government and politics, nonetheless can be aroused when things go awry. If there is a major scandal, or if policy fails in a dramatic way, as in a prolonged and unsuccessful war, public opinion can be aroused. In such unusual cases, leaders suffer politically for their failures and are called to account for them, as the instrumental model of elections anticipates. Normally, however, the connection between leaders and followers in elections is fuzzy and hard to define. The public's apathy may even be desirable because it gives leaders freedom to experiment with policy options without fear of electoral reprisal for every failure or deviation from a platform or campaign promise.[39]

How, then, is representative government to be realized? The short answer (expanded in Chapter 5) is that citizens are linked to government and politics by much of their "nonpolitical" life. If people are not very political in elections, they are actually much more political than they realize in their social, economic, religious, and professional lives. Just as Madison understood, these spheres of activity are all important sources of "faction." Pluralists emphasize group involvement, not "faction," but the result is similar to Madison's conclusions. By joining a social organization, by belonging to a union or professional organization, by attending church, citizens

---

[38]Dahl, *Who Governs?* has a chapter titled "Citizenship without Politics." Compare Bernard Berelson, Paul F. Lazarsfeld, and William N. McPhee, *Voting* (Chicago: University of Chicago Press, 1954), chap. 14, which documents low levels of political information and involvement and presents the pluralist interpretation of these findings.

[39]"Low interest provides maneuvering room for political shifts necessary for a complex society in a period of rapid change. Compromise might be based upon sophisticated awareness of costs and returns—perhaps impossible to demand of a mass society—but it is more often induced by indifference. Some people are and should be highly interested in politics, but not everyone is or needs to be": Berelson et al., *Voting*, pp. 314–315.

unwittingly introduce a significant political dimension to their lives. Consider the case of Brian:

Brian regularly attends the Lutheran church in his neighborhood. He was raised as a Lutheran and is a committed Christian. He has made friends in his church, he volunteers for various church activities, and he subscribes to several church-related publications. He also belongs to a labor union because he has a job as an electrician on the staff of a large shopping mall. When elections take place, Brian sometimes votes and sometimes does not. He is a registered Democrat but he is not very interested in politics, and he readily admits he does not watch closely what is going on in his state capital or in Washington.

Brian is a free rider when it comes to electoral politics. He votes occasionally because he has the feeling he should, but he does so without much information. He joined his church and his union for essentially personal reasons. If he had not joined the union, he could not keep his job at the mall. If he stopped going to church, he would lose touch with many of his friends and he would not be able to satisfy his commitment to Christianity.

Pluralists would see Brian as one of the many people who are not political when it comes to elections, but whose involvement in organized groups (his church and union, not to mention the neighborhood homeowners' association, the parent-teacher organization at his children's school, and the local tennis club) and family life (he and his wife own a home in a middle-class neighborhood and he has a close relationship with his retired father) have important political consequences. Brian walks out of church one morning and encounters a table set up by some of his friends urging him to sign a nuclear-freeze petition. The newsletter published by his union informs him that a bill in the state legislature may weaken his union as the bargaining agent for electricians. His neighborhood organization is worried about the city's proposal to widen the major thoroughfare just two blocks from his home. The PTO at his children's school is starting a campaign to publicize a bond issue to permit the school district to raise teachers' salaries and provide more classroom space.

Brian not political? Brian a free rider? Pluralists would beg to differ. Brian is very political, although if an interviewer were to ask him, he would say he is "not very interested in politics." He doesn't always vote, but he puts $15 in the collection plate every Sunday. His contribution helps the church pay the minister's salary. The minister is active in the local peace movement and therefore serves as a representative of Brian's views on the nuclear-freeze issue. Moreover, the church is part of a national organization of Lutheran churches, which in turn is part of an organization of churches of many denominations, which hires lobbyists in Washington to (among other things) press for a nuclear freeze. Representation is possible through channels other than the electoral process.

So pluralists would argue that we should look at the full complexity of Brian's social life before we conclude he is not very political. What he does in the "nonpolitical" spheres of his life can have political consequences both for him and for others. Pluralists contend that virtually all citizens and all interests are encompassed by the group system, whereas many citizens are left out of the electoral system. Therefore we must look to social, economic, and political interest groups to provide the bulk of political representation.[40]

Party Theory: Elections Can and Should Be Enough

Pluralists respond to the evidence about citizen participation in elections by looking elsewhere for the basis of representation. Party theorists refuse to look elsewhere. They insist that if elections are not working, something must be done to make them work. According to **party theorists' understanding of the citizen,** voters will vote for their self-interest if they can easily see where their interest lies. Party theorists are committed to arranging things so that political responsibility is easy for voters to determine. If the economy is suffering, who's to blame? If voters know whom to blame, they will be "in charge," because they can easily vote accordingly.

Party theory (discussed in more detail in Chapter 4) does not deny that politics is remote from the concerns of most people most of the time. Nor does it deny that citizens have little incentive to bear the significant information costs associated with casting an informed vote. The problem, then, is to create a situation in which voters can decide how to vote in an instrumentally self-interested way without prohibitive cost. By focusing on outcomes, party theorists think they have found a solution.

Think of the person about to purchase an automobile. The average consumer cannot be expected to understand the intricacies of automotive engineering. He is unlikely to know the advantages and disadvantages of fuel injection as opposed to carburation, nor are the details of the suspension system of particular relevance to his decision as to what car to buy. If an interviewer were to ask him about his interest in and knowledge about automotive engineering, the typical consumer would prove to be uninterested and poorly informed. But once he has owned the car for a time, he can judge its performance. He knows he gets better (or worse) gas mileage than

---

[40]This is the central conclusion to pluralist thought, and it bears close scrutiny. That analysis is taken up in Chap. 5, which deals with interest groups in American politics.

he expected. He knows the car regularly starts on cold mornings, and he likes the way it handles. If he is happy with the result of his purchase, he buys from the same company when it is time to buy a new car again. Knowing this, automobile manufacturers have powerful incentives to produce a car that gets good mileage, starts on cold mornings, and handles well. And of course, they do understand the intricacies of automotive engineering.

In the same way, voters do not need to understand the difference between Keynesian and supply-side economic theory to know they want prosperity. The experts—those in and close to government—can debate the best ways to achieve prosperity in much the way automotive engineers debate the best way to increase gas mileage. The question of *means* is complex, and the information costs associated with entering the debate over how best to bring about prosperity are high. But the question of *ends* is simple, and the information costs associated with knowing whether or not the economy is prospering are low.

So party theorists want to fix responsibility on political decision makers in much the way that brand names fix responsibility in economic exchange. In this way, the ideal of political accountability in the instrumental model of elections can be realized. Why not simply devalue the electoral process as the pluralists do and look elsewhere for a way to achieve representation? The short answer is that the electoral process is the one point in politics where power is allocated equally. Every citizen gets one and only one vote. The longer answer is that party theorists do not believe there is any other way to achieve true representation. So, among other things, they reject the pluralist view that groups provide adequate political representation.

The debate between pluralists and party theorists is relevant to the rest of this book. It will take a while to spell out the theories and the differences between them. But you should recognize at this point that a central difference between them turns on the way they see the citizen in elections. Pluralists argue that we must look elsewhere for the mechanisms that produce representation because the instrumental model fails to describe citizens' behavior. Party theorists argue that the failures of the instrumental model only indicate that we must find ways to make it work. There is no other way to achieve truly representative government.

Who's in Charge Here? Some Concluding Remarks

Who's in charge here? The question is much easier to ask than it is to answer. In the Republic, self-interest is supposed to give each faction a piece of the action so that interests will check one another.

No single interest is in charge, but all are involved in the "necessary and ordinary operations of government." Yet the key ingredient, instrumental self-interest, is seriously problematic. Participation is costly. Participation in ways that will promote representation is even more costly. As a result, the instrumental model of elections, whereby citizen-voters watch what is going on in government and pass judgment through their choices in elections, is not an adequate description of the way voters behave. Politics is remote and ambiguous. Voters need a way to vote which does not require them to get much information. Yet, at the same time, the cues they rely on can distort their understanding of the choices they are offered. And this distortion can push their behavior even further from their instrumental self-interest.

Madison's Republic, like any other political theory, must be evaluated in light of the evidence. The theory can be right, wrong, or somewhere in between. Certainly in a narrow sense, the theory is wrong. Citizens are not politically self-interested. What to do? Some people argue that the Republic is wrong enough to warrant significant constitutional reform, and they propose alternatives that would reorganize American government in fundamental ways. Some party theorists take this approach.[41] Others suggest that reforms short of a revamping of the Constitution should take place in order to correct the theoretical oversights of the Republic. Many party theorists and some pluralists take this approach. Still others believe that reform is unnecessary and even dangerous.[42] The Constitution justified by the Republic works quite well, and fundamental reform is difficult to justify, even though some of the theoretical propositions of the Republic are found wanting. Many pluralists adopt this last position.

Who's in charge here? It *is* a difficult question, and an answer requires much more than a mere examination of the citizen in politics. Indeed, the question motivates the rest of this book. Inevitably there are many shades of difference in the responses at which thoughtful people arrive. Pluralist theory and party theory form clusters of answers so that some of the alternatives can be brought forward. The answers they offer are not exhaustive, nor are they

---

[41]For examples, see Charles Hardin, *Presidential Power and Accountability* (Chicago: University of Chicago Press, 1974); Lloyd N. Cutler, "To Form a Government," in *Reforming American Government*, ed. Donald L. Robinson (Boulder, Colo.: Westview Press, 1985), pp. 11–23.
[42]Robinson, *Reforming American Government*, and James L. Sundquist, *Constitutional Reform and Effective Government* (Washington, D.C.: Brookings Institution, 1986), provide excellent discussions of the issues involved in constitutional reform.

always mutually exclusive. But the two theories are useful in the stimulation they provide to critical thinking about the American system of government.

Key Concepts

accountability

ambiguity of politics

cognitive balance theory

cost-effective way to vote

electoral mandate

ideology

incumbency effect

information costs

instrumental model of elections

party identification

party theorists' understanding of the citizen

pluralists' understanding of the citizen

rationalization

salience

selective perception

symbolic model of elections

Political Parties
An Alternative to the Republic?

We want Dutch! We want Dutch! We want Dutch!
>—Dutch's Dollies,
>Republican State Convention,
>Cedar Rapids, Iowa,
>June 1980

The people are involved in public affairs by the conflict system. Out of conflict the alternatives of public policy arise.
>—E. E. Schattschneider

. . . the essence of democracy can best be established by the popular choice between and control over alternate responsible political parties; for only such parties can provide the coherent, unified sets of rulers who will assume collective responsibility to the people for the manner in which government is carried on.
>—Austin Ranney

In presidential election years the party faithful convene throughout the nation to help choose their party's nominee for president. In 1980 Ronald Reagan was a candidate for the Republican party's presidential nomination. He was shortly to address the delegates to the Iowa state nominating convention in Cedar Rapids. Suddenly at the front of the hall appeared about a dozen women dressed in red satin tutus, blue-and-white hats, white stockings, and red shoes. After prancing about in a seemingly random fashon, they led the assembled delegates in a chant: "We want Dutch! We want Dutch!" The women—"Dutch's Dollies"—got a rousing response from the throng. Delegates stood on chairs and slapped each other on the back, all the while hooting and hollering for "Dutch" Reagan. They did not have long to wait. The candidate strode across the dais to

87

the cheers of the delegates and delivered a stirring speech exhorting the activists to work hard against the Democrats in the fall campaign, urging party unity, and reciting a list of ills he attributed to mismanagement in the White House under the incumbent president, Jimmy Carter.

I was at the Iowa Republican convention collecting data for a research project. As I left the hall with my research assistants, I asked them to reflect on their experience. One student made a sarcastic comment about Dutch's Dollies. Another topped it by reminding us all about the little old lady with blue hair who was covered with "Bush for President" buttons. Another student was impressed by all the men in light-green leisure suits and white patent-leather shoes. No one seemed to be able to be serious. And to be truthful, party conventions (Democratic ones as well as Republican ones, state and even national ones) do not inspire serious reflection on the role of the political parties in American politics. There are too many people in funny hats behaving in strange ways.

Yet somehow such party theorists as E. E. Schattschneider and Austin Ranney see the political parties as the best hope for American democracy. Beneath the veneer of hoopla, balloons, and cheerleading, something very serious is going on. Parties attract dedicated followings of activists committed to candidates and policies that they believe can improve the nation's welfare. One of the most important things parties do is to nominate candidates for local, state, and national offices. They generate enthusiasm for those candidates and they try to persuade people to vote for them. Since both the Democratic and Republican parties do these things, they are constantly competing with each other. That competition is important to Schattschneider, who argues that the conflict between the parties is a principal means by which democratic ideals can be realized.[1] Ranney agrees and emphasizes the link between party competition in elections and the parties as they function in government.[2]

This chapter has two major goals. The first is to examine party theory in some detail. We need to understand party theory because it offers an extensive critique of the Republic and the contemporary pluralist defense of Madison. Moreover, party theory goes beyond the critique to suggest an alternative way of doing things. The second major goal is to survey the American two-party system, the

---

[1]E. E. Schattschneider, *The Semisovereign People: A Realist's View of Democracy in America* (Hinsdale, Ill.: Dryden Press, 1975), p. 135.
[2]Austin Ranney, *The Doctrine of Responsible Party Government* (Urbana: University of Illinois Press, 1962), p. 12. Ranney provides an excellent and very readable summary of the essence of party theory in his chap. 2.

factors that contribute to it, and some of its major consequences. The chapter concludes by returning to party theory and raising questions about it in light of the actual functioning of the parties in America.

Getting Started

What Is a Political Party?

A political party is *an organization whose purpose is to monopolize governmental power by winning as many elections as necessary to control the principal institutions of government.*[3] This definition highlights some important aspects of political parties.

First, parties are more or less organized teams whose unabashed goal is legitimate political power. At root, then, parties are factions that attempt to mobilize a majority in order to dominate government. As such, they are certainly at war with the goals of Madisonian theory. Madison feared any concentration of power, and the Republic is quite explicit in organizing things so that a majority faction will be unable to control government. As a result, it is not uncommon for one major party to control Congress while the other occupies the White House. Separate institutions responsive to different constituencies frustrate the parties' attempts to mobilize a single national majority and translate it into control over the institutions of government.

Second, political parties are "linkage" institutions connecting citizens to government. Parties organize the choices that are offered to the electorate in elections by nominating candidates, by defining platform issues that spell out the program of the party, and by distributing resources in the electoral process. They mobilize the electorate through the appeals they make. The electorate is an extremely ungainly actor in politics which must find ways to channel its preferences so that government has some idea of what it wants and has an incentive to respect its wants. As Schattschneider put it, "the people are a sovereign whose vocabulary is limited to two words, 'Yes' and 'No.' This sovereign, moreover, can speak only when spoken to."[4]

Where Are the Political Parties?

One prominent accounting of the parties holds that they are found at three levels of the political system: the electorate, the party organizations outside of government, and official positions in gov-

---

[3]The definition is closely related to Anthony Downs's in *An Economic Theory of Democracy* (New York: Harper & Row, 1957), p. 25.
[4]E. E. Schattschneider, *Party Government* (New York: Rinehart, 1942), p. 52.

ernment.[5] Most citizens identify with a political party, and we shall not dwell further on the "party in the electorate." We shall focus rather on the parties as institutions that seek to control government, and therefore serve as a bridge between citizens and government.[6]

The party organizations outside the formal institutions of government are complex and vary considerably across the fifty states. A description of this organizational complexity is beyond the scope of this chapter. However, the activities of the party organizations (including such activists as Dutch's Dollies) are extremely important both in the reality of the American party system and in the ideal expressed by party theory. The boundaries of the party organizations are difficult to identify, but they certainly encompass the people who hold formal party offices, such as state and county party chairs, precinct leaders, and members of the staffs of the national party headquarters, as well as candidates for office.

The parties are also found in government. Almost all officeholders in the national government have clear ties to a political party, and often their involvement in party affairs has been an important part of their political careers. There are also organizations of officeholders, such as the Democratic Caucus in the House of Representatives, to facilitate partisan interaction and to promote shared partisan interests. As this chapter is concerned with parties as potential bridges or links between the public and the government, we shall consider governmental activities only insofar as they help us comprehend this aspect of party.

Party Theory

Party theory begins with a set of values and finds the American political system, including the Republic as the founding theory, seriously wanting. That is, the American system of government fails to measure up to the values that help define party theory. Recognizing the failure of the American system to approximate its values, and given its understanding of the theoretical weaknesses to be found in the Republic, party theory offers an alternative "founding theory." Party theorists, given the chance, would reorganize American governmental institutions to bring them into line with their theory. Here they differ from pluralists, who see some difficulties with the Republic as a theory but generally do not argue for major governmental reforms.

---

[5]Frank J. Sorauf, *Party Politics in America*, 4th ed. (Boston: Little, Brown, 1980), chap. 1.
[6]This is not to prejudge the issue of how well parties can link the people to government. That is an open question which demands critical analysis every bit as much as the theory offered in the Republic.

Party theory begins with a set of values that most Americans would find quite acceptable. It must be said, however, that party theorists see these values as strongly dictating much of their analysis. Taking these values seriously *and* finding the real world of politics quite at odds with their ideal, they are strongly motivated to change the political world to conform with those values. It is worth keeping in mind that while these values sound quite conventional, party theory is capable of supporting conclusions that, if also accepted, would amount to extensive reform of American political life.

Political equality. Political equality, perhaps the most fundamental value held by party theorists, exists when each citizen has equal influence over the political process. Equal influence can never be achieved in practice, but some patterns evident in American politics are so contrary to the ideal of political equality that party theorists seek to rectify them. For example, party theorists are distressed by the costs of participating in the electoral process. The failure to vote of large numbers of citizens is troubling because people who do not participate cannot exert direct influence. Especially to the extent that nonparticipation results from the costs of participating, the bias that results favors people with more resources and excludes from the political process those with fewer resources. For party theory, voting is of special interest because everyone is precisely equal: in an election, every citizen has one and only one vote.

Electoral democracy. Party theorists reject the pluralist position that elections can be deemphasized in view of evidence that the citizen is poorly informed and apathetic, and participates in politics only sporadically. They disagree with pluralists not because they disagree with the evidence reviewed in Chapters 2 and 3 but because they believe it is only through elections that their ideal of political equality can be realized. **Electoral democracy** is based on the idea of one citizen, one vote. When each citizen has an equal part in deciding the fundamental direction of society through elections, formal equality is protected.

If party theorists are not willing to look beyond the electoral process for the cornerstone of representative democracy, and if they see substantial evidence of bias, nonparticipation, and confusion in the electoral process, what follows? Elections must be invigorated. The instrumental model of elections presumes a voting citizenry in command of enough information to communicate its preferences and to hold leaders accountable for their failures. Thus party theorists seek to arrange things so that the instrumental model of elections is put in practice. In this way, the people would be in charge, and each citizen would have an equal say as part of the people. Elections are not working the way they should? Many citizens are not participating? The costs of information are too high? Politics is remote and ambiguous? These serious flaws in the electoral process must be remedied. The answer is not to "devalue" the electoral process; the answer is to fix it.

Responsibility. Leaders who occupy positions in governmental institutions must bear **responsibility** for their actions. This ideal applies both to the individual officeholder and to the institutions of government as a whole.

Consider an example that will become key to our analysis of Congress. An individual senator is responsible to the extent that voters in his state can determine what he has done to and for them, and vote accordingly. Here responsibility is equivalent to accountability. Assume for a moment that senators are perfectly responsible in this sense. They cannot do anything that hurts their home state without incurring the voters' wrath, nor can they do anything that helps their state without receiving from the voters the credit they deserve. Is this enough? Party theorists do not think so. They also want to promote "collective responsibility."[7] Senators' self-interest should be directly connected to the performance of the institution. If Congress passes legislation that ends up hurting the national interest in some way, who's responsible? Individual senators can easily point to their votes against the legislation, or to their preference for another version when the legislation was in committee. As we will see when we examine Congress, individual senators and representatives usually are not held responsible for the failures of the institution as a whole. This failure of collective responsibility leads to serious political mischief. So in addition to wanting individuals in government to be held accountable for their personal actions, party theorists very much want members' political careers to be linked to the failures and successes of the institutions in which they serve.

There is yet another way in which party theory is concerned with promoting responsibility. This form of responsibility is close to what we often mean by the term in everyday discourse. Someone is "irresponsible," for example, when he does not live up to his commitments, or when he is not dependable. Party theorists want lead-

---

[7]A good analysis of collective responsibility is offered by Morris P. Fiorina, "The Decline of Collective Responsibility in American Politics," *Daedalus* 109 (1980): 25–45.

ers to promote "responsible" action in politics and government.
Candidates for office should not promise more than they can deliver. They should not generate false expectations in the public, nor
should they criticize the opposition in ways that are unfair. Once in
government, leaders should make every effort to make good on their
campaign promises. They should also behave in ways that are consistent with the law, with broad constitutional doctrine, and with
the canons of justice, morality, and fair play.

Equality, electoral democracy, and responsibility are values at
the heart of party theory. Party theorists may argue among themselves about the best way to achieve these values, or what the
proper mix should be when they come into conflict with one another. But they are united in their belief that these values are
fundamental to their theory. If the political world does not conform
to these values, then it must be changed or improved until it more
closely approximates these ideals. Party theorists are not blind to
the complexity of the world, nor are they indifferent to the fact that
whereas theories can be stated relatively simply and purely, the
social world is messy and always imperfect. They do not think that
any of the three values can be realized fully in American politics,
but they are convinced that we could get much closer. To the degree
that it would change the way Americans conduct their public
affairs, then, party theory is frankly political. Many party theorists
strive to change American government and politics not just by
writing about them but also by engaging in direct political action,
as by testifying before congressional committees or pushing for
constitutional change. In doing so they are implicitly or explicitly
confronting some of the most basic tenets of Madison's theory.

Party Theory's Critique of the Republic

We have summarized Madison's Republic as follows: Self-interest
→ representation → conflict and dispersed power. Party theory
disagrees with every step of the argument either on descriptive
grounds (the way things are) or for normative reasons (the way
things should be). Let us consider party theory's critique of each
step in the Republic.

Self-interest. The first objection to the Republic is purely descriptive. Party theorists do not think human nature can be characterized as politically self-interested in the manner described by
Madison. Madison worked with an instrumental concept of self-
interest, which ignored the costs associated with political participation and the paradox of collective action. Party theorists recognize
that individuals make at least rough calculations of costs and benefits, and that as a result, citizens do not expend much effort to learn

about politics or pursue many of their political goals. They argue that any theory of representative government must explicitly acknowledge that most citizens' commitment to politics is quite limited. Politics is not salient, though it can be made more so. Politics is ambiguous, though it can be made less so. Citizens can be better informed, but not because they will bear higher information costs. If citizens are to pursue their interests in politics, they will do so because the political process alerts them to the stakes involved and provides channels through which self-interest can readily be expressed. Once that self-interest is expressed, the process itself can register and respond to it.

In short, then, party theorists do not take self-interest as a given, nor is it something that must be controlled. If a theory is to be based on instrumental self-interest, it must include some way of stimulating self-interested behavior, because it will not occur as a result of "human nature." Party theorists do not expect altruistic behavior from citizens or leaders. But instrumentally self-interested behavior must be aroused in citizens before it can produce political representation.

Representation. Representation will not occur with certainty in the absence of self-interested behavior. Party theorists would have no trouble with such a statement as "*If* self-interest, *then* representation." Leaders indeed want power and can be depended on to behave in ways that increase their chances of attaining and holding attractive positions in government. But the "if" is a very big hurdle. So if citizens are not naturally self-interested, if many of them are more or less free riders, leaders may find ways other than representing the people to hold on to power. And, party theorists argue, this is exactly what they do. They manipulate the electoral process (witness the incumbency effect in House elections), they gather resources, they make appeals on the basis of image, fear, or the anxieties of the electorate, and generally distort the purposes of the electoral process. They are able to hold power without satisfying the interests of the people who elected them because efforts to satisfy those interests are not especially relevant to victory in elections.

So once again, the failure of Madison's Republic is a failure of descriptive theory. Because self-interested behavior by the public is problematic, so is representation. Party theorists want representative government. They do not believe the argument embodied in Madison's Republic is the way to achieve it.

Conflict and dispersed power. Just as representation is problematic, so is the conflict in government which, according to Madison, results from representation. For Madison, representation would bring "the spirit of faction" into the "necessary and ordinary operations of government." Each faction would have a share of governmental power and would use that power to check other factions. Hence power would be dispersed and tyranny avoided. But this is unlikely to be the result unless representatives indeed represent. And representation in the absence of a politically interested citizenry is doubtful. So party theorists doubt the conclusions first on grounds that follow from their doubts about the Republic's faith in self-interest.

But party theorists have a more profound objection to Madison's argument about conflict and power. The dispersal of governmental power is not a solution to the problem of self-interest; it contributes to the problem. Here party theorists engage the normative conclusions in the Republic. The dispersal of governmental power violates all three of the party theorists' fundamental values. The dispersal of power destroys political responsibility. Therefore, the dispersal of power undermines electoral democracy and thwarts the hope for political equality. So not only is conflict in government unlikely to occur in the measure hoped for by the Republic, it is also highly undesirable.

In essence, the dispersal of power raises information costs well out of the range of the typical citizen. A government based on this principle is necessarily complex. There are indeed "separate institutions sharing power," and citizens have great difficulty determining who is responsible for what results. When inflation rages or a budget deficit threatens economic ruin, how are presidents likely to respond? By pointing out the failure of Congress to pass the programs necessary to solve the problem. How do members of Congress cope? By pointing out the misguided programs of the president or of their colleagues in Congress. When power is shared, responsibility is inevitably also shared. And responsibility for failures, when shared, can be difficult or impossible to place. Certainly for citizens who do not research the problem closely, the fixing of responsibility will be impossibly difficult and costly. Therefore, dispersal of power increases the ambiguity and distance of politics, removing citizens from effectively engaging in the political process in a manner based on political interests.

Dispersal of power undermines the personal responsibility of leaders because citizens cannot judge the role the individual plays in determining governmental policy. Dispersal of power undermines collective responsibility because no one claims credit for failures and all claim responsibility for success. Dispersal of power undermines responsible government because the electoral process is severed from the governmental process. Candidates have every incentive to promise more than they can deliver because they can always point to others' failures when government cannot fulfill those promises.

Party theorists' rejection of the dispersal of power is the key to their concerns about equality and electoral democracy. Electoral democracy is possible only when voters can cast a self-interested vote without expending much effort or other resources. Voting itself is pretty cheap. We have seen that although voting is, strictly speaking, against the self-interest of the citizen, the very small costs associated with going to the polls can be overcome by a sense of duty. And of course, anything that draws citizens into politics, encourages them to vote, or reduces the costs of voting will increase electoral participation. The real catch is not in getting people to vote. The most serious block to electoral democracy is getting people to vote with enough information so that their votes reflect their political interests. This task requires that information costs be lowered so that politics will be more salient and less ambiguous. According to party theory, the political parties are the best means to mobilize the electorate and to focus both individual and collective responsibility in the political process.

It is all well and good to criticize the political theory offered by James Madison in the Republic. Any political theory can be subjected to extensive criticism. The real test is whether the critics have an alternative that promises to solve more problems than it creates. Party theorists think they have such an alternative, and we turn to it now as an option to the Republic.

The Program of Party Theory

Both Schattschneider and Ranney are leading party theorists, and the statements that introduce this chapter provide helpful hints about their programs. Schattschneider emphasizes that conflict has certain properties desirable in a democracy. He highlights what he calls the **contagion of conflict**[8] and emphasizes that a good fight draws a crowd. In a democracy, the people are a "crowd," and they must be attracted before they will enter the fight (that is, politics). Involvement in politics is desirable to party theorists because popular participation is an important part of their definition of democracy. In any conflict, some participants want to limit the fight to just a few because when the "crowd" gets involved, the outcome of the fight can change dramatically. Schattschneider, like other party theorists, believes that strong political parties are the best means to

---

[8]Schattschneider, *Semisovereign People*, chap. 1.

ensure that the fight will engage the people, because strong parties will alert them to the stakes involved in political choices.

Austin Ranney's statement spotlights the way parties involve the people in politics. The choice should be between two parties in competition for power. The competition between the parties is the conflict Schattschneider is depending on to be contagious. Ranney wants each of the parties to be "coherent" and "unified" so that the implications of the fight will be obvious to citizens and the choice between the parties reasonably clear. In that case, what parties promise when they compete in elections and what they do when they govern are plain to voters, and "collective responsibility" results. Let us examine in more detail the changes party theorists would like to bring about.

Strengthening of party organizations. Party theorists uniformly call for strengthening of the party organizations. This task could be accomplished in a variety of ways, but the essential idea is to give the party organizations more control over the resources candidates need to get elected and reelected to public office. For example, candidates almost always must have a major party's nomination to win a seat in Congress or the White House. One way to strengthen the party organizations, then, might be to give the national party organizations copyright control over the use of the party label. Another would be to require that all money spent in campaigns must come from the political parties.[9] Strengthened party organizations are absolutely essential to the rest of the party theorists' program of reform. In fact, it could be said that strengthening of the party organizations is their *complete* program. Everything else either is a result of strengthened parties or would contribute to their strengthening.

Imposition of party discipline. Party organizations must be strengthened so that they may have the resources to discipline the people who serve in government and run as candidates on their behalf. **Party discipline** is important because it promotes party responsibility. Party theorists disagree with Madison's idea that individual officeholders should represent particular factional interests. Legislators such as members of Congress should be committed to the national political party rather than to their local constituencies. They should represent the party's program to the

---

[9]Under current constitutional interpretation, a strict requirement that all money spent in campaigns must come from the party organizations would probably be unconstitutional. Nonetheless, some variant could be mandated that would give the parties the upper hand in the distribution of campaign funds.

constituency and they should support the program when they are in office. Constituencies, then, are simply collections of citizens who choose between party representatives in elections rather than factions with unique interests.

A system that ties candidates to the national party differs markedly from one that links candidates primarily to the local constituency. Consider the situation in the Republic, where no party organization imposes discipline on candidates for the national legislature. People competing for votes in a particular constituency tailor their appeals to the interests of the legislative district or state. The result is a plethora of unique concerns brought into government. Party theorists find this arrangement objectionable on several counts. The legislature will have no coherent program to guide its deliberations following an election, nor will it be able to act on national problems in a sustained or coherent fashion. Legislative politics will be devoted to efforts to redeem the many commitments individual candidates (now legislators) have made to their constituencies. Some form of individual responsibility may be achieved, but collective responsibility will go begging. As the analysis of Congress in Chapters 6 and 7 attests, the party theorists have a point.

Of course, candidates and legislators must have an incentive to follow national party policy rather than attend to narrow constituency interests. To link each individual candidate's and legislator's career fortunes firmly to the destiny of the party is the purpose of party discipline. A candidate who did not reflect the party program or a legislator who refused to support the party's commitments could be denied renomination. Someone else would be chosen to run in the constituency on behalf of the party. Thus the self-interest of the legislator is tied to the interests of the party.

Parties capable of imposing this kind of discipline produce two important consequences, according to party theory. First, a party has a powerful incentive to fashion a program that addresses pressing national problems *and* appeals to a majority of the nation's citizens. It must put together such a program in order to win control of government. The parties' programs, or platforms, are prominent in the competition between them. Debate rages over the best way to handle unemployment, budget deficits, international tension, inflation, racial unrest, poverty, educational decline, or whatever the issues happen to be. Because parties are responsible, they will not make rash promises. They must live with the promises they make if they win, so programmatic appeals will be realistic and reasonable.

Second, individual candidates play the role of salesman to the constituencies. They present and defend their party's program because if they don't, they will be disciplined. If they do a good job, they will win in their constituency and gain a seat in the legislature. If they are part of the majority, they will participate in governing. Their careers are inextricably linked to the success of their party (much as a salesman's career depends on the success of his company in developing sellable products), so they will work hard to promote the party's success.

Provision of a clear choice. Because party organizations are strong, they can discipline. Because they can discipline, they will offer to voters clear, coherent, and probably different choices in their platforms. Candidates will do everything possible to make the platform attractive to voters, and the conflict between candidates in any particular constituency will closely approximate the conflict between the parties nationally. In this way, choices made in local constituencies directly relate to national issues and the debates between the parties which occur in government. As Schattschneider put it, "the people are involved in public affairs by the conflict system." Conflict is contagious, and citizens are aroused to grapple with the issues that inevitably must occupy governmental officeholders.

In other words, the relatively simple choice presented to the voters when candidates represent their national party platforms puts the people "in charge." Information costs are low, and ordinary people, who cannot be expected to watch public affairs closely, can make a choice that approximates their political interests. Party theorists argue that this logic will work itself out in two ways, both of which are part of the ideal expressed in the instrumental model of elections.

First, voters will be able to *communicate* their preferences by choosing between the parties. The election outcome will represent a mandate. When candidates run on their party's platform, voters become reasonably well informed about the differences between the parties. The parties have an incentive to help their candidates compete successfully, so voters will normally experience a balanced, vigorous campaign. Campaigns turn less on differences between the individual candidates, such as incumbency, experience, and personality, and more on the issues that divide the parties. The debate between candidates will inform voters, who respond in a way that reflects their instrumental self-interest.

Voters will also have a much easier time holding parties *accountable*. Here the most important difference between the parties is simply the difference in names. The voter is like a consumer choosing between two makes of automobile. If the consumer has driven a Ford lately and had a good experience with it, he probably will buy another. The Ford name tells him that the Ford Motor Company is responsible for his good experience, and he rewards the company by purchasing another of its products. If his experience is a bad one (the car won't start on cold mornings, handles poorly, gets poor gas mileage, and so on), he knows whom to blame, and he tries a different make.

In like manner, if voters experience peace, prosperity, and other good things under the Democrats, they have no reason to switch. Provided there is some reason to think the Democrats are *responsible* for these happy results, voters will reward their success. If, in contrast, things are not going well under the Democrats, voters will switch to the Republicans.

The point of emphasizing the choice offered by competing parties is to reduce information costs for the voter and to provide party organizations with a powerful incentive to improve the "product" they offer to voters. Voters cannot communicate their preferences unless the choice is clear and their votes (cast without much effort on their part) bear a close relation to their political interests. Information costs must be drastically reduced if this outcome is to be achieved. Even if voters are not aware of the differences between the party programs, many party theorists stress that the "brand name" accountability is enough to produce party responsibility.[10] This logic creates a powerful incentive for parties to satisfy voters by producing the good *results* by which they will be judged.

Concentration of governmental power in the hands of the winning party. It is in the matter of the concentration of power that party theorists most clearly and radically depart from Madisonian theory. Power must be concentrated if responsibility is to be fixed. Imagine the situation if an automobile manufacturer could say to the consumer: "Had trouble with your transmission? Sorry, it was made by Mitsubishi. Trouble with the engine? Too bad, that was made by General Motors." Despite the fact that there is a fair amount of component swapping in the automotive industry, the name affixed to the car identifies the company responsible for putting the thing together. Consumers don't have to keep track of all the subcontractors who contributed various parts.

Neither should voters have to monitor all the individual decisions that go into an economic policy. Dispersal of power and

---

[10]"Our survival depends on our ability to judge things by their results and our ability to establish relations of confidence and responsibility so that we can take advantage of what other people know": Shattschneider, *Semisovereign People*, p. 134. In chap. 8 Schattschneider makes a powerful argument that voters need not be well informed about the details of governance or party differences in order to exercise significant control over what government does.

therefore dispersal of responsibility requires the citizen to do such monitoring. This is an impossibly expensive exercise, so most citizens don't do it. That is the failure of the Madisonian system, according to party theorists. It is only when power is concentrated that voters can determine who is responsible. Dispersal of power, by destroying responsibility, severs the connection between the people and government. It prevents electoral democracy.

How might concentration of power actually work in American politics? Because the American constitutional system is based on the principle of dispersed power, many party theorists argue for fundamental constitutional reform.[11] Many proposals for reform have been advanced, some much more extensive than others. At the minimum, some party theorists would be satisfied to give parties more control over the nomination of candidates and over money spent in campaigns so that they could impose more discipline. This measure would "concentrate power" only in that it would make the party organizations stronger players in the political game. It would not change the underlying constitutional principle of dispersed power. It would make parties better able to compete in the constitutional framework, however, and it would make the competition between them more prominent. Political conflict would center less on individual candidates in competition for specific offices and more on the national parties in a fight for control of government.

Many party theorists favor more fundamental reform to create a **parliamentary system.** In such a system the national legislature (the parliament) would have but one house, and it would have the power to organize the executive branch. The party that wins a majority of seats in the parliament controls both the legislative and the executive branches. Indeed, the executive branch is chosen from among the majority party leaders in parliament. Members of parliament who have been active in support of the party program gradually gain stature within their party. Their ambition is to join the executive team (or cabinet) when their party is in the majority. The ultimate goal of the politically ambitious is to lead the party and, when the party wins a national majority, to serve in the executive leadership position (prime minister).

The parliamentary system is very clearly at odds with Madi-

---

[11]See Charles M. Hardin, *Presidential Power and Accountability: Toward a New Constitution* (Chicago: University of Chicago Press, 1974); Donald L. Robinson, ed., *Reforming American Government* (Boulder, Colo.: Westview Press, 1985); James L. Sundquist, *Constitutional Reform and Effective Government* (Washington, D.C.: Brookings Institution, 1986); and James MacGregor Burns, *The Deadlock of Democracy* (Englewood Cliffs, N.J.: Prentice-Hall, 1963) for analysis of the issues surrounding constitutional reform in accordance with the party theorists' ideal of concentrated power.

son's Republic in the most basic way possible. Madison feared concentration of power anywhere, but more than anything he dreaded governmental power in the hands of a majority. As a result, government in the Republic is divided against itself in many ways, inaction is likely, compromise among a broad array of interests is necessary. In a parliamentary government, the majority controls governmental institutions and need not compromise in a direct way with the minority party. It can put its program into effect and be held responsible for its failures and successes.[12]

To concentrate power in ways consistent with party theory is not to give absolute power to the majority party. Various checks on power could be incorporated, such as constitutional restrictions defining fundamental rights that no government could violate. The party holding power would have control of government for only a limited time. Parties must compete vigorously, and the party in power must govern in the context of an active minority opposition. We have now arrived at the final plank in the party theorists' platform.

Party competition in and between elections. Once again Professor Schattschneider defines the issue for party theorists: "Above everything, *the people are powerless if the political enterprise is not competitive.* It is the competition of political organizations that provides the people with the opportunity to make a choice."[13] Competition between parties, each striving with all its might to occupy or retain power, with the people retaining the final say, is the essence of democracy for party theorists.

Power in a parliamentary system is given to the winning party, but only for a period of time between elections. Elections *must* be held regularly, and the party out of power must have a reasonable chance to win power in the next election. Ideally, power rotates on a fairly regular basis between the competing parties. The fact that elections are held regularly and that the **governing party** is vulnerable to defeat serves as a powerful check against it. If it is tempted to use its power in arbitrary ways or unfairly to trample the rights of the minority or **opposition party,** it knows it may be subject to the

---

[12]Needless to say, a government based on parliamentary principles would be much more energetic than one based on separated powers. Indeed, for some people this is the primary reason to support parliamentary government. They argue that modern governments must be able to react quickly to changing world events. They must be effective in times of crisis and cannot be hamstrung by the checks and balances built into the American system. See Burns, *Deadlock of Democracy,* and Robert A. Goldwin and Art Kaufman, eds., *Separation of Powers: Does It Still Work?* (Washington, D.C.: American Enterprise Institute, 1986).

[13]Schattschneider, *Semisovereign People,* p. 137.

same treatment when the opposition wins control of the government.

The opposition party plays a critical role between elections. When a party wins a majority of the seats in parliament, it controls the government. It retains control of parliament and of the executive so long as a majority of its members vote with it, but at all times the opposition party also holds seats in parliament. It simply lacks the majority necessary to seize control. So the opposition party is very well placed to criticize what the government is doing. It votes against the majority party's programs, speaks against the policies of the government, and in general calls the majority party to task for its failures to live up to its promises or to produce adequate results. Always it is trying to persuade enough people to join it in the next election so that it can win a majority of seats and take over government.

Just as Madison argued that conflict is essential, party theorists rely on conflict in their ideal government. But Madison depended on conflict among many factions to check governmental power, whereas party theorists look to conflict between two competing parties to define alternatives, raise issues, and mobilize interest. Party theory seeks ways to make the parties the focus of conflict because party organizations are uniquely situated to expand the scope of conflict. Because the minority party has an overwhelming interest in becoming the majority, it must follow an expansive strategy. It must attract newcomers to politics or (less probably) seduce followers of the other party. Anticipating this strategy by the opposition, the majority party too must mobilize new followers, appeal to a broad array of interests, and exhort its following to hold fast in their support. The result is an expansive form of conflict that is highly visible, mobilizes citizens to engage in electoral politics, and informs them about the stakes involved in the conflict.[14]

In contrast to parties, other contestants in politics do not have an interest in expanding the scope of conflict. Interest groups often have compelling reasons to restrict the visibility and extent of political conflict, especially if their membership is relatively small. Likewise, senators and representatives in Congress often seek to limit the scope of electoral conflict in their districts. An increase in the visibility of the campaign or in the rate of participation may only increase the chances that they will suffer defeat. Party theorists argue that the Madisonian system favors groups that would restrict

---

[14]One study of voter turnout found that the weak American party system accounts for about a 13 percent disadvantage in turnout in comparison with other Western democracies: G. Bingham Powell, Jr., "American Voter Turnout in Comparative Perspective," *American Political Science Review* 80 (March 1986): 17–43.

the scope of conflict because it multiplies the number of decision makers, disperses power, raises information costs, and generally increases complexity. All of these things tend to exclude the people for whom politics is remote and ambiguous, thereby undermining democracy as party theorists understand it.

Party Theory Summarized

By now it should be (perhaps distressingly) clear that party theory is markedly different from Madison's Republic. It begins with a set of values that probably would strike most people as eminently reasonable and even conventional. These values lead party theorists to a thoroughgoing critique of the Republic both as theory and as it works out in contemporary American public life. Party theorists, given the nature of their criticisms, are quite naturally given to stating alternatives. These alternatives vary in their effects, from fairly modest proposals that would strengthen the parties to a wholehearted junking of the American constitutional order in favor of some variant of parliamentary government. Party theory is summarized in Table 4-1.

Party theory, like Madison's Republic, is "only" a theory. It may be right, it may be wrong, or it may be somewhere in between. Again like the Republic, it is based on certain assumptions and evidence, and it would have powerful consequences if it were put into effect. Consider the value of individualism, discussed at the close of Chapter 1. Individualism is a value firmly embedded in the Republic and in American society. One reason Madison's theory "feels right" to many Americans is that it accords with this value.

Party theory would depart rather significantly from a normative emphasis on individualism. Take party discipline, for example: once a party program was established, individual candidates and officeholders would not be free to deviate from that program. They could not serve the folks back home in Indiana if doing so were contrary to party policy. At present each member of Congress is able to pursue constituency interests. Individualism makes collective responsibility very difficult, though a theory that celebrates individualism accommodates diversity much better than one that attempts to realize more collective values. Thus party theory is often criticized because it would reduce political conflict to an overly simple choice between two broad coalitions. If power were concentrated in the parties and the governmental structure simplified to reduce information costs and fix responsibility, the diversity in government would necessarily be reduced. A simplified government, then, would also simplify the complexity and diversity found in modern American society.

So party theory is a political theory that offers an extensive

Table 4-1 Values, Critique of the Republic, and Alternative Program of Party Theory

→Values	→Critique of Republic	→Alternative program
Political equality. All citizens are equal and should have equal influence over government.	Self-interest. Not automatic in politics. Theory must take into account costs of participation and paradox of collective action. Resource bias seriously distorts equality.	Strengthened party organizations. If parties had control over the resources necessary to gain public office, they could use those resources to discipline members and promote party coherence.
Electoral democracy. Elections are designed to promote political equality because each citizen has one vote. Elections should be organized to approximate the instrumental model, whereby citizens use their votes to communicate their preferences and hold leaders accountable.	Representation. Problematic. Many interests are seriously underrepresented because of nonparticipation, bias, information costs. Interests with more resources are more likely to be heard and represented.	Concentration of power in hands of winning party. Give winning party control over government. For some party theorists, this goal requires restructuring of American government into a parliamentary system.
Responsibility. Both individual officeholders and governmental institutions must be responsible for political outcomes and for the conduct of public affairs.	Conflict and dispersed power. Problematic and inappropriate. Representation does not produce conflict. Dispersal of power undermines responsibility, especially collective responsibility, thereby subverting electoral democracy.	Party competition and provision of a clear choice. Electoral competition between parties gives voters a meaningful choice, thus putting people in control, as in the instrumental model. Elections determine who governs, thus promoting equality and electoral democracy.

blueprint for the conduct of our politics. One may subject its propositions to careful evaluation by appealing to evidence or to values. It may be insightful and worth adoption in whole or in part, or it may be wrongheaded and dangerous. It is a coherent and intelligent enough alternative to Madison and pluralism to be taken seriously. With party theory well in hand, then, we can move to an analysis of the way the parties actually operate in contemporary American politics.

The Parties in American Politics

Why Only Two?

The fact that there are only two major parties in competition for power in American elections is important. As most party theorists would like, it makes the choice between the parties simple. It also guarantees a legislative majority to the victor so long as the two parties are the only competitors. At the same time, the broader range of choice offered by multiparty systems is not available when there are only two parties.

Several factors help explain why there are only two parties in America.[15] First, most national institutions are based on a **winner-take-all system of representation.** Thus disgruntled factions have powerful incentives to remain within the party. In congressional elections, for instance, only the winner in each district or state gets the seat in the House or Senate. The losing party or parties, even if they lose by a narrow margin, get no representation from that district. The presidency is based on a similar principle. Presidential candidates who have failed to capture a majority in the Electoral College cannot combine their support to form a coalition government. Therefore losers in a party's nomination campaign have little reason to split off and run their own independent campaigns.

In contrast to a winner-take-all arrangement, a system of **proportional representation** allocates seats in the legislature in proportion to the votes each party receives. Minority parties have little incentive to cooperate with their competitors in order to build a majority in the election. If a faction splits off from a party, nominates candidates, and attracts votes, it is rewarded with a number of seats in the legislature roughly proportional to the percentage of the vote it received.

A second explanation for the dominance of two major parties in America is that various policies at the state and national levels

---

[15]See Sorauf, *Party Politics in America*, pp. 38–41, for a fuller discussion of the two-party system.

discourage minor parties. For example, most states have require-

ments that restrict a would-be candidate's ability to have his or her
name listed on printed ballots and on voting machines, so that the
Democratic and Republican nominees have a relatively clear field.
Insurgent candidates such as John Anderson in 1980 have to collect
signatures on petitions in many states in order to be listed on the
ballot. Laws vary, but it is true that minor parties that remain
active from election to election usually have access to the ballot.
Another explanation is based on national campaign finance policy
as it applies to presidential elections.[16] Major-party nominees are
eligible to receive federal funding for their campaigns, whereas
minor-party candidates must attract a minimum level of voter support before they can be reimbursed for their expenses.

Finally, popular attitudes tend to favor the idea of a two-party
system (which may help account for the policies that hinder minor-
party candidates). Some people have also argued that the relatively
limited range of opinion in American politics leaves room for only
two parties. In other systems where opinions range from those of
Marxists and socialists on the left to those of nationalists and
monarchists on the right, more than two parties may exist to
accommodate them.[17] At the same time, it is entirely possible that
when several parties are encouraged to flourish, public opinion
expands to cover a broader range in response to the more extensive
menu of choice offered by candidates and parties.

Is There a Difference Between the Parties?

Do the parties differ in any substantial way? The short answer is
yes. The longer answer is that it depends on where you look and
what the issue is. But a safe generalization is that the Republican
and Democratic parties differ in the issues supported by their adherents, and the differences grow larger as one compares more
active segments of the parties. Consider Figure 4-1. In their detailed
comparison of the public with convention delegates of both parties,
Warren Miller and Kent Jennings found that the differences in
opinion between Democratic and Republican national convention
delegates tend to be greater than the differences between citizens
who identify with the two parties.[18] The data in Figure 4-1 support
this generalization by comparing the four groups (along with independents) on the same general issue scale. The most liberal group

---

[16]See Herbert B. Asher, *Presidential Elections and American Politics*, 4th ed. (Chicago:
Dorsey Press, 1988), pp. 211–224, for a discussion of presidential campaign financing.
[17]Downs, *Economic Theory of Democracy*, chap. 8.
[18]Warren E. Miller and M. Kent Jennings, *Parties in Transition* (New York: Russell
Sage, 1986).

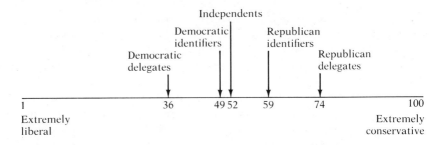

Figure 4-1 Locations of Convention Delegates and Party Identifiers on Liberal–Conservative Issue Scale, 1980. SOURCE: Data from Warren E. Miller and M. Kent Jennings, *Parties in Transition* (New York: Russell Sage, 1986), p. 197.

in 1980 was made up of Democratic delegates to the Democratic nominating convention. As a group they were more extreme in their views than Democratic identifiers, a finding that was mirrored on the Republican side. As one might expect, independents were almost squarely in the middle of the 100-point scale.[19]

Figure 4-1 presents a summary picture based on a wide range of issues. The differences between the parties tend to be greatest on economic and welfare issues; they are less marked on some foreign policy issues, domestic issues unrelated to economic welfare, and such moral issues as abortion. But the general picture is clear: there is a good deal more than "a dime's worth of difference" between the Democratic and Republican parties.[20]

These differences between the two parties demonstrate that ideology is a powerful motivator among the people who are most active in American politics. We have seen that citizens do not usually think in ideological terms about politics. But among those who contribute substantial amounts of their time to party and candidate organizations, many are powerfully motivated by ideological principles. They strongly desire to change things in ways consistent with their ideological values, even though an expenditure of considerable time and effort in an attempt to do so is not strictly in their self-

[19]Numerous studies report similar findings. Activists and officeholders are usually more extreme than members of the public who identify with the party, but they are on the same side of the liberal–conservative scale as their followers. For an early study, see Herbert McClosky, Paul J. Hoffman, and Rosemary O'Hara, "Issue Conflict and Consensus among Party Leaders and Followers," *American Political Science Review* 54 (1960): 406–427. For evidence on the differences between Democrats and Republicans in Congress, see Table 7-1 in Chap. 7.

[20]George Wallace claimed there was not when he ran as an independent in the 1968 presidential campaign.

interest.[21] Such activists, if they work to attract voters to the causes of the candidates they support, can collectively make a great deal of difference. And their willingness to devote substantial personal resources to the effort is a cornerstone of the American party system.

Strategic Differences Between the Parties

Something of a puzzle presents itself when we ask whether the parties differ. First, the evidence is clear that the parties do differ, especially when activists and officeholders in the two parties are compared. But when we turn to the incentives and behavior of candidates as they compete for votes on the campaign trail, evidence indicates that the differences are muted. Why is this the case?

The answer is seen most clearly in a simple economic analogy.[22] Two nacho stands are competing for customers on a beach-front boardwalk (see Figure 4-2). The price of nachos is fixed, and the two stands compete only by means of the locations they select on the boardwalk. Salt air makes people hungry, and the sun worshipers on the beach will go to the nearest nacho stand to satisfy their craving for junk food. The nacho stands cannot simply move up and down the boardwalk with ease—they can move, but not easily.

A commission, charged with regulating the concessions on the boardwalk, might well decide that the two nacho stands should be located midway between the center of the boardwalk and each end. Nacho stand a would be midway between the end of the boardwalk (A in Figure 4-2) and the center, C. Its competitor, stand b, would be

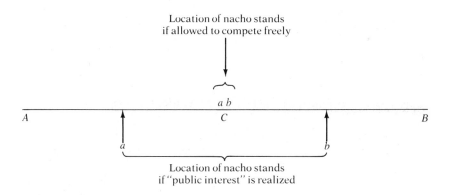

Figure 4-2 Competition Between Nacho Stands on Boardwalk

---

[21]For a collection of recent essays dealing with the motivations of party activists, see Ronald B. Rapoport, Alan I. Abramowitz, and John McGlennon, eds., *The Life of the Parties* (Lexington: University of Kentucky Press, 1986).
[22]The following analysis depends heavily on Downs, *Economic Theory of Democracy*, chap. 8.

located midway between B and C. In this way, no one would have to walk more than one-quarter of the length of the boardwalk to buy a nacho. If the stands were located anywhere else on the boardwalk, the maximum distance some people would have to go would be greater. Keeping this maximum distance as small as possible would reasonably satisfy the "public interest" in this simple case. If the nacho stands remain at their assigned locations, and if consumers are spread pretty equally over the distance of the boardwalk, each nacho stand should attract about half of the market.

But someone on the boardwalk commission might object to requiring the vendors to occupy assigned locations. After all, isn't free competition the American way? What happens if the nacho stands are permitted to relocate on the boardwalk? One of them will surely recognize that if it moves toward the other, it has nothing to lose and everything to gain. For example, if nacho stand a relocates at point C, it retains all of the market it had before and it cuts significantly into b's sales as well, because the boardwalkers who are to the right of C but closer to a will now purchase from that stand. Nacho stand b is not run by an idiot. Having lost part of the market to his competitor's wily ways, b inevitably will respond by moving toward the center. In fact, the equilibrium point in this example—the point at which neither vendor has any incentive to move—is reached when both are occupying positions cheek by jowl in the center of the boardwalk. This result of permitting the nacho vendors to locate themselves in the market does not appear to be consistent with the public interest. The maximum distance one must go in order to buy a nacho is now one-half the length of the boardwalk. And the vendors are no better off than before because each still ends up with half of the market.

Anthony Downs applied the logic of two vendors in a market space to the competition between two parties for votes in an ideo-logical or issue space (see Figure 4-3).[23] He argued that when most citizens are at or close to the center of the ideological space and only a few are at the extremes, the two parties will pursue a **strategy of convergence.** The liberal party will occupy a position very close to the center of the distribution (but to the left of center), while the conservative party will be just to the right of center. The votes each party gains by occupying a centrist position more than offset the losses it may suffer from disenchanted citizens at the extremes. Put another way, the best way to lose the election would be to abandon the center to the opposition and occupy a position distinctly off-center.

Just as one could conclude that the nacho stands' convergence

---

[23]Ibid.

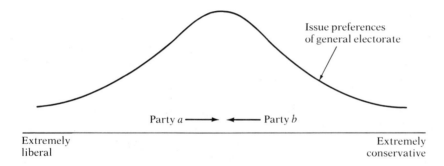

Figure 4-3 Party Location in Two-Party System with Normal Distribution of Voter Preferences

at the center of the boardwalk is contrary to the public interest, Downs argued that party convergence creates a **rationality crisis** in a two-party system. That is, rational party behavior (seeking to win the election) makes rational voting behavior (voting for the party closest to one's position on the liberal–conservative scale) more difficult. When parties and candidates converge, voters have trouble perceiving the differences between them, and so they may vote without information or for a candidate who does not represent their interests.

Many close observers of presidential candidates in national elections have been impressed by the logic of Downs's argument and have found evidence that candidates tend to follow a strategy of convergence in elections.[24] Parties may converge by adopting similar positions on specific issues, as on the advisability of a tax hike, or by failing to distinguish themselves in a broader ideological sense. Candidates also emphasize purely symbolic issues, such as an affinity for the pledge of allegiance or for "competence." Since no one is against the pledge or competence, emphasis on these issues does not really serve to distinguish the candidates. To some extent, the exceptions prove the rule. When a candidate differentiates himself from his opposition, as the liberal George McGovern did in 1972 and as the conservative Barry Goldwater did in 1964, voters perceive the differences and vote accordingly. But in both of these elections the candidates who abandoned the strategy of convergence lost dramatically, just as Downs would have expected.

---

[24]An excellent study of the problem is Benjamin I. Page, *Choices and Echoes in Presidential Elections* (Chicago: University of Chicago Press, 1978). Even a highly salient issue about which voters are well informed cannot motivate "rational" voting behavior if candidates converge. See Benjamin I. Page and Richard A. Brody, "Policy Voting and the Electoral Process: The Vietnam Issue," *American Political Science Review* 66 (September 1972): 979–995.

Are there any reasons to believe that Downs's logic in regard to the strategy of convergence is flawed? One important reason that candidates may *not* converge is that before they can compete in a general election they must secure their party's nomination. And, as we have already seen, party activists (such as delegates to the national nominating conventions) are not typical of the general electorate. Figure 4-4 illustrates the problem in simple form. Candidates for the Democratic party's presidential nomination must appeal to the party's **nomination activists,** from Democrats who vote in the primaries to national convention delegates. Their position on the "boardwalk" is distinctly left of center. Likewise, Republican candidates for the presidential nomination must compete in a right-of-center market. The visibility of today's nomination races may freeze the nomination winners away from the center and limit their ability to follow the strategy of convergence. The most successful candidates, then, are those who can balance their appeals to ideological activists with the need to occupy a centrist position in the general election.[25]

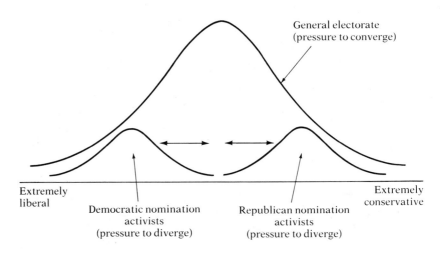

Figure 4-4 Issue Preferences of General Electorate and of Party Activists

---

[25]See Walter J. Stone and Alan I. Abramowitz, "Winning May Not Be Everything, but It's More than We Thought," *American Political Science Review* 77 (December 1983): 945–956. Much of Reagan's success turned on his ability to appeal to his party on ideological grounds while building a popular following based on his personal qualities and image. Despite his relatively extreme conservatism, Reagan convinced Republican activists in 1980 that he was the nomination candidate with the best chance of winning in the general election.

If parties follow the strict logic of the nacho-stand example, one of the implications could easily be that voters would fail to perceive the differences between the parties. Figure 4-5 shows popular perceptions of the parties and presidential candidates in recent presidential election years.

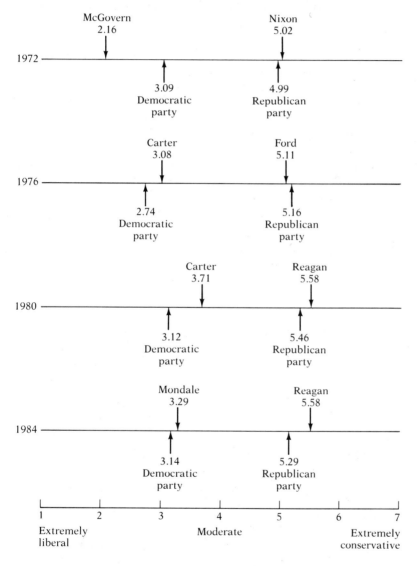

Figure 4-5 Median Estimates of Placement of Major Parties and Presidential Candidates on Liberal–Conservative Scale, 1972–1984. SOURCE: Center for Political Studies, University of Michigan, American National Election Study, 1972, 1976, 1980, 1984 (Ann Arbor: Interuniversity Consortium for Political and Social Research, 1975, 1977, 1982, 1986 respectively).

Most striking are the indications that the differences between the parties and candidates in presidential election years are understood by the electorate as a whole. As we saw in Chapter 3, misperception is possible and even likely under some circumstances, but on the whole, the electorate correctly places the Democratic party and its presidential candidates on the liberal side of center and the Republicans to the right of center. For the most part, candidates are seen as pretty close to their party. The biggest exception can be seen in 1972, when McGovern was perceived as almost a full unit more liberal than the Democratic party. Latter-day Democratic candidates have all been perceived as being to the right of their party.

Care must be taken not to make too much of the differences represented in Figure 4-5. Calculations of respondents' estimates of the parties' and candidates' locations exclude the substantial numbers of respondents who are not sure where to place them on the liberal–conservative scale. Of course, such uncertainty is very likely to result from the convergence strategy. Candidates may also deemphasize their differences on some issues (perhaps the most important ones) or stress positive aspects of their personal image in such a way as to render differences between the candidates and parties less relevant than they would be if they were stressed during the campaign. Despite these qualifications, however, it does appear that at least the broad cast of party differences is understood by much of the electorate.

But assume for a moment that candidates and parties follow a strategy of convergence in campaigns. From one perspective, such a strategy is not only rational for candidates, it is perfectly consistent with the public interest. Consider again the example of the nacho stands. The beach commission, if it had the power to do so, would place the stands at equal distances between the ends of the boardwalk and the center. But what if the nacho stand that sells the fewest nachos must leave, and the "winning" stand is left alone on the boardwalk? Where should the commission place that stand? By the public-interest criterion that the greatest distance anyone walks to buy a nacho should be minimized, the ideal location of the one stand is at point C, at the center of the boardwalk. That, of course, is exactly where the stands go if they converge toward the equilibrium point.

A similar argument can be applied to candidates and parties.[26] If the distribution of public opinion on the liberal–conservative scale clusters around the middle, with relatively few voters at the extremes, where should the parties ideally locate themselves? By

---

[26]Page, *Choices and Echoes*, chap. 2.

the **criterion of choice** they should differentiate themselves clearly so that voters can choose between them without incurring substantial information costs. When parties take clearly different stands, voters come to see the differences between them and can communicate their preferences with respect to those differences. But by the **optimum outcome criterion,** the candidates should be located right at the center. For it is the case that one party will win and one will lose, and the winner controls government (occupies the White House, say) more or less as a monopoly. Therefore, the optimum location for both contenders is as close to the center of the distribution of public opinion as possible.

Whether party systems should be judged by the degree of choice they offer voters or by their approximation to an optimal position in the political space is a question that raises difficult issues of democratic theory. A full airing of these issues would range well beyond the scope of this chapter. However, in closing our discussion of party theory as an alternative to the Republic, we can link our analysis of the way parties actually function in American politics to some fundamental issues in party theory. Party theorists are not unanimous in their responses to these questions, but the questions must be raised (and worried over) if we are to continue to think of party theory as an alternative to the Republic and pluralism.

Three Issues in Party Theory

How Much Choice Must There Be Between the Parties?

The bulk of opinion among party theorists is in favor of ideologically coherent and distinctive political parties. The argument by now is familiar. Voters cannot be expected to take on the costs of ferreting out information relevant to their voting choice. If such information is readily available, they pick it up. Thus most party theorists believe that if political conflict can be organized more visibly around the differences between the parties, voters will appreciate the differences and use their votes to communicate their preferences.

What of the strategy of convergence? Some party theorists simply deny that the nacho-stand situation is analogous to party competition. They argue that if party organizations are strengthened and party discipline is thereby promoted, the minority party will differentiate itself from the majority party and come up with innovative policy alternatives in order to win votes. To be sure, the parties will not differ on everything. But the differences between them will become the focal points of political conflict so long as the parties are given the resources they need.

Another response to the problem posed by party convergence is to deny its importance. This is tantamount to saying that the ideological differences between the parties need not be visible to the voter. What is important, in this view, is the ability of voters to fix responsibility for the results of public policy; it is not important that voters participate in the debate over means. Ideological differences between the parties often speak to means rather than results. Thus a conservative may believe the best way to achieve prosperity is to let the market work unfettered by government manipulation, whereas a liberal may think the government must interfere quite substantially with the market if the nation is to achieve prosperity. But so long as both can agree on a definition of prosperity, the argument is about how best to achieve what everyone agrees is a good thing. Voters can base their choices, then, on their assessment of the job the party in power has done in its efforts to promote prosperity. Let the experts debate about how much market regulation is required, just as automotive engineers debate the best way to increase gas mileage.

The answer to the problem of how much difference there should be between the parties, then, depends in large part on how informed one believes voters can and should be. Some party theorists believe that voters need very little information to make reasonable choices between parties so long as they know whom to blame for nasty outcomes. They argue that party organizations need to be strengthened so that responsibility may be fixed; for them the issue and ideological differences between the parties are not very important. For others, an electorate informed about the differences between the parties is important because voters then become involved not only in the business of judging results but also in the choices of the means best calculated to achieve the desired results. From this perspective, participation in the choice among means is an important part of the democratic ideal. People who take this view deny the relevance of the consumer analogy to voters because it ignores the involvement of citizens in critical political debates about the course of national policy.

How Many Parties Should There Be?

All party theorists agree that one party is not enough. Defenders of the two-party system argue that the virtue of having two and only two parties is that the winning party automatically has a majority and thus can organize the government. This is a desirable feature because responsibility for the conduct of government can be clearly fixed: the governing party is responsible. Proponents of a two-party system are willing to acknowledge that the parties may converge in elections and thus reduce the visibility of the choice offered to voters. Moreover, when the options are reduced to a simple choice between two parties, the system fails to capture the diversity of interests in society, the shades of opinion found among all factions, and the differences of emphasis that diversity implies. Nonetheless, given the importance they attach to political responsibility, many party theorists strongly prefer a two-party system over a multiparty system.

Those who would like to see more than two parties usually argue that the complexity of modern society demands more choices than two contenders alone can offer. Inevitably, multiparty systems offer those choices. People who take this position usually emphasize the importance of choice over responsibility because in multiparty systems several small parties often must form a coalition *after* the election in order to organize the government. Such coalition governments can be faulted for the difficulty of fixing responsibility, since parties in the coalition have the opportunity to claim credit for successes and shift blame for failures to their partners.

How Much Democracy Should There Be Within the Parties?

The question that party theorists find most difficult to resolve is: how democratic should the parties be? Party theorists are committed to the ideal of democracy. Yet many devices for promoting democracy *within* the parties have the effect of weakening the party organizations. And, of course, party theorists are committed to strengthening party organizations as the surest way to promote democracy. Take the direct primary as an example. The **direct primary** is an election to determine which of several nomination candidates will receive the party's nomination, and it is designed to introduce more democracy into the nomination process. Direct primaries have become a prominent feature of American politics, and winning a primary is an essential first step toward winning most political offices at the state and national levels today.

Despite the fact that primaries dramatically increase participation in nominations and are on this count more democratic than closed systems of nomination, it can be argued that they are quite undemocratic in their effects. The people who vote in primaries are not typical of voters in the fall. To the extent, then, that they make choices that represent their own views rather than anticipate the interests of the broader fall electorate, the results may be quite unrepresentative of the desires of the voting public.[27] Primaries may encourage a proliferation of candidates. They may lead to highly visible and divisive contests within the parties which have

---

[27]Nelson W. Polsby, *Consequences of Party Reform* (New York: Oxford University Press, 1983). Polsby is quite critical of the proliferation of the direct primary in contemporary presidential nominations.

negative effects that carry over to the fall, and which encourage candidates to establish personal organizations independent of the party. By removing control over nominations from the party organization, primaries weaken the parties. Party theorists who oppose the direct primary and similar attempts to promote intraparty democracy usually conclude that democratic ideals are most likely to be realized in the competition *between* the parties rather than by efforts to promote democracy *within* the party organizations.

Some party theorists are quite supportive of efforts to increase democracy within the parties. They argue that party leaders (including candidates) must be accountable to the membership of the party, but that means other than the direct primary are available. Caucuses of activists, for instance, could select candidates for nomination and determine the party's policy commitments. A linkage of nominations and party platforms to party activists might discourage party convergence, since activists are usually strongly committed to ideological positions. Parties might also be more sensitive to changing social and economic conditions if they were subject to greater control by active members.[28]

Conclusion: Are the Parties in Decline?

The American political parties are at best weak reflections of what party theorists would like to see. They do not go very far toward controlling the resources that would enable them to discipline their members and use nominations to promote broad policy goals. They must operate within a constitutional environment that is hostile to their very existence. Many observers believe that the parties are at an even greater disadvantage now than they were in the past, and as a result are in a period of decline. This idea worries party theorists, for obvious reasons, and it even troubles many pluralists. Pluralists do not believe that the American government should be reorganized around party theory, but neither do they want to see the parties wither away.

Are American parties, never very strong, actually in decline? As usual, the answer is not altogether clear. Observers who see decline point to several factors that support their pessimism. One of the most important developments is "dealignment" in the electorate. In 1952, only about 6 percent of the electorate declared itself "strictly independent" of party identification. By the early 1970s that figure had more than doubled, to over 14 percent, though it has dropped some since then. Dealignment may contribute to party decline be-

---

[28]For a particularly good defense of intraparty democracy, see Alan Ware, *The Logic of Party Democracy* (New York: St. Martin's Press, 1979).

cause the electorate is more fluid, more subject to appeal by independent candidates and interest groups, and less susceptible to the major parties' appeals.

Party organizations may also be in decline, particularly if one looks at their ability to influence nominations. The proliferation of direct primaries is one reason. In 1952, seventeen states held Democratic primaries during the presidential nomination campaign. By 1988, the number had jumped to thirty-five. A similar increase occurred on the Republican side.[29] Since primaries are not known for encouraging candidates to be loyal to the party organization once they are nominated and elected to office, this development is generally seen as weakening the parties. Along with weakened parties, many observers see increased involvement by special interests in nominations and general election campaigns. Since parties no longer have so many of the resources necessary for election, candidates turn to interest groups for money, volunteers, and endorsements in order to wage their campaigns. This development may help account for decreasing party cohesion in government.[30]

Not everyone accepts the thesis that the parties are in decline,[31] but it worries those who look to the parties to provide some coherence to American national politics. Of course, the decline of party would not trouble a strict defender of Madison's Republic. For Madison, fragmentation was desirable. Power should be dispersed among many factions, and any organization that sets out to shape a majority into a faction capable of controlling government, as a party does, should be allowed to decline, if it were ever permitted to exist in the first place. Yet parties today are a familiar and important part of the political scene. Almost all close observers of politics see the parties' historical development as significant in the growth of modern democratic institutions. The debate, as we have seen, is not over whether parties should exist. The question is whether government and politics should be organized around party conflict, or whether the pluralists' vision of politics should prevail.

We turn next to an analysis of pluralism as the contemporary version of the Republic and the principal rival to party theory in our

---

[29]Polsby, *Consequences of Party Reform*, p. 64.
[30]Melissa P. Collie and David W. Brady, "The Decline of Partisan Voting Coalitions in the House of Representatives," in *Congress Reconsidered*, ed. Lawrence C. Dodd and Bruce I. Oppenheimer, 3rd ed. (Washington, D.C.: Congressional Quarterly Press, 1985), pp. 272–287.
[31]Joseph A. Schlesinger, "On the Theory of Party Organization," *Journal of Politics* 46 (May 1984): 369–400. Schlesinger argues, for instance, that dealignment should strengthen the party organizations because it creates a more open market in which they can compete. With more independents, a party can hope to attract voters who are not locked in to support of the opposition party.

analysis. The choice between them turns ultimately on the issue of whether power should be concentrated or dispersed. Party theorists have taken their stand for concentrated power and in doing so reject a conclusion fundamental to Madisonian theory. What to do with power is a serious question. The answer offered by party theory demands that we look beyond the antics of Dutch's Dollies to the serious purposes that parties can serve in a contemporary democracy. Pluralists would have us look to interest groups as the principal vehicles of political representation, and side with Madison on the issue of political power. This debate invites us to examine one of the most fundamental questions political theory is capable of raising.

Key Concepts

contagion of conflict

criterion of choice

direct primary

electoral democracy

governing party

nomination activists

opposition party

optimum outcome criterion

parliamentary system

party discipline

political equality

proportional representation

rationality crisis

responsibility

strategy of convergence

winner-take-all system of representation

Factions Revisited

Interest Groups in American Politics

Recall Brian, whom we met in Chapter 3. He is a Lutheran and an electrician. He belongs to a union and to a neighborhood association, and he is quite active in his church. He is also a problem. He is a problem, that is, from the perspective of two of the theories we have been discussing. He is a problem for Madison's Republic because he is not self-interested when it comes to politics. He does not think of himself as politically interested or active, he often does not vote, and he is not very well informed about public affairs. So Brian does not meet the expectation of a self-interested citizen actively pursuing his interests through political participation.

"But," you may say, "what about Brian's factional interests?" Madison is keenly aware that religious affiliations and economic activities give rise to factions "united by some common impulse of passion, or of interest, adverse to the rights of other citizens, or to the permanent and aggregate interests of the community." And Brian belongs to religious and economic groups. But neither he nor anyone else would mistake his motives for belonging to the Lutheran church or to a union for an "impulse of passion." Neither could we say he is politically motivated. He did not join the church with any intention of confronting the interests of any other group, to say nothing of the "permanent and aggregate interests of the community."

So if we want to link faction to political self-interest in a direct way, Brian and the millions of citizens like him present a problem to the Republic. Of course, he is also a problem for party theory. His political self-interest is not well formed and often it is not expressed in elections. It is not so much that party theory fails to anticipate citizens like Brian. Rather, party theory despairs of achieving its democratic values unless something can be done first to inform citizens like Brian and then to activate them.

Brian is not a problem for pluralists. In fact, he was introduced in Chapter 3 to provide a preview of pluralist theory. The purpose of this chapter is to spell out pluralist theory in as complete a way as possible. Keep in mind that pluralists agree that Brian is not self-interested in the way Madison expected of citizens in the Republic. Keep in mind also that pluralists recognize the tensions we have explored between the instrumental and cost-benefit concepts of self-interest. Nonetheless, pluralist theory is remarkably close to the argument found in the Republic. It must modify the expectation of self-interest, and it does not see elections as the only (or even the principal) means by which citizens' interests are linked to government activity. But pluralists do not believe that these modifications of the Republic undermine its central conclusions. And they certainly do not accept the party theorists' contention that the American government must be fundamentally reformed.

The Pluralist Theory of American Democracy

The central insight of pluralism gives the theory its name and echoes themes prominent in *Federalist* 10 and 51. American society is complex and embodies many (plural) interests. Therefore, a complex, pluralistic government is necessary. Just as Madison argues in *Federalist* 10 that society contains many factions that check one another, so pluralists argue there are many "interest groups" clamoring for attention, making claims, and influencing policy and one another. Just as Madison contends in *Federalist* 51 that the government must be complex, with many centers of power, each responsive to different, offsetting interests, so pluralists maintain that governmental power must be dispersed, with "multiple points of access" for groups' claims on government. The language has changed but the ideas are similar. Indeed, many pluralists approvingly cite Madison's arguments, and *Federalist* 10 and 51 serve as a kind of manifesto for pluralist thinkers.[1]

Pluralist Theory and Interest Groups

The pluralist conception of an interest group is very closely related to Madison's understanding of a faction but with much of the sting removed: "As used here 'interest group' refers to any group that, on the basis of one or more shared attitudes *[By a faction I understand a number of citizens . . . actuated by some common impulse of passion or of interest]*, makes certain claims upon other groups in society *[adverse to the rights of other citizens, or to the permanent and aggre-*

---

[1]See David B. Truman, *The Governmental Process* (New York: Knopf, 1951).

gate interests of the community] for the establishment, maintenance, or enhancement of forms of behavior that are implied by the shared attitudes."[2]

Like Madison, pluralist theorists see interest groups as a natural consequence of social living. Differences in occupation, economic status, religious tradition, geography, status, and political preferences give rise to interest groups in American society. People join interest groups because they have something in common—a "shared attitude." Because there are so many sources of differences in contemporary society, there are thousands of interest groups. These groups are not necessarily overtly political in character. In fact, David Truman describes an interest group as political "if and when it makes its claims through or upon any of the institutions of government."[3] Thus Brian is in an interest group when he goes to church because a shared attitude binds the group together (religious tradition, commitment to certain practices and beliefs, and so on). The church is not primarily a political group, but it becomes one when it participates in a lobbying effort in Washington for a nuclear freeze, or when the deacons of the church petition the city council for a Sunday-morning noise ordinance.

Like factions in Madison's Republic, interest groups are the building blocks of the pluralist theory. A group helps to define political interests by informing citizens of policy debates relevant to the group. Thus political action is often facilitated by group membership. Brian leaves church and is presented with the opportunity to sign a nuclear-freeze petition. Most college students, by virtue of being in a group identified by the name of their college or university, are bombarded with politically relevant information. Groups represent the political world to their membership through newsletters and other publications, bulletin boards, political action units, telephone networks, and the like. The information costs associated with monitoring what is going on in the political system are, to some degree, defrayed by the group.

Groups also play a critically important role in the representation of interests to the government. As a result, according to pluralists, government is sensitive to a much broader array of interests than it could become aware of through the simple mechanism of elections. Groups present claims before government by lobbying the Congress, by pressing the bureaucracy for favorable rulings, and by taking their cases to the courts. The claims that interest groups bring to government more or less reflect the shared attitudes that

---

[2]Ibid., p. 33.
[3]Ibid., p. 37.

are the basis of the groups' existence. Hence, when an official of the Sierra Club issues a press release to try to influence public opinion, when an attorney for the National Association for the Advancement of Colored People testifies before a congressional subcommittee, when a university president helps make a case before the National Institutes of Health for a research grant, representation is taking place. Group leaders represent group interests. They may do so imperfectly (much as representatives in a legislature imperfectly reflect the interests of their constituents), but they are providing political representation nonetheless.

In short, interest groups are "linkage" organizations for pluralists, much as political parties are for party theorists.[4] Groups link the interests of ordinary citizens to government, and they help citizens understand how government activity affects their interests. They reduce information costs and they mobilize citizens for political action. Because a wide variety of interests in society are clamoring for satisfaction from government—because society is, in a word, pluralistic—groups inevitably come into conflict with one another. No group has a monopoly on the truth and no group monopolizes political power. The NAACP may win a court case involving discrimination in the armed services but lose in its attempt to get Congress to extend affirmative action policy. College students may catch the attention of the nation when they protest against a war yet be unable to prevent the government from reducing the amount of money available for student loans. Conflict among groups is as important to an understanding of the way the system works as the role any particular group plays in representing specific interests. Let us examine more closely how pluralists see the interest-group system as working.

Resources and Strategies of Interest Groups

In order to get heard, groups must participate in politics. And in order to participate, groups must pay. Participation is costly for individuals, and it is costly for groups.[5] If a group is going to be organized with a staff, a membership, perhaps a newsletter, and an attorney on retainer in Washington, the costs are obvious. Organizations must be maintained, staff must be paid (or induced to volunteer their time), membership lists must be updated, the rent must

---

[4]Pluralists agree that parties are linkage organizations, and party theorists grant that interest groups also serve that function. The issue is how much one can depend on the two kinds of organizations to promote representative democracy.
[5]It is difficult to calculate the precise costs of participation for groups. For an interesting attempt to do so, see Kay Lehman Schlozman and John T. Tierney, *Organized Interests and American Democracy* (New York: Harper & Row, 1986), pp. 107–109.

be paid, and on and on. Organization is important because it enables groups to monitor what government is doing and to alert the membership when political action (such as a petition drive or a letter to a legislator) is called for.

Some pluralists have argued that "potential groups" can have an effect on government even if they are completely unorganized.[6] For instance, even if retired people had no formal, organized group representation in Washington (as in fact they do), politicians would have to consider their potentially negative reactions to public policy. Retired people would organize if they became disturbed enough, and besides, they vote.

Even if we grant some merit to the case for potential interest groups, there can be no doubt that organization is a central resource. After all, if unorganized interests are in conflict with well-organized interests, no one will be surprised to learn that the interests of the unorganized get short shrift. Just getting policy makers' attention is difficult when there is so much activity in the centers of government. To expect decision makers to take into account the interests of those who are not around to press their demands is to expect a lot.

So organization is important. Groups may be more or less organized, they may have a large or a small staff, they may store their membership files in computers or in shoeboxes. But some degree of organization is an essential resource.

If resources are necessary and if participation is costly, does it not follow that a resource bias is at work in the interest-group system just as it is in the electoral system? Pluralists do not deny that some groups have more resources than others. They also realize that resources can be used to further a group's interests and increase its chances of success. But a critical element in the pluralist argument is that an interest group's resources are not cumulative. Therefore, the resource bias in the interest-group system, though it exists, is not crippling to their argument. Groups relatively poor in one resource can cast about for strategies and tactics that reflect their particular resource base. Indeed, sometimes strength in one resource almost necessarily implies weakness with respect to another. We can see this **noncumulative nature of group resources** in the kinds of resources groups draw upon when they enter the political arena.

Size. The relevance of size to a group is obvious in a system that allocates power in part on the basis of the ability to win elections. A

---

[6]Truman, *Governmental Process*, p. 35.

group that could speak authoritatively on behalf of American women, for example, would have tremendous influence because millions of women vote. Size is also a resource that can be converted to strength in other ways. A group that enrolled as dues-paying members even 2 percent of American consumers could afford a huge and highly professional staff.

Geographical dispersion. Like size, geographical dispersion is an important resource because of its fit with the electoral system. John Kingdon found in his study of congressional decision making that interest groups frequently attempt to influence legislators through their constituencies because they know that that tactic enhances their chances of success.[7] Thus a group such as the National Education Association, with a membership consisting of teachers, principals, PTO leaders, and superintendents in every congressional district, has a resource it can exploit when the issue is important enough to warrant mobilization of its members.

Cohesiveness. Cohesiveness enables the leadership of a group to speak with confidence on behalf of the group's interests. If the group is divided, the leadership may have difficulty making statements on controversial policy issues without alienating some part of the membership. One of the problems for a group such as the U.S. Chamber of Commerce is the difficulty of maintaining group cohesion in the face of a large and diverse membership. The Chamber devotes considerable resources to the effort to reconcile differences among its members. Nonetheless, because of its diversity, it can run into trouble. For example, the Chamber has stood foursquare in favor of government deregulation of business. But in successfully pressing that interest during the Carter years, it lost the membership of several airlines, which opposed deregulation of their industry.[8] Similarly, one business may stand to benefit from barriers to the importation of goods produced abroad while others would suffer from such a policy because it would increase their costs. As a result, it is not uncommon for smaller, more cohesive groups to win important policy concessions while groups with large and dispersed memberships stand mute on the issue. Hence cohesiveness is a resource often unavailable to large, geographically dispersed interests.

---

[7]John W. Kingdon, *Congressmen's Voting Decisions*, 2nd ed. (New York: Harper & Row, 1981), pp. 154–158.
[8]W. Douglas Costain and Anne N. Costain, "Interest Groups as Policy Aggregators in the Legislative Process," *Polity* 14 (Winter 1981): 260.

Social status. Included in social status are such resources as the wealth and prestige of the membership or occupation represented and the skills the group is able to call upon. Wealth is an important resource because it can be put to so many uses. It can purchase expertise in the form of attorneys, public relations professionals, and advertising agencies. Status often translates into influence because high-status interests are granted legitimacy by decision makers and public opinion alike. When the American Medical Association weighs in on an issue, the high status of the medical profession lends to its cause a credibility not enjoyed by such low-status occupational groups as morticians and used-car salesmen.

Intensity. "Intensity" refers to the salience of the group's interest to the membership. An intensely concerned membership is more likely to contribute funds and effort to the cause, whether the tactic is flooding Congress with mail expressing a preference on pending legislation, working in a political campaign for or against a particular candidate, or protesting government policy with respect to the family farm, abortion, or registration for the military draft.

Intensity is a resource that supports the pluralists' contention that group resources are not cumulative. A large or geographically dispersed group faces immense barriers in its efforts to elicit a very high level of commitment from its membership. Intensity also can be the basis of successful group action outside the conventional channels of political participation, which tend to reward high social status. For example, the American civil rights movement in the 1960s and the movement in opposition to American involvement in Vietnam at the close of that decade were both fueled by a willingness on the part of many people to become intensely involved in protests. Students do not enjoy high status, nor do they as a group command large amounts of wealth or related resources. But their willingness to take a semester off to protest segregation laws in the South and their participation in countless protests against the Vietnam war called attention to their cause and helped produce significant policy changes.

Certainly this is not a complete list of the resources groups draw upon when they approach government. The major point to grasp is that anything that can be converted into political influence may be considered a resource. And there are many ways of trying to influence political outcomes, from capturing some part of the public's attention to getting the right people elected, from defining an issue in a favorable way to making one's case in the privacy of a representative's office, from filing a brief before an appeals court to persuading an agency head to increase the amount requested for research in a particular area. Resources may be as tangible as a large staff and budget or as impalpable as a good sense of timing. Table 5-1 lists some common tactics groups employ in their attempts to influence political outcomes and some resources useful in their efforts.

Pluralists attribute great importance to interest groups as means by which citizen interests are represented. Even citizens like Brian, who do not participate regularly in electoral politics or who participate without information, can achieve substantial representation through the interest-group system. Yet aside from their representative function, groups support American democracy in another fashion. For Madison, factions are an inevitable expression of the "nature of man." One could destroy factions (and the problems associated with them) by destroying liberty. But this would be a "remedy . . . worse than the disease." Pluralists also see a close relationship between liberty and interest groups. Group conflict provides citizens with alternative views of public issues and insulates the citizen from totalitarian influences.[9] In a society with

Table 5-1 Typical Tactics and Resources of Interest Groups

Tactic	Resources
Individual contact with decision makers through hearings, lobbying, personal contacts	Knowledgeable staff skilled in research and interpersonal relations; legitimacy of cause
Letter-writing campaign by membership	Intensity of commitment by members; size; geographical disperson
Legal action; e.g., class-action suit, "friend of the court" brief in a case of interest	Legal skills, wealth
Campaign contributions, volunteers to work for or against candidates targeted by group	Wealth, intensity, geographical disperson
Public endorsement of candidates for office	Size, geographical disperson, legitimacy of group interests to voting public
Creation of climate of opinion favorable to group	Wealth, public relations and advertising expertise
Protests and demonstrations to call attention to demands and interests	Intensely committed membership, cohesiveness, legitimacy of cause

[9]William Kornhauser, *The Politics of Mass Society* (New York: Free Press, 1959). The concern with a "mass society" is with a society in which the citizenry and the state stand in an unmediated relation to each other. The state, therefore, can dominate the political consciousness of the citizenry without interference from competing opinions expressed by other groups.

many groups in conflict, the individual retains choices and is offered competing perspectives. Group conflict, in short, limits the exercise of public power. Group conflict constrains the institutions of the state, much as Madison hoped that factional conflict would frustrate the arbitrary use of power. Both for Madison and for the pluralists, the absence of group conflict would be a cure far worse than any of the diseases associated with group activity in politics.

Much of what we have said so far is entirely consistent with Madison's understanding of factions. One difference should be noted, however. In the opening paragraphs of *Federalist* 10 Madison laments the "violence" of faction. He associates factions with danger to society and explicitly argues that these dangerous tendencies must be curbed. Pluralists have a much more benign, less threatening view of interest groups. One reason is historical. Madison was writing at a time when the legitimacy and authority of governmental institutions were fragile. Indeed, he wrote to defend a marked strengthening of national institutions and, of course, a new constitutional order. Without that order, he feared, factions would not have a stable, constraining framework within which to pursue their interests. Pluralists, writing in the mid-twentieth century, were less fearful of governmental collapse. They were more concerned to explain the unusual stability and order they saw in American society in comparison with the situations in many other countries.

But aside from the differences in the historical contexts in which they wrote, pluralists conceive of groups as less threatening than Madison's factions because of the moderating pressures of overlapping memberships, or **cross-pressures.** A state chamber of commerce pushing for reduced taxes on corporations and a pro-growth policy to stimulate new industry is composed of many members, some of whom also belong to their local parent-teacher organizations (which seek higher taxes for education) and to environmental groups adamantly opposed to a pro-growth policy. The cross-pressures experienced by most group members have the effect of moderating the group's demands, according to pluralists, because the group leadership cannot afford to alienate important segments of the membership. Since virtually all groups have members who belong to other groups, interest groups are not made up of single-minded individuals "actuated by a common impulse of passion or of interest." Rather, interests are complex—even pluralistic—and their complexity tends to moderate the positions groups take in pursuit of those interests.

The Pluralist Conception of Government

Madison's theory of government reflected his understanding of faction. Government had to be strong in order to subdue the violence of faction. Government's power had to be dispersed and checked in order to prevent one faction from controlling government and perpetuating a tyranny. Pluralists' idea of government is in accord with the Republic, although the terms used to justify it are a bit different. In essence, the argument is that a pluralistic society requires a pluralistic government. Any attempt to organize government around a single principle of power, such as majority rule, will fail. It will fail because it cannot accommodate the complexity of American society. It would also be dangerous because, in failing to reflect society's complexity, it would inevitably lead to something very like Madison's tyranny.

Truman's concept of a government that provides **multiple points of access** for groups complements the pluralists' notion of groups as major channels of representation in society:

> A characteristic feature of the governmental system in the United States is that it contains a multiplicity of points of access. The federal system establishes decentralized and more or less independent centers of power, vantage points from which to secure privileged access to the national government.[10]

Truman goes on to praise a party system that plays an important role in the nomination and election of officeholders but only a weak one in the determination of policy. He also applauds the system of "separation of powers" as providing alternative "lines of access."[11]

Pluralists' acceptance of the governmental framework provided by the Republic is a logical consequence of their argument about interest groups. Because there are many groups with competing interests and differing resources, the well-constituted government provides "privileged access" or representation to these groups. The complexity of government permits different groups to find access at different centers of decision making. Thus a large, poorly organized group may best serve its interests by pursuing them directly through elections and the party system. A group that has little electoral clout may find it advantageous to approach government through the courts. Thus the National Organization for Women and the National Education Association endorsed the Democrat Walter Mondale in his campaign for the presidency in 1984, whereas Jehovah's Witnesses, a small religious minority, is not active in electoral politics but has enjoyed considerable success in protecting its interests through the Supreme Court.

---

[10]Truman, *Governmental Process*, p. 507.
[11]The concluding chapter of Truman's book, "Group Politics and Representative Democracy," is an excellent summary of the pluralist theory of groups and the American system of government.

To Madison, the separation of powers in American national government was a mechanism designed to frustrate majority rule and other sources of tyranny; pluralists see it as a device to ensure that different kinds of interests get heard. It amounts to the same argument. The interests that have leverage in the House are not necessarily the same interests that have clout in the Senate. The congressional committee system favors well-organized interests capable of monitoring what Congress is doing, whereas presidential politics is much more visible than congressional politics to large, poorly organized interests. The kinds of resources groups can call upon are varied and the complexity of the governmental process rewards that variety. The "checks and balances" in government work in such a way that a group resource that is valuable in the House of Representatives is not necessarily important to a case before the Supreme Court. Presidential candidates are attentive to some kinds of interests, but bureaucrats may be responsive to an entirely different set of groups.

So, pluralists conclude, power in government must be dispersed. They reject the party theorists' argument for concentrated governmental power for reasons that, again, closely parallel Madison's reasons for abhoring any scheme that concentrates power. Pluralists argue that concentration of power in American government won't work because it is unrealistic to expect a pluralistic society to reduce its political conflicts to a single choice. Party theory, according to Truman, would reduce "the diversity of lines of access to governmental decisions."[12] In reducing access, it would necessarily reduce representation. In organizing itself around a single principle for the control of governmental power—majority rule—it would deny the eclectic nature of political influence in the current system. Interests not capable of playing the electoral game successfully would be shut out. A majoritarian system would respond to interests with resources that are convertible in that exchange, and would destroy the noncumulative nature of interest-group resources in the current system. The mechanism of electoral choice reduces political conflict to a much too simple choice between alternatives that cannot hope to match the diverse social, economic, and political interests found in American society.

---

[12]Truman, *Governmental Process*, p. 528. Truman, like many pluralists, is extremely skeptical about the possibility of reforming the American system on the principles of party theory: "Nothing seems more certain than that peaceful constitutional change in the United States will take place only in such fashion as to permit the continued existence of the fiction that the system remains essentially as it came to us from the Founding Fathers. A crisis so severe as to permit a wholesale revamping would be revolutionary in the most complete sense. . . . The stubborn facts of diversity always constrict the sphere in which co-ordinated access and party discipline can operate" (pp. 530, 533).

Pluralism, it should now be clear, is a theoretical variation on themes already stated in Madison's Republic. Pluralist theory departs most clearly from Madison in its understanding of the citizen. But the theory's dependence on interest groups is closely related to the centrality of factions in Madison's thinking. And the pluralists' acceptance of a government based on dispersed power is identical to the Republic's insistence that the institutions of government be constituted in such a way as to respond to different interests, but with overlapping powers, or "checks." Dispersed governmental power, in short, is the operative principle both in the Republic and for the pluralists. Pluralism can be summarized in six propositions that begin with the theory's understanding of the citizen and end with government:

1. *Citizens are not politically self-interested.* This, admittedly, is an overstatement. Some people are intensely concerned about politics some of the time. And almost everyone may in some way be characterized as politically self-interested. But politics is remote from the concerns of most people most of the time. Most people are not well informed, they are not active. Thus pluralists beg to differ with the Republic's understanding of the citizen.

2. *Elections are not the only or the most important means of linking citizens to government.* Because citizens are not politically self-interested, the instrumental model of elections does not do a very good job of describing how elections function. Elections can neither communicate citizens' interests effectively nor enforce leaders' accountability to the citizens. Elections and political parties serve as *one* means to connect citizens to government, and together with the interest-group system they help to produce a government responsive to the public. So pluralists do not claim that elections are irrelevant or merely symbolic. And for interests whose resources are most conducive to mobilization through the electoral process, elections are critically important. The key point, however, is that the success of representative government does not depend on the success of the instrumental model of elections. Elections are a necessary but not a sufficient condition for representative government.

3. *Citizens participate widely in the interest-group system by virtue of their economic, social, religious, and political interests.* Involvement in interest groups does not spring primarily from political interests, although the "shared attitudes" that form the basis of group involvement may be political. To say that citizens are not politically self-interested is only to say that people do not generally become intensely concerned about political affairs. But the vast majority of citizens are socially active through their occupations,

religious affiliations, hobbies, neighborhoods, educational pursuits, and the like. These activities connect them to politics and government because the interests that bring people together sometimes are affected by what another group or government is doing. Moreover, from the perspective of the politically interested citizen, it often makes more sense to pursue political ends through an interest group than through a political party. Parties, because they must strive to attract a majority, face powerful pressures to be ambiguous on the issues. Groups, however, can be associated with precise policy goals because they need not attract majority support. As Jeffrey Berry puts it, "the appeal of the American Soybean Association, the Veterans of Foreign Wars, and the Independent Truckers Association is that each works only on the problems of soybean farmers, veterans, and independent truckers, respectively. A dollar donated to these groups is a dollar spent on their narrow set of issues."[13]

4. *Political action by interest groups is costly.* The principal costs of participation in the political process through interest groups are associated with organization. Organization is essential to a group's efforts to inform its members of the stake they have in political action and to monitor government behavior. It is also important to most of the strategies groups pursue in their efforts to influence public policy.

5. *Despite the costs of participation, the group system is reasonably inclusive and balanced in the interests it represents before government.* Whereas the electoral system fails to carry the full array of interests in society to governmental councils, the interest-group system is more inclusive and balanced. Whereas many citizens do not vote, very few are excluded altogether from participation in the group system. Pluralists recognize the presence of bias in the interest-group system, but they contend that the group system is more inclusive and better captures the diversity of American society than a system that depends primarily on two parties in competion in an electoral arena. Government that reflects the diversity of American society is an important value to pluralists. It addresses not only the vast array of specific and often quite narrow interests in society but also the intensity with which those interests are pursued. Thus, for pluralists, the simple fact that a majority loses to a minority is not evidence that the system is "unrepresentative" or "undemocratic." It may simply mean that the minority cares much more deeply and is therefore more willing to pay the costs associated with efforts to influence government. Intensity, remember, is one kind of resource—a resource that is more likely to be associated with small groups than with large ones.

---

[13]Jeffrey M. Berry, *The Interest Group Society* (Boston: Little, Brown, 1984), p. 56.

6. *Governmental power should be fragmented and dispersed.* The constitutional system based on separate institutions sharing power is completely consistent with pluralist theory. It provides "multiple lines of access" for groups so that interests with different resources and different claims to make on government can get representation. Pluralist theory, at bottom, shares with Madison a skepticism about governmental power: it cautions against investing too much power in a single institution or organizing governmental power around a single principle, such as majority rule.

Party Theory's Critique of Pluralism

To be blunt, party theory charges pluralism with resting its case on a pipe dream. Pluralists agree with the evidence that most citizens are not politically self-interested, yet they believe that political representation nonetheless occurs through interest groups. In one important respect, party theorists want to hold to a fundamental Madisonian proposition: political self-interest leads to representation. Without self-interest, representation will not occur except by happenstance. No one should base a political theory on happenstance.

The pluralist case rests on positive answers to two questions: (1) Do groups represent the interests of their members? and (2) Is the interest-group system reasonably complete in the range of interests included within it? The evidence that speaks to these questions is not complete by any means, and many complexities and difficulties have to be smoothed over. The critics of pluralism believe that the evidence is sufficiently strong to warrant negative answers.[14] Pluralists, obviously, think otherwise.

The Logic of Individual Participation in Groups

One of the cornerstone insights for pluralism's critics comes with a reexamination of the reasons that people support (and fail to support) interest groups. The pluralist position is that shared attitudes motivate people to support groups. According to pluralist thinking, a shared preference for higher soybean prices motivates farmers who grow soybeans to support a group lobbying for public policy designed to increase the market price of soybeans. But we have seen since Chapter 2 that although people may have an instrumental

---

[14]For a supremely confident statement criticizing pluralist theory, see E. E. Schatt-schneider, *The Semisovereign People: A Realist's View of Democracy in America* (Hinsdale, Ill.: Dryden Press, 1975). Another work sharply critical of pluralism but less closely associated with party theory is Mancur Olson, *The Logic of Collective Action* (New York: Schocken, 1968).

self-interest in something, they nonetheless may have no interest in helping to pay for it. According to Mancur Olson, the paradox of collective action applies to members and potential members of interest groups: the collective good is available to all who stand to benefit from the group's success.[15] Thus soybean farmers share a collective interest in higher prices for their product, but if they act in accord with their self-interest, they remain free riders. So long as the group is reasonably large, according to the familiar logic, the contribution of one farmer more or less to a group's effort to influence policy will not affect the group's chances for success. So the individual farmer who decides not to help pay for the group's efforts (by contributing his time, membership dues, and so on) still benefits from whatever success the group enjoys.

Olson uses this logic to question the pluralist conclusion that groups will naturally form when an interest is shared and when some political action is implied by that shared interest. He suggests that many times groups do not form even though every potential member of the group has a shared and strongly held interest in some outcome. If every soybean farmer behaved as a free rider, the American Soybean Association would not exist. But a group able to overcome the paradox of collective action still may not be able to organize all of its potential members because many remain free riders. Thus, according to Olson, benefits that otherwise might accrue to the group are provided at a less than optimal level.

Olson's argument has encouraged a reconsideration of the reasons people participate in interest groups. And while it is clear he has a point, it is equally evident that the paradox of collective action cannot fully explain why people do or do not participate in interest groups. Still, we can gain some useful insights by pursuing the question. Let us make a simple distinction between **political groups,** the bulk of whose members are motivated by political concerns, and **nonpolitical groups,** most of whose members give their support for nonpolitical reasons.[16]

The paradox of collective action simply does not apply to many nonpolitical groups. Members join and support the group because they receive some private benefit from membership, and there is no temptation to be a free rider. When Brian joins his union, he does so primarily because his job depends on union membership. He cannot get or keep his job as an electrician unless he joins the union. A student who supports a university by paying tuition does so because

---

[15]Olson, *Logic of Collective Action.*
[16]See Robert H. Salisbury, "An Exchange Theory of Interest Groups," *Midwest Journal of Political Science* 13 (February 1969): 1–32, for a discussion of the reasons people actively support interest groups.

the university offers a private benefit—an education, a diploma—which is unavailable unless tuition bills are paid. A physician who joins the American Medical Association has access to professional information and networks via journals and conventions sponsored by the association. If the doctor fails to pay her dues, the publications of the association stop coming. And of course, "members" of a corporation such as Lockheed or General Electric must support the corporation's activities by contributing their time and efforts as employees if they expect to continue to receive a salary. The Brians of the world belong to a church for religious and social reasons. Although there usually is no material reason for church involvement, if their primary religious and social needs are not satisfied, presumably churchgoers look elsewhere.

Political groups must rely primarily on political incentives for support. Even if such groups provide some personal benefits (such as a membership card, a letter of thanks from a visible national leader, or the opportunity to associate with like-minded people), those benefits usually do not directly compensate the members for the time or dues they contribute. Political groups are distinguished from nonpolitical groups by their dependence on their members' commitment to their *political* purposes. The members share the goals of the group, are active on the group's behalf because they are commited to the group's purposes and do not consider the personal costs of their support to be relevant.

Many groups associated with a cause plainly fall into this category. When Brian's neighborhood association mobilizes to oppose the city's plans to widen the thoroughfare through the neighborhood, it depends heavily on Brian and his neighbors not to be free riders. Brian may be active in the group simply because he shares its goals and does not even consider sitting out the group's campaign. Members of his church who oppose abortion are active in the pro-life movement out of a strong moral and ideological commitment to their cause. So are others active in the pro-choice movement. Countless other groups, from student public-interest coalitions to the American Civil Liberties Union, from the Moral Majority to anti-capital punishment groups and environmental groups, depend on some degree of "irrationality" in their members. If all who shared their political goals were strictly self-interested free riders, the groups would not be able to exist.

The point of distinguishing between political and nonpolitical groups is not to argue that groups organized for other than political purposes are outside of the political arena. Indeed, the pluralists are correct when they point out that corporations, universities, churches, and labor unions often are quite active in politics. Party theorists emphasize the distinction between political and nonpolitical groups because the members' reasons for their group activities have important effects on how adequately groups represent their members' interests. The distinction between political and nonpolitical groups also is important in understanding the adequacy of the group system to capture the range of interests in society. Critics argue that nonpolitical groups cannot be depended on as adequate channels of representation and that severe biases are associated with the group system. Therefore, the electoral system must be energized in accordance with the program of party theory described in Chapter 4.

Implications for Group Representation

The point here is a simple one: groups that rely on material and other nonpolitical benefits to motivate their members' support will be less likely to represent their political interests than groups that rely on political incentives.

Consider the case of a student who adamantly opposes the arms race. His university regularly seeks funds from the government for research that contributes to the United States' military readiness. The student opposes such research. He may join a protest against the research, he may write a letter to the regents of the university or to state legislators. Does he continue to support the university by paying tuition? Probably. He has a bargain with the university which has nothing directly to do with research for the military. He pays tuition, the university supplies him with instruction and ultimately a diploma. If the university were to renege on that bargain by eliminating his major or by hiring incompetent professors, the student would withdraw his support from the university. But so long as the student is receiving what he came to the university to get, he continues to pay tuition. Of course, it need hardly be pointed out that by paying tuition he is supporting the organizational resources of the university, including those that it uses to persuade government decision makers to fund research relevant to the military.

In general, groups that can provide nonpolitical benefits that adequately compensate their members for their support may be relatively free to pursue political goals contrary to the interests of their members. This is not to say that there are no constraints on group leaders, or that there are no mechanisms that can produce representation of the members' interests. Certainly when Brian's union opposes legislation that would make it more difficult for it to bargain on his behalf with his employer, the union is representing Brian's interests. But when the union joins a lobbying campaign to promote affirmative action, Brian may feel much less certain that it is representing his preferences.

Now consider Terry, a medical doctor in a large northwestern city. Terry actively supports Physicians for Social Responsibility because he agrees with their position on the nuclear arms race. Every year he sends a $60 check for his membership dues. Terry has not read Olson's book, and if he did read it, he would not be impressed by it. He knows that in a strict economic sense he is not getting anything like his money's worth from PSR. The occasional book discounts, the conventions, the newsletter, and the membership card are worth much less than $60 in strictly material terms. In fact, Terry would send his check even if PSR stopped providing any of these private benefits. Terry belongs to Physicians for Social Responsibility for political reasons. He wants to support the group's efforts to stop the arms race.

What would cause Terry to stop supporting Physicians for Social Responsibility? He would stop if he thought it was not being aggressive enough in opposing the arms race, or if the group took a stand on another issue of major importance to him with which he disagreed. Groups such as Physicians for Social Responsibility rely on a strong commitment by their members to their political purpose. They know their members are motivated by the political goals of the group, and they base their appeals for support on explicitly political goals (see Figure 5-1). If the National Abortion Rights Action League failed to oppose the nomination of a Supreme Court justice dedicated to the reversal of the ruling that asserted women's right to abortion, its membership would be appalled. Significant numbers of them would probably withdraw. Just as surely, if the National Right to Life Committee failed to support the nomination, many of its members would withdraw their support.

Therefore, there is good reason to believe that groups that rely on political incentives represent their members' political interests. However, when pluralists make their case for interest groups as important conduits for representation, they do not emphasize groups whose members are politically motivated. In order to get past the lack of political interest in many citizens, pluralists must stress the importance of nonpolitical groups in the lives of millions of people like Brian. But in the absence of political interests, party theory asserts, it is folly to expect political representation. No amount of wishful thinking in an effort to escape the consequences of Madison's failure to appreciate citizens' indifference to politics can change that fact.

Implications for the Interest-Group System

Is the interest-group system reasonably inclusive of the range of interests in society? Evidence on the question is not so clear as we would like, but there is reason to believe that a crippling resource

Pₕysicians for Sₒcial Rₑsponsibility

The United States' Affiliate of International Physicians
for the Prevention of Nuclear War, Recipient of the
1985 NOBEL PEACE PRIZE

Dear Member,

As I write, we have before us an opportunity to help our nation and the world take an important step back from the nuclear abyss. But we must act. Now.

This spring, the House of Representatives and the Senate will be voting on military funding that the Administration has requested for 1988. And may -- depending on the work of Physicians for Social Responsibility in the next eight weeks -- for the first time in history, eliminate the funding for further nuclear testing.

Last year the House of Representatives voted to cut off funding for nuclear testing. The Senate did not. When the President went to the Iceland summit, the House relented and nuclear testing continued.

Now there is a more sympathetic Senate and more support than ever in the House -- there is a real possibility that testing can be stopped. Now.

But it will take pressure to bring about this halt. As concerned physicians and supporters of PSR, we have a special obligation to use the attention accorded us in Congress and to help create that pressure.

During the 19-month Soviet nuclear testing moratorium the U.S. tested 25 times. While the Soviets have recently resumed testing, they have announced their willingness to halt testing again whenever the U.S. is ready to join them. The timing could never be better for PSR to focus attention on this critical issue and really make a difference.

And we need your help.

We know that the administration will fight this legislative effort with everything they've got. To stop this administration in its nuclear tracks it will take the kind of resources that only our members can supply. That is why I am asking for your special financial support.

● ● ●

Stopping testing is just one step, but it is a crucial one. We must take that step now. Our leaders must realize that we will not follow them into the nuclear abyss willingly.

Please help now. There is no time to waste.

Sincerely,

Victor Sidel, M.D.
President

Figure 5-1 Sample Membership Appeal Letter from a Political Group

bias operates in the interest-group system. One way to see this resource bias is to consider who participates in groups. Many studies have reported evidence that the people who participate in voluntary membership groups are more educated and have higher incomes than those who do not participate.[17] Participation in groups is costly in time and money, and those with the resources will be better able to bear the opportunity costs involved. This observation may be especially relevant to groups that rely on political incentives. A political interest group that depends on its members' contributions of dues or other resources to support its efforts to attain shared issue goals is asking its members to forgo the self-interested stance of a free rider. People with substantial resources will be better able to do so.

Common Cause is a national interest group devoted to government reform. It also apparently depends on its members to share in the group's political goals. A membership survey found that substantial proportions joined Common Cause because they wanted to help it achieve its goals. Yet the membership of Common Cause is not at all typical of the general population. In 1982, for example, the median family income of members was almost twice the national norm.[18] Table 5-2 compares the levels of education among Common Cause members and the national population. Striking evidence of bias can be seen. Whereas only 19 percent of the population in 1982

Table 5-2 Level of Education of Common Cause Members and National Population, 1982 (percent)

	Common Cause members	National population
Some high school	2%	23%
High school graduate	6	34
Some college	15	24
College graduate	19	12
Graduate education	57	7
No response	1	–
Total	100%	100%

SOURCES: For Common Cause, Andrew S. McFarland, *Common Cause: Lobbying in the Public Interest* (Chatham, N.J.: Chatham House, 1984), pp. 48–49; for national population, Center for Political Studies, University of Michigan, *American National Election Study, 1982* (Ann Arbor: Interuniversity Consortium for Political and Social Research, 1984).

---

[17]Schattschneider, *Semisovereign People;* Schlozman and Tierney, *Organized Interests,* p. 60.
[18]Andrew S. McFarland, *Common Cause: Lobbying in the Public Interest* (Chatham, N.J.: Chatham House, 1984), pp. 47–48. Of members surveyed, 27 percent "wanted to feel [they] had a say in government," 26 percent joined because they believed in the aims of the group, and 12 percent mentioned national issues.

had graduated from college, fully 76 percent of Common Cause members had at least a bachelor's degree. Other studies find similar patterns among other political groups.[19]

The ability of a resource bias to determine in large part who joins political interest groups may be especially damaging to the pluralist argument. There is good reason to believe that the bias is much greater among groups that depend on political motivations than among groups that can compensate their members with material benefits. If political groups are more likely than nonpolitical groups to represent the interests of their members to government, the bias is compounded. The interests that are most likely to be heard by policy makers are those of people rich in resources, who can afford to be politically active.

Critics who question the pluralist hope for representation through the interest-group system attack the question from another perspective as well. Because the free-rider problem is especially difficult for political groups to overcome, they are less likely to form, less likely to endure, and less vigorous in their political action than groups that rely on material incentives. All of the factors that make organization possible and that are costly can be labeled **organizational overhead.** Depending on the group, these factors may include everything from staff salaries to rent, from newsletters to expense allowances, from computer time to stationery.

How does a group pay its organizational overhead? Most groups that can afford to offer their members material incentives are directly or indirectly engaged in economic activity. Corporations, labor unions, universities, and professional associations do not face the free-rider problem. Their primary reason for existence is economic, and they pay their organizational overhead out of the proceeds of their economic activities. If they are not successful in the marketplace in which they compete, they cannot survive as organizations. But if they are successful, most of the organizational costs associated with political activity are already paid when it comes time to act as a political interest group. A large state-supported university pays for the staff it retains for legislative liaison in the state capital out of its general operating budget. Students' tuition helps to support that activity. For such groups, attempts to influence government can be considered a by-product of their primary activities.[20] Even a group such as a church or a fraternal organization, whose purpose is not primarily economic,

[19]Schlozman and Tierney, *Organized Interests*, pp. 58–63.
[20]Olson, *Logic of Collective Action;* Robert H. Salisbury, "Interest Representation: The Dominance of Institutions," *American Political Science Review* 78 (March 1984): 64–76.

nonetheless pays its organizational overhead out of the income derived from its nonpolitical activity. If it is successful, the organizational apparatus is available for political action, again as a by-product of the group's primary reason for existence.

A group whose primary reason for existence is political must pay its organizational overhead out of income derived from its political efforts. By definition, it must attract its membership from among politically interested citizens who share its goals. The fact that the bargain between the group and its membership is a political one makes the group more likely to represent its members' interests. But it also makes it more difficult to pay the costs of organizing. Whereas individuals can quite rationally exchange their time and efforts for a salary when they go to work for a corporation, they must have surplus time and energy, or a very strong commitment to the cause, or (probably) both, before they can afford to contribute substantial personal resources to a political group.

This argument has several implications for the pluralists' contention that the interest-group system is inclusive. Groups with explicitly political goals may have more difficulty organizing and entering the interest-group system. Since interests that do not enjoy an organizational base from which they can draw resources face serious barriers in their efforts to enter the political fray, it is no surprise that corporate and producing interests are overrepresented in Washington circles. Kay Schlozman and John Tierney estimate, for example, that about 7 percent of the U.S. population in 1980 was engaged in managerial and administrative occupations, but a whopping 71 percent of the organizations with Washington representation were classified as corporations, trade and business associations, and associations of business professionals. The 9 percent of the population who were engaged in professional and technical occupations were represented by 17 percent of the Washington organizations. The bias in favor of these sorts of by-product organizations can be seen also in the underrepresentation of interests less able to call upon existing organizational structures. Whereas Schlozman and Tierney estimated the unemployed portion of the population to be about 4 percent, they could find only one-tenth of 1 percent of Washington organizations to classify as "unemployment organizations." And while 12 percent of the population was retired, only 0.8 percent of organizations looked after senior citizens' interests.[21]

Such calculations indicate only roughly the degree of represen-

---

[21]Schlozman and Tierney, *Organized Interests*, pp. 69–71.

tation various interests actually realize, but the patterns the investigators found have been confirmed by similar studies.[22] Moreover, there is some evidence that political groups may not have the staying power that economic groups have. Schlozman and Tierney found that political groups appear to be less enduring members of the Washington community than other kinds of groups. And a recent increase in corporate representation outstrips any growth in the total number of corporations.[23]

All of this evidence points to bias in the kinds of interests that get represented by organized groups. Party theorists find the evidence so compelling that they believe the interest-group system can *never* be as inclusive as the party and electoral system.[24] Politics will always favor people with more resources over those with fewer resources, but the interest-group system, with the premium it puts on organization, compounds the bias inherent in the electoral system. There is real reason to hope that the bias in the electoral system can be reduced; such a hope is not realistic in regard to the group system.

Party theorists also contend that groups, by their nature, are exclusive. They restrict their activities to limited agenda, although of course some are more "special" in their interests than others. Indeed, the bias against political groups undermines the ability of the group system to represent claims for broad, collective benefits and favors those groups that seek narrowly selfish economic goals. Thus it is not uncommon for a relatively small group seeking a particular benefit, such as a tax loophole or a product subsidy, to have its way over much larger, more diffuse interests soliciting benefits that would accrue to the general population. A corporation seeking a defense contract may be in a much stronger position politically than a peace group interested in reducing the defense budget.

Political parties, according to party theorists, are political organizations uniquely capable of offsetting this restrictive, exclusive nature of the group system. The power that parties mobilize can dominate the group system because access to formal, institutional power is directly linked to victory in elections. And parties, not interest groups, mobilize the forces necessary to win elections. They do so, that is, if they are strong enough to monopolize the resources necessary to gain nomination and election to public office. And so party theory returns to the argument spelled out in Chapter 4.

---

[22]Salisbury, "Interest Representation."
[23]Schlozman and Tierney, *Organized Interests*, p. 79.
[24]Schattschneider makes this argument most forcefully in *Semisovereign People*.

The Pluralist Response

The evidence in favor of either the pluralists' or the party theorists' positions on the issues discussed in this chapter does not lead to anything like closure. We do not wish to go back and forth endlessly between the two theoretical camps, but since this is a chapter on interest groups, it is only fair to give the pluralists one chance to respond to the serious charges leveled by their theoretical antagonists.

Are Groups Representative of Members' Interests?

Pluralists contend that groups are adequate channels of their members' interests, although no pluralist thinker argues that they are perfect. And it may be true that political groups are better than nonpolitical groups at representing their members' political views. But that is almost a truism and not necessarily a very interesting one. A pro-life group is good at representing its members' views on abortion, a university is good at representing its members' interest in a strong university, and a union can pursue the interests of its members as wage earners in a particular trade or industry. The broader the political agenda of any such group, the more likely it will stray from the interests of its membership. Thus if a union joins a civil rights effort or if a pro-life group joins a coalition of groups supporting a strong defense establishment, it may be less representative of its membership. And it may suffer consequences dangerous to its organizational health. The strength of the union (along with other groups whose purpose is primarily economic) lies in its ability to compensate its members for their support by providing job security and other material benefits. The strength of the pro-life group (along with many other groups whose purpose is primarily political) lies in its ability to summon the faithful with a clarion call to do battle for its version of the public good.

In a word, political resources are noncumulative. Economic activity brings some kinds of resources, political activity brings others. Groups exploit their resources as best they can. A dedicated membership fired by a moral cause may well be more than a match for groups fueled by narrowly selfish economic interests. At least it should be an interesting fight.

From the perspective of the individual citizen seeking political representation, interest groups provide many opportunities, but no single group is likely to be fully adequate. The student opposed to military research has two interests. His interest in a university with the resources to provide him with a quality education may at times conflict with his interest in stopping military research. It would be unrealistic to expect a single group to represent both interests. To get an education, he joins the university. When the university supports policies that strengthen it and higher education, his interests are often well served. But to pursue his interest in reducing military research, he may need to join a peace group. The peace group cannot be expected to reflect the student's interest in higher education, but it does a first-rate job of representing his views on the arms race.

Is the Group System Seriously Biased?

Again, pluralists don't deny the existence of biases. But party theorists overstate the degree of bias, they contend, and party theory's alternative to reliance on groups as an important source of political representation is unrealistic.

While it is true that political groups must pay the costs of organization out of income derived from their political activity, that necessity is not the obstacle that Olson supposes. Again, it is a matter of exploiting the resources available to the group. If a group cannot compensate its members with material benefits, it must motivate people to support it in other ways. Political groups concerned with environmental issues, the arms race, consumer interests, abortion, capital punishment, civil rights, women's rights, prayer in schools, civil liberties, and much more manage not only to form but to thrive. They do so by making strong ideological and issue appeals, by appealing to moral and religious traditions, and by drawing upon visible, charismatic leadership. They also attract support (and organizational resources) from nonpolitical groups. The peace and pro-life movements have relied heavily on churches, and many "public interest" groups depend on grants from foundations, government, and business.[25]

Here we see but a variation on the theme of noncumulative resources. But it is important, according to pluralists, to recognize the diversity and extensiveness of the group system. Some interests may be underrepresented, others may have more extensive representation, but very few interests are excluded altogether. And of course parties and elections are an important part of the process. Thus interests that have difficulty organizing can find access to power through the party system.

The fluidity of the group system also must be understood. Broad classifications of groups such as corporations and business associations fail to recognize that business is anything but a unified

---

[25]Jack L. Walker, "The Origins and Maintenance of Interest Groups in America," *American Political Science Review* 77 (June 1983): 390–406.

interest. Business interests are often in conflict with one another; they seldom present a united front on public policy issues. Some businesses oppose environmental regulations because such regulations will subject them to more government control and increase their costs, but other businesses (such as those that provide alternative energy sources) thrive under pollution-control policies. Conflict among groups is an important check on any interest's ability to monopolize governmental power, just as Madison argued.

Conclusion

The differences between pluralists and party theorists are sharp and extensive. The two schools debate how best to organize citizen interests, how to represent those interests before government, and how to organize government itself. The differences span the full range of questions addressed by Madison's Republic. Therefore, let us review these differences in the context of the three major themes of Madison's Republic (see Table 5-3).

Neither pluralists nor party theorists question the evidence that shows the average citizen to be largely indifferent to much of what happens in public affairs. The clash between the theories turns on what that indifference signifies. For pluralists, the evidence indicates that elections are necessarily of limited usefulness as channels of political representation. Madison's erroneous belief that citizens are self-interested is not a crippling blow to the theory because citizens are not socially inert beings. They are connected to the political world through their social and economic life, even if strictly political concerns can fairly be described as remote from their immediate concern. Party theorists argue that the citizen can be enlisted in the political process. Indeed, they go further: citizens *must* be enlisted in the political process if the system is to be characterized as democratic.

The perspective taken on self-interest is the key to the rest of the debate. Will citizens' interests be sufficiently well represented in government in the absence of political self-interest? Pluralists think so; party theorists think not. Here pluralists rejoin the Madisonian argument, having demurred only on the question of self-interest. Citizens' interests are represented because citizens participate in groups. These groups have the resources necessary to monitor what government does, to mobilize their membership when necessary, and to pressure government on behalf of their members' interests. Even if the individual cannot say what the political implications of being a student are, leaders of the university have a very good idea what the interests of the university are, and they actively seek policy that reflects those interests. Party theorists are skeptical. They see groups as effective in seeking group interests, but that is a good part of the problem. Too many interests are excluded from the "interest-group system" and resources are distributed very unequally among groups. Interest groups provide representation, yes. But groups do not represent the full range of interests in society, and they are

Table 5-3 Pluralism vs. Party Theory
on Central Themes of Madison's Republic

Theme	Pluralism	Party theory
Self-interest	Not an accurate description of the citizen, especially in political context. People are not active in or well informed about politics.	Not an accurate description of the citizen in electoral politics. People are not politically active or well informed, but, if information costs were low, could be expected to act in their political self-interest.
Representation	Interests get represented through a multitude of channels. Elections are only one such channel, and not necessarily the most important one. Madison is right to emphasize factions, or interest groups, as a critically important means by which interests are represented before government.	Political representation will not regularly occur without political self-interest. The group system is too biased in favor of people with resources to be an adequate channel. If energized by self-interest, the electoral system is the best hope because it is based on equality.
Conflict/ dispersed power	There is significant conflict among the thousands of organized interests in society. Power in government must be dispersed and fragmented to accommodate societal complexity and facilitate access by as many different interests as possible. Groups do check one another, as do government institutions. Only a pluralistic government representing a pluralistic society can be truly democratic.	Conflict between the parties which draws citizens into politics and informs them of the stakes involved is desirable; but conflict in government defuses responsibility and raises information costs. Governmental power must be granted for a limited time to the winning party. Then, and only then, can responsibility be fixed and the system be truly democratic.

severely biased in favor of some kinds of interests and against others.

With the question of conflict and dispersed power, the argument between the two theoretical camps moves us neatly to Part III. For the pluralists, the institutions of American government are based on sound principles. Those principles are adequately defended by James Madison. Each institution is sensitive to a different cluster of interests. Therefore the conflict that necessarily arises among factions and groups in society can be expected to invade government. That is a good thing, because that conflict guarantees that power will not be exercised on behalf of a limited set of interests.

Party theorists see conflict in government and dispersed power as part of the problem, not the solution. To be sure, there are many conflicting interests in a society as complex as ours. But the political process exists because those differences are recognized. Ultimately it produces winners and losers. Most important, if political processes are to work properly, winners must know they are winning, and losers must know when they have lost. In short, politics cannot be remote. People must be conscious of their political interests. Dispersal of power raises the costs of knowing who's winning and who's losing. For most citizens, the costs are way out of line, so they don't know. The political process must be reshaped so that those costs are reduced, so people will know when they are winning and when they are losing. Ordinary citizens (not just such people as public affairs officers in universities) must know where their political interests lie. Concentration of power fixes responsibility so that citizens can tell relatively easily whether they are being helped or hurt, and by whom. They can also do something about it.

Self-Interest? Representation? Conflict and dispersed power? The answers are complex and unsettled. Madison poses and answers the questions raised by the Republic quite confidently, and his answers constitute a broad-ranging and extremely influential political theory. At the same time, the root concept of self-interest in the Republic proves to be an inadequate description of what motivates people in politics. Pluralists recognize that fact and strive to correct the oversight in the theory without altering the major conclusions. Party theorists argue that the self-interest problem undermines the foundations of the Republic and therefore destroys the entire edifice. We turn next to an examination of the institutional structure of American government. In doing so, we take the opportunity to explore in detail the implications of self-interest for the operation of representative government.

Key Concepts

cross-pressures

multiple points of access

noncumulative nature of group
  resources

nonpolitical groups

organizational overhead

political groups

The Problem with the Solution III

Part III examines the Madisonian solution by analyzing the two principal representative institutions of American national government: the Congress and the presidency. If representation is to be found, the Congress is surely the place to look. Congress is important (and complicated) enough to require two chapters. Chapter 6 looks at the relationship between individual members of Congress and their constituencies. It considers congressional elections from the lawmaker's point of view, and asks how well members of Congress represent their constituencies' interests. Chapter 7 continues the analysis by exploring the implications of representatives' interest in satisfying their constituents for the way Congress as a whole represents the nation. Together these two chapters embrace the central themes in Madison's Republic:

Theme 1, *self-interest*. Citizens in the Republic are self-interested in their political action. They select members of Congress who share their interests and who will help them get those interests satisfied by government. Hence

Theme 2, *representation*. Because representatives are self-interested (they want to remain in Congress), they represent the interests of their constituencies. To do otherwise would be to invite the self-interested citizens who elected them to vote them out. Many constituency (factional) interests are brought into the national legislature in this way. The presence of these diverse interests of course leads to

Theme 3, *conflict*. Because so many different interests are represented in Congress, conflict among them is inevitable. Conflict is further ensured between the Senate and the House of Representatives because the two chambers are based on different constituencies and different principles of apportionment.

Conflict, then, is Madison's solution to the problem of self-interest. Conflict protects against the arbitrary use of power on behalf of one or a coalition of interests against others. Conflict protects against tyranny.

The presidency, considered in Chapter 8, is also an important part of representative government. Its role in the solution is to introduce more conflict by virtue of its unique constituency and institutional makeup. It was to have a different "ambition," which would check that of the legislative branch. The way the aggregation of national interests was represented in the Congress, then, was to differ from the way the nation was represented by the presidency. Chapter 8 treats representation in the presidency as the question of presidential leadership.

The problem with the solution is closely related to the problem with the problem. The problem with the problem was that Madison's understanding of self-interest was incomplete. The problem with the solution is that the complications surrounding citizens' political interests, discussed in Part II, keep representative government from neatly following from self-interest. Self-interest among the people does not have a consistently instrumental quality because individual citizens lack the resources and incentives to pursue political goals. Citizen participation often falls prey in one way or another to the paradox of collective action. The people who occupy positions of governmental authority, candidates for office, and other "elites," however, usually have both the resources and the incentives to pursue their self-interest. They are not tempted to be free riders because, unlike voters, they pursue private in addition to collective goods. The private benefits associated with public office are prestige, status, and power. These private benefits create a fundamental imbalance between the interests of citizens and those of officeholders which strains the Madisonian link between self-interest and representation. Citizens' self-interest lies in the collective benefits associated with governmental policy and representation. The self-interest of elites lies in the private benefits associated with positions in government.

The imbalance between the interest of the citizen in collective goods and the interest of representatives in private goods is the problem with the solution. Because of this imbalance, officeholders can entertain the possibility of retaining their positions of power without providing representation. If voters can be satisfied in ways that are more easily accomplished than providing representation, self-interested representatives can be expected to resort to them. A major problem with the contemporary Congress, then, is that individual members of Congress have found ways to insulate their interest in maintaining their careers from popular dissatisfaction with the institution. A similar escape is not readily available to the president, a fact that has important implications for the kinds of representation offered by the two branches.

As usual, things are complex and answers are not always clear. Pluralists continue to hold a reasonably optimistic view of representative government in America, while party theorists maintain their critical stance. Party theory's response to the "problem with the solution" is to look for ways to reconnect leaders' interest in the private goods associated with positions of power and citizens' interest in the collective goods that national representative institutions are supposed to provide. Pluralism's response is to argue that the institutions have done a good job of adapting to twentieth-century realities and of meeting the fundamental demands of representative government.

Getting Elected and Reelected to Congress

Self-Interest Run Amok?

Congressman David Skaggs represents the Second Congressional District in Colorado, where I live. He works very hard at his job, and in that respect he is fairly typical. Very few of his colleagues are slackers. Members of Congress (MCs) spend long days in Washington working at various legislative tasks, attending meetings, and meeting constituents. They travel home to their districts and states frequently to discuss the issues with the people who elected them, to deal with problems that constituents bring to their attention, and to listen.[1] David Skaggs is energetic, visible, and eager to serve his constituents. He assigns seven and one-half out of a staff allocation of eighteen full-time positions to his Washington office, and ten and one-half to his district office in Colorado.[2] Between his election to the House in 1986 and the early summer of 1988, he made no fewer than thirty-seven trips home to visit with constituents.[3]

Newsletters are another means by which Congressman Skaggs demonstrates his commitment to his constituents. Figure 6-1 shows the front page of one newsletter sent to all postal patrons in the district. It alerted them to several opportunities to meet Mr. Skaggs personally at "town meetings" held at convenient locations throughout the district. Constituents were invited to contact the congressman's office "when you have a problem with your Social Security check, veterans' benefits or other government services." Inside the newsletter, the names and telephone numbers of local and Washington staff members were provided, along with an issues questionnaire and an article about recent bills providing "jobs and help for Colorado" which had been passed by Congress.

---

[1] For an excellent account of MCs' activities in their districts, see Richard F. Fenno, Jr., *Home Style: House Members in Their Districts* (Boston: Little, Brown, 1978).
[2] Interview with Carol Byerly, district director for Congressman Skaggs.
[3] Correspondence with Representative Skaggs.

Inside. . .

- Clean Water Bill passes
- Help for the Homeless
- Skaggs Staff List
- Issues Questionnaire

April 1987 • 9101 Harlan #130, Westminster, CO 80030 • 1723 Longworth, Washington, DC 20515

AN INVITATION TO MEET WITH YOUR CONGRESSMAN

During the coming months, I will be holding town meetings and branch office hours throughout the Second Congressional District. These sessions are designed to give me and my staff a chance to hear from you and your neighbors about the issues facing our country and any problems you may be having with federal government offices. They provide an opportunity to find out what's on your mind. The next town meetings will be held:

SATURDAY, APRIL 11
10:30 a.m. to Noon
National Bureau of Standards
   Auditorium (main entrance)
325 Broadway
Boulder

SATURDAY, APRIL 11
2 to 2:30 p.m.
Thornton High School Auditorium
9351 North Washington
Thornton

SUNDAY, APRIL 12
2 to 2:30 p.m.
United Church Social Hall
14th and Colorado
Idaho Springs

MONDAY, APRIL 13
7:30 to 9 p.m.
Broomfield City Council Chambers
Municipal Building
6 Garden Office Center
Two blocks east of Hwy. 287 and
   north of Midway
Broomfield

Dear Friend,

When you have a problem with your Social Security check, veterans' benefits or other government services, or need help tracking down information about a federal program, my Colorado and Washington offices are available to help you. A list of the staff is included inside this newsletter, along with phone numbers and addresses.

The questionnaire inside will help me learn your views on some of today's most pressing issues. It will provide important information — please take a few minutes to fill it out and mail it back.

On **April 11, 12 and 13,** I will be holding town meetings in Boulder, Thornton, Idaho Springs and Broomfield. (See adjoining column.)

Similar meetings will be held throughout the year, including "branch office hours" at local shopping centers.

I hope you'll join me at one of these upcoming events.

Sincerely yours,

David Skaggs

Figure 6-1 Front Page of Representative David Skaggs's Newsletter

The kind of attention Representative Skaggs and most of his colleagues lavish on their constituencies is to be expected, since members of the House must be reelected every two years. The question of concern to us here is what the implications of this attention are for constituency representation. (Chapter 7 examines the implications for the institution of Congress as a whole.) In order to proceed, we must return once again to Madison's Republic to get our bearings.

157
CHAPTER 6
Getting
Elected and
Reelected to
Congress

Two Levels of Representation

Representation in Congress operates at two related levels. The first is the constituency or "micro" level of representation. **Micro representation** defines the relationship between the individual member of Congress and his or her constituency. In the Republic, for example, it is in the self-interest of the MC to pursue constituency policy interests. Thus Madison's theory of micro representation links the self-interest of the representative or senator to the self-interest of citizens in the district or state. When we address the problem of micro representation, we ultimately are interested in how *responsive* individual lawmakers are to the needs and wants of their constituents.

But individual representatives do not exist in a vacuum, nor is adequate micro representation the final goal of representative government. Hence we need to consider the second, or "macro," level of representation. **Macro representation** defines the relationship between the Congress and society as a whole. The question then becomes not "How well does Congresswoman Smith represent her district?" but "How well does Congress represent the nation?" Here we are ultimately drawn into a discussion of the power of Congress. Congress cannot be a truly representative institution without also being an effective one. Congress must exercise significant power, or any responsiveness that individual MCs exhibit to their constituents will have no real meaning.

Many close observers of Congress argue that MCs spend too much time providing benefits to their districts (micro representation), to the detriment of the national good (macro representation).[4] Among these critics are party theorists, who, remember, worry about promoting responsibility in Congress. They are most concerned about Congress's failure to achieve collective responsibility—a concept closely related to macro representation.

The major theme of this chapter and the next, then, is the fundamental tension between the two levels of representation. We must understand the way the contemporary Congress copes with this tension if we are to understand representative government as it functions in the home stretch of the twentieth century.

Madison, writing at the end of the eighteenth century, un-

---

[4]For a very readable criticism of Congress along these lines, see Morris P. Fiorina, *Congress: Keystone of the Washington Establishment* (New Haven: Yale University Press, 1977).

derstood the tension between the two levels of representation as a creative solution to the problem of tyranny. Micro representation is supposed to produce macro representation more or less automatically. If micro representation ensured that each representative faithfully represented his constituency's interests, the process by which those interests were brought together and reconciled would constitute macro representation. The payoff would be the policy that emerged from Congress. Tyranny would be avoided because individual policy makers would be strongly linked to their constituencies. Since MCs must work with many other legislators, each responsible to a different constituency, conflict inevitably would characterize the policy process. Thus macro representation is achieved when many different interests are involved in the making of policy. As Madison puts it in *Federalist* 10, "the regulation of these various and interfering interests forms the principal task of modern legislation and *involves the spirit of party and faction in the necessary and ordinary operations of government.*"

In this formulation the link between self-interest and the exercise of governmental power in the public interest is found. The public's interest in avoiding tyranny is protected when self-interest checks self-interest. Under these conditions, government, and specifically Congress, can be given significant power to control the governed. Even a cursory reading of Article I of the Constitution impresses one with the powers assigned to Congress. In the scheme of things, in fact, the Congress was to be the most powerful branch. And it was to have this power because it was also to be the most responsive, inclusive branch.

Self-Interest and Micro Representation

Since the Republic is based on self-interest, it is fair to ask whether members of Congress actually represent their constituencies. Is it in their self-interest to produce policy that reflects their constituents' wishes? If Congress is to work the way the Republic anticipates, reelection of its members must turn on their provision of this representation to their constituencies. Micro representation is the place to start because in the theory constituency representation produces institutional representation.

Getting Reelected to Congress

It is when MCs run for reelection that citizens have an opportunity to pass judgment on the quality of representation they have received from their legislators. Chapter 3 described this kind of accountability as an important part of the instrumental model of elections.

But as we also saw in Chapter 3, the instrumental model of elections, at least as it applies to citizens, is in trouble. It demands that citizens have information about the choices they make in elections. However, citizens have little incentive to gather this kind of information, and the political process itself does a very uneven job of informing them. When congressional elections roll round, people typically know little about what their MC has done during the past two years. As a result, voters often rely on shorthand cues, such as partisanship, to decide whom to vote for; their choice may not be based on much information at all about the actual choice the election is giving them.

Even more troubling from the perspective of the Republic is the evidence of a powerful incumbency effect. Campaigns for office may inform the uninterested citizen, since candidates seek voters' support through various kinds of appeals. But in the case of congressional elections, we have seen evidence of a biased process that strongly favors incumbents and works against challengers. Citizens are much more likely to have been contacted by incumbents than by challengers (Table 3-5). And that is no accident, as we shall now see.

Assume for the moment that members of Congress do everything in their power to get reelected. This assumption is not very different from Madison's supposition that they will be "ambitiously contending for power," since in order to keep power, MCs must get reelected. David Mayhew argues that MCs engage in three activities designed to help them get reelected: advertising, credit claiming, and position taking.[5] These activities not only affect members' chances of reelection and their ability to represent their constituencies (micro representation), they also have powerful effects on the functioning of the institution as a whole (macro representation).

Advertising. According to Mayhew, **advertising** is getting one's name out, usually in a way that associates it with a positive symbol. For example, the slogan "Congressman Jones works for Massachusetts" on a bumper sticker or billboard tells us the name and associates it with something positive (working for the district). A newsletter story showing the incumbent greeting local high school students on a visit to the capital gets the MC's name and picture before the folks in the district and again associates the incumbent with something positive (friendliness, hospitality, responsiveness). The prominent display of David Skaggs's picture and name on the masthead of his newsletter in Figure 6-1 is another example. Notice what

---

[5]The following discussion relies heavily on David Mayhew's brilliant *Congress: The Electoral Connection* (New Haven: Yale University Press, 1974).

advertising is *not:* it is not information about the policy-making behavior of the representative in Washington. It really does not inform citizens at all, except to make the incumbent's name more visible. Name recognition is important in congressional elections.

Credit claiming. A second way MCs help themselves get reelected is by **credit claiming**: they do something pleasing for someone and then take responsibility for it. Credit claiming helps win support in the form of votes or other resources necessary for reelection (such as campaign contributions). Nothing wrong with that—the Republic is based on just such quid pro quos: self-interested leaders have something to offer self-interested constituents, who show their satisfaction by returning the incumbents to office. But consider how these exchanges work in practice. Imagine you are in an audience listening to a congressman telling you and your neighbors why you should vote for him. He claims credit for reducing national unemployment, which, it happens, has recently dropped 2 percentage points. He indicates that because of his efforts, Congress has passed legislation that has created jobs, lowered investment taxes, and reduced the pressure on American industry from foreign manufacturers. Do you believe him? Maybe. But think how much more plausible it would be if your representative claimed credit instead for reducing unemployment in your hometown by fighting hard to keep the local military base open when the president wanted to close it down. The difference between reducing national and hometown unemployment is largely a matter of scale, and people generally find it easier to believe that one representative out of 435 could have an impact on the economy of his district than that he could influence the national economy.

This matter of scale is important to an understanding of the way incumbents get reelected. Mayhew refers to policies at the local or small end of the scale as producing **particularized benefits.** These policies benefit *particular* localities, groups, or even individuals. In some respects, the more particularized the benefit, the better for the incumbent. The more the benefit is limited to a small group, the more plausibly the MC can claim credit for having a hand in producing it. Particularized benefits also have the happy consequence of *not* generating opposition. As Morris Fiorina put it, particularized benefits "are nonpartisan, nonideological, and most important, noncontroversial."[6]

What might some particularized benefits be? Keeping the local military base open is one. Building a post office branch or a VA

---

[6]Morris P. Fiorina, "The Decline of Collective Responsibility in American Politics," *Daedalus* 190 (1980): 37.

hospital or an irrigation project are others. Answering requests for
information about child care, social security benefits, and passport
rules are even more particularized benefits. If an MC helps a constituent get her passport application through government red tape
in three days, he has made a friend without risking opposition in the
district. He can hope she will tell her friends how helpful he was,
and his reputation for being "responsive" will grow. If producing
particularized benefits for grateful constituents helps incumbents
get reelected, producing benefits for grateful constituents is what
they will do.[7] If they spend their time and staff resources producing particularized benefits, the production of collective benefits
may lag.

Position taking. The third activity identified by Mayhew as important in helping incumbents get reelected is **position taking.** To take
a position is to speak out on an issue in a way that is pleasing to
constituents and others who can help or hurt the MC's career. A
statement in a newsletter against high unemployment, a response to
a constituent's letter in which the MC agrees with the constituent
that prayer must be allowed in schools, or a speech before a group of
mayors defending sources of local tax revenues against proposed
changes in the federal tax code—all are instances of position taking.
Position taking has symbolic rather than instrumental value; it does
not actually produce public policy. Mayhew argues that members of
Congress have little incentive to help produce public policy, as they
are unlikely to be able to claim credit for it. MCs do have a reason to
be on the right side of issues, to avoid taking stands on issues that
are unpopular. In Mayhew's words, "we can all point to a good
many instances in which congressmen seem to have gotten into
trouble by being on the *wrong* side in a roll call vote, but who can
think of one where a member got into trouble by being on the *losing*
side?"[8]

MCs' pursuit of reelection by advertising, credit claiming, and
position taking have important implications for micro representa-

161

CHAPTER 6
Getting
Elected and
Reelected to
Congress

---

[7]Casework makes up a huge portion of the congressional work load. Roger H. Davidson and Walter J. Oleszek report that in 1977 the estimated work load for members of
the House was 10,000 cases per year, while that of Senators varied between 1,000 and
70,000 cases, depending on the size of the state (*Congress and Its Members*, 2nd ed.
[Washington, D.C.: Congressional Quarterly Press, 1985], p. 134).

[8]Mayhew, *Congress*, p. 118. "A decade ago the Southern senators took a last-ditch
stand on civil rights; they lost heroically, but at no time were their jobs in danger."
Political careers can be built on position taking, whether the issue is the communist
menace, Central America, or abortion. As long as the correct position is taken,
constituent pressure to win may be minimal or nonexistent. "That the pressure to
win is only modest is an enormously important fact of life in Congress," says
Mayhew.

tion. Note that these methods of getting reelected to Congress presume a poorly informed constituency. Constituents respond favorably to content-free advertising. Constituents react positively to visible, particularized benefits without considering the costs of such benefits. And constituents are impressed by symbolic position taking without much concern for what the MC is actually *doing* to make his or her pleasing positions a reality. The evidence in Chapter 3 is consistent with this understanding of the citizen, and therefore with Mayhew's pessimistic view of what it takes to get reelected. So the powerful link between the self-interest of legislators and the self-interest of constituencies in the Republic is in trouble again.

An "Everyone-Can-Win" Congress?

There is more. One of the most important conclusions Mayhew drew from his analysis is that a **norm of universalism** prevails in Congress. In a nutshell, the activities in which MCs engage to get themselves reelected do not usually hinder other members' attempts to get reelected. This is a radical departure from the Congress anticipated by the Republic. In that theory, each legislator's reelection depends on his ability to satisfy factional policy interests. Inevitably the MC will be in conflict with other legislators representing other factions with different interests. But the norm of universalism indicates that this kind of conflict does not normally occur. It says that conflict among legislators may even make their individual reelections more difficult. Conflict would hinder the ability of Congress to distribute particularistic policy. Conflict occurs when there are winners and losers. Under the norm of universalism, everyone can win. When everyone wins, what is there to fight about?

How is it that MCs need not fight with one another? Curiously, the most important reason is the same thing that led Madison to expect so much conflict in Congress: each MC is reelected by a different constituency.[9] Therefore the principal source of competition for reelection is not inside the chamber but back home in the district, where any number of politically active residents may be gearing up to mount a challenge. Legislators can protect themselves against such challenges by cooperating in the distribution of particularized benefits to each other's districts, by granting to themselves and their colleagues in Congress resources necessary to advertise, and by promoting a policy process that facilitates posi-

---

[9]Senators, of course, share a constituency with one other colleague in the same chamber. Interestingly, Mayhew argues it is this sharing of the constituency that creates conflict between two senators from the same state.

tion taking without personal responsibility for what Congress actually does.

163
CHAPTER 6
Getting
Elected and
Reelected to
Congress

The evidence in favor of this argument is circumstantial but strong. Consider first what lawmakers have done to help them advertise their names back home in their states and districts.

Incumbent "perks" and advertising. Every member of Congress has valuable **incumbent perquisites** of office (or "perks") which amount to important resources convertible into name recognition and, happily for them, votes. Pity the challengers who must pay for their advertising out of their own campaign chests. Members of Congress receive paid trips home to their states or districts, personal staff who work in Washington and in home offices, virtually unlimited free mailing privileges (the "frank"), assorted office expenses, and a subsidy to help pay for newsletters mailed to constituents.[10] The money for all of these things comes from the public treasury, for use by the MC at his or her discretion. Madison would probably say that incumbents use these resources to help themselves "ambitiously contend for pre-eminence and power."

Consider Figure 6-2, which presents the cost of franked mail sent out from congressional offices between 1980 and 1986. It shows

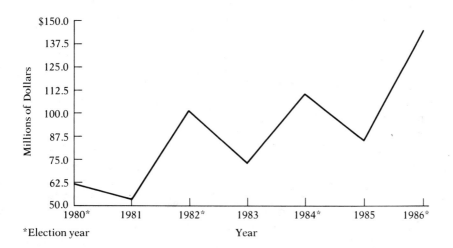

Figure 6-2 Cost of Franked Mail Sent from House of Representatives, 1980–1986 (millions of dollars). SOURCE: From data in *Congressional Quarterly Weekly Report*, October 19, 1985, p. 2110.

---

[10]See Davidson and Oleszek, *Congress and Its Members*, pp. 132–133.

that the volume of franked mail follows the electoral calendar very closely.[11] Mail is sent out at dramatically higher rates in election years than in nonelection years, and peaks just before the election. Members of Congress are not stupid. They send out mail because it will increase their name recognition and thus their support in the district. Morris Udall, a member of Congress who attempted to halt the increasing amounts of money spent on franked mail, said, "Members really like the frank. . . . It's effective. It's worth a couple of hundred thousand dollars to incumbents."[12]

Evidence in Chapter 3 supports the conclusion that use of the frank and other perquisites increases constituency support for the incumbent. So does careful research by scholars interested in the effects of congressional mailing.[13] Most important, note that if challengers nationwide were to match the flood of mail sent free by incumbents, they would have to pay for it themselves. The frank, along with the other resources incumbents have voted themselves, is a perquisite of *holding* office, not of *running* for office.

Reelection and campaign finance law. Perhaps the most dramatic evidence for the norm of universalism as it relates to congressional elections is seen in what Congress has done (and not done) in the area of campaign finance law. In the wake of the Watergate scandal, which led to the resignation of President Richard Nixon, Congress passed legislation providing for the use of U.S. Treasury funds by presidential candidates in both nomination and general election campaigns. Why not do the same in congressional elections? After all, there have been any number of scandals involving money illegally raised and spent in congressional campaigns. The problem with financing campaigns with public money is that challengers would then have a minimum guaranteed war chest to use against incumbents. Their campaigns would be more effective and the advantage incumbents enjoy over challengers would be reduced. Conflict in the average district would increase. The norm of universalism would be violated.

Not content with refusing to grant challengers this minimum

---

[11]This pattern is evident in earlier, comparable data. See *Congressional Quarterly Weekly Report*, April 16, 1980, p. 2387.
[12]*Congressional Quarterly Weekly Report*, October 19, 1985, p. 2110.
[13]Thomas E. Mann and Raymond E. Wolfinger, "Candidates and Parties in Congressional Elections," *American Political Science Review* 74 (1980): 617–632. An ingenious experiment shows that direct mail by incumbents increases name recognition and favorable evaluations of MCs, at least up to a point. See Albert D. Cover and Arthur S. Brumberg, "Baby Books and Ballots: The Impact of Congressional Mail on Constituent Opinion," *American Political Science Review* 76 (1982): 347–359.

amount to wage campaigns against them, members of Congress have limited the amount of money they can accept from any one contributor. This limitation, in addition to warding off attempts to buy candidates and elections by unscrupulous "fat cats," increases the difficulty of raising large amounts of money. Though the limitation applies to all candidates, incumbents and challengers alike, and so appears to be admirably evenhanded, it is remarkable how neatly it serves the interests of incumbents. Figure 6-3 shows that as challengers' expenditures increase, so does recognition of their names—dramatically at first, then more gradually. This finding accords with our expectations. We would naturally anticipate that candidates' expenditures on advertising and other campaign activities would increase their visibility among the electorate. But the same does not hold for incumbents. As their expenditures increase, their recognition among the electorate does not tend consistently to grow. It doesn't have to. House incumbents are very well known in their districts whether they spend much or little. They have already used the perquisites of their office to saturate the market. The current campaign finance law is in perfect accord with incumbents' self-interest because it does not provide challengers with federal funds and it makes it difficult for them to raise large amounts of money by forcing them to attract many small donations. Incum-

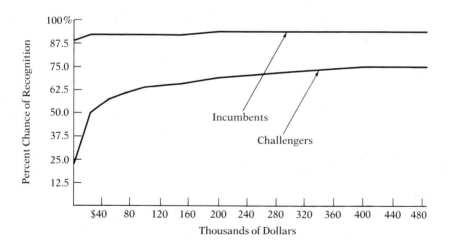

Figure 6-3 Chance that Voters Will Recognize Names of Congressional Incumbents and Challengers by Thousands of Dollars Spent on Campaigns. SOURCE: Gary C. Jacobson, *The Politics of Congressional Elections,* 2d ed. (Boston: Little, Brown, 1987).

165

CHAPTER 6
Getting
Elected and
Reelected to
Congress

bents campaign with their perquisites, challengers are left to fend for themselves.[14]

As a result, most House challengers are woefully underfunded. Table 6-1 shows that in recent years incumbents have been able consistently to raise more money than challengers. Contributors want to give to winners, and most incumbents are very likely to win reelection. Indeed, according to Gary Jacobson, incumbents normally do not spend money in order to become better known; they spend money because they are being seriously challenged in their districts. Hence "for incumbents, spending a great deal of money on the campaign is a sign of weakness rather than strength."[15] The strongest incumbents are those who are able to discourage strong challengers from running. Campaign finance legislation is one of the most impressive weapons in the incumbents' arsenal. One can easily imagine that much stronger candidates would run for Congress

Table 6-1 Average Amounts of Campaign Money Raised by Congressional Incumbents and Challengers, 1976–1982

	Incumbents	*Challengers*
1976		
House	$ 91,094	$ 49,600
Senate	677,278	440,461
1978		
House	120,596	55,039
Senate	1,322,450	355,925
1980		
House	180,000	61,716
Senate	1,351,688	425,411
1982		
House	285,015	74,825
Senate	1,871,212	526,977

SOURCE: Edie N. Goldenberg and Michael W. Traugott, *Campaigning for Congress* (Washington, D.C.: Congressional Quarterly Press, 1984), pp. 78–79.

---

[14]Much evidence supports the contention that increases in campaign spending help challengers but not incumbents. See Gary C. Jacobson, *Money in Congressional Elections* (New Haven: Yale University Press, 1980) and *The Politics of Congressional Elections*, 2nd ed. (Boston: Little Brown, 1987).

[15]Jacobson, *Politics of Congressional Elections*, p. 52.

and that they would succeed more frequently in unseating House incumbents were the odds not so firmly stacked against them.[16]

If we assume that a well-funded challenger is likely to have a significantly better chance of unseating an incumbent than one who is forced to run an underfinanced campaign, things may be going from bad to worse. Figure 6-4 shows the amounts that House and Senate challengers spent between 1976 and 1982 as percentages of the amounts spent by incumbents. The downward trend in both the House and the Senate indicates that although the absolute amounts that challengers are spending is increasing (Table 6-1), their expenditures are declining in comparison with those of incumbents.

Under the norm of universalism, then, members of Congress have more in common with each other than with the people who would challenge them from outside the institution. One MC's reelection does not generally threaten any other's reelection. All can satisfy this most basic need, and conflict among them need not occur. It is easier to help each other than it is to hurt each other. Everyone can win.

167

CHAPTER 6
Getting
Elected and
Reelected to
Congress

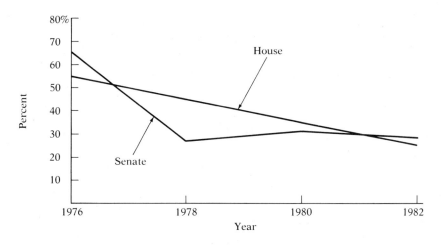

Figure 6-4 Challenger Spending as Percentage of Spending by Senate and House Incumbents, 1976–1982. SOURCE: Calculated from data in Table 6-1.

[16]Senate races generally attract much stronger challengers than House races, because senators cannot create as great an advantage over their challengers as their colleagues in the House are able to do. As a consequence, Senate challengers are much more visible and better liked than House challengers. See Alan I. Abramowitz, "A Comparison of Voting for U.S. Senators and Representatives in 1978," *American Political Science Review* 74 (1980): 633–640.

Actually, this is not quite an "everyone-can-win" Congress. There are real losers. One loser, quite obviously, is the underfunded, outgunned challenger in most congressional elections. Another loser is the average citizen. Citizens' interests are served by elections in which competition between candidates is strong, information is available and cheap, and choices are reasonably clear. Under these conditions, the instrumental model of elections is most likely to work: self-interested citizens will be linked to self-interested leaders. In the absence of competitive and informative congressional elections, the process is tilted against the kind of micro representation anticipated by the Republic. Ordinarily, citizens will be unable or unwilling to bear significant costs to get the information they need if they are to correct for the bias institutionalized by incumbent members of Congress in pursuit of their self-interest.

Constituency–Representative Policy Agreement

Thus far we have seen that incumbents have ways of getting reelected which do not depend directly on their willingness or ability to satisfy their constituents' policy preferences. They advertise. They use their perquisites, and they exploit the fact that no other member's reelection fundamentally threatens their own. Thus they ward off the common foe, the challengers real and potential back home. Does constituency opinion then go unrepresented in the halls of government in Washington?

The answer is plainly no, although the degree of representation is less than Madison anticipated. Political scientists have devoted considerable energy to the task of measuring how well individual representatives reflect constituency interests in their opinions and in their roll-call votes.[17] Perhaps surprisingly, given the failure of voters to measure up to the ideal of an informed, active citizenry, constituencies and their representatives are almost always in agreement, and sometimes quite substantially so.[18]

Why do legislators represent constituency interests? In the first place, if one were to suggest to the average representative or senator that the folks back home are not watching what is going on in Congress, the response would likely be "So what? I still have to worry because I never know when my constituents *might* become informed about what I'm doing." That potential is most likely to be realized when the MC does something that is unpopular back home. Constituents *could* become informed and vote against the incum-

---

[17]The classic study is Warren E. Miller and Donald E. Stokes, "Constituency Influence in Congress," *American Political Science Review* 57 (1963): 45–57.
[18]Walter J. Stone, "Electoral Change and Policy Representation in Congress: Domestic Welfare Issues from 1956–1972," *British Journal of Political Science* 12 (1982): 95–115.

bent if he were to make a major mistake, or if he were consistently to vote against their preferences.[19] Challengers, dissatisfied interest-group leaders, newspaper editors and reporters all have an interest in providing the constituency with information if the legislator steps out of line. The self-interested incumbent uses perquisites to build a following in the constituency and to insulate himself against this potential for negative reactions, but he ignores his constituents' policy preferences altogether at his peril.

169

CHAPTER 6
Getting
Elected and
Reelected to
Congress

A second factor, quite apart from the threat of defeat embedded in the electoral process, is the fact that most lawmakers share important characteristics with their constituents. These shared characteristics make it likely that the opinions of legislators will agree with those of their constituents even in the absence of communication between them. Imagine a Congress in which the members were selected by lot from the 435 districts and the 50 states. Imagine further that these randomly chosen MCs always voted their own policy preferences in Congress without a thought to what the folks back home want. Particularly in the House, where the districts represented are relatively small and homogeneous, at least a modest amount of agreement between legislators and their districts would be found. An MC chosen at random from an inner-city district would be quite different from one chosen from a rural midwestern district. And both would differ from a representative chosen from a middle-class suburban district.

Members of Congress therefore can be expected to act in ways broadly consistent with constituency opinion. There is a link between the interests of constituents and the interests of those who represent them, although that link is not so powerful as the instrumental model of elections might lead us to expect. Despite the fact that voters do not conform to the instrumental ideal, MCs must be concerned about straying too far from constituency preferences. Incumbents devote a great deal of effort to protecting their positions, but they nonetheless often share the policy objectives of their constituents, and thus provide representation.

Conclusion

Notice that we have two potentially contrary propositions before us as we close this discussion of micro representation. First, the norm

---

[19]See John W. Kingdon, *Congressmen's Voting Decisions*, 2nd ed. (New York: Harper & Row, 1981), especially chap. 2. Scholars have found that incumbents who consistently depart from constituency opinion suffer such consequences as a strong challenge or a loss of support. See, for example, Jon R. Bond, Cary Covington, and Richard Fleisher, "Explaining Challenger Quality in Congressional Elections," *Journal of Politics* 47 (1985): 510–529.

of universalism suggests that MCs do not have to fight because their need for reelection does not bring them into conflict with one another. They cooperate to pursue their common interest in reelection against the threat of significant challenge back home in their constituencies. This situation would lead us to expect, for example, that incumbents of different parties have more in common with each other than do incumbents and challengers of the same party. By this reasoning, Democrats and Republicans in Congress should cooperate with one another on matters that serve their common interests as incumbents even though they are of different parties.

The second proposition recognizes that MCs do not run for Congress just to run for Congress. That is, they have genuine policy preferences that they would like to see become law.[20] These policy preferences, we have seen, are likely to be similar to those of their constituents because both representatives and constituents come from similar socioeconomic, political, and ethnic environments. Districts and states differ, and members of Congress are likely to mirror (imperfectly, to be sure) these differences. This second proposition suggests that MCs have conflicting interests. The policy preferences of MCs from inner cities differ from those of members from rural districts, whose views differ from those of members from suburban districts. Democrats' preferences differ from those of Republicans.[21] These differences are not necessarily consistent across all issues and they do not always result from the MCs' need to get reelected, but they nonetheless occur. Indeed, they occur for the very reason suggested by the Republic: members of Congress are elected from different constituencies.

The two apparently contrary propositions—that MCs will not fight because their reelection needs do not threaten one another and that MCs will fight because they have differing policy preferences— reflect a genuine ambiguity in the nature of Congress. On some matters of central concern to political theories such as the Republic, the conflict expected among lawmakers does not materialize. At the same time, members of the House and Senate have genuine and strongly felt policy goals. On many issues, differences in policy *goals* can be resolved with surprisingly little conflict because MCs also differ in the policy *areas* they consider most important. On other issues, however, these differences erupt into conflict. We must un-

---

[20]An important theoretical argument based on the supposition that MCs seek to build power in the Congress is Lawrence C. Dodd, "Congress and the Quest for Power," in *Congress Reconsidered*, ed. Lawrence C. Dodd and Bruce I. Oppenheimer (New York: Praeger, 1977).

[21]See Julius Turner, *Party and Constituency: Pressures on Congress*, rev. ed., ed. Edward V. Schneier, Jr. (Baltimore: Johns Hopkins University Press, 1970).

derstand how Congress as an institution manages conflict if we are to understand the second, or macro, level of representation.

171

CHAPTER 6
Getting
Elected and
Reelected to
Congress

Key Concepts

advertising

credit claiming

incumbent perquisites

macro representation

micro representation

norm of universalism

particularized benefits

position taking

Congressional Representation

A Response to Self-Interest?

Had every Athenian citizen been a Socrates, every Athenian assembly would still have been a mob.

—James Madison, *Federalist* 55

Representative Michael Synar, of Oklahoma, swears that this actually happened: He was addressing a Cub Scout pack in Grove, Oklahoma, not far from his home town of Muskogee. Synar asked the young boys if they could tell him the difference between the Cub Scouts and the United States Congress. One boy raised his hand and said, "We have adult supervision."

—Gregg Easterbrook

Congress, it seems, takes it on the chin from everyone. To say the least, Madison reached an uncharitable conclusion about popular assemblies. And we chuckle at the cub scout's response because there is a ring of truth to it. As we shall see, most Americans give Congress a pretty low rating as a political institution. The reasons for their low opinion will take a while to spell out, but when the national legislature is a national joke, it is worth the effort to understand what's going on.

Congress often appears to be in need of "adult supervision." How can an august body of the United States government vote in favor of a president's plan to double the number of nuclear warheads in the U.S. arsenal and shortly thereafter vote in favor of a freeze on those same nuclear weapons?[1] How can individual members stand in front of the chamber decrying "special favors" to "pressure groups" and then return to their committees and subcom-

---

[1]Gregg Easterbrook, "What's Wrong with Congress?" *Atlantic Monthly*, December 1984, p. 57.

173

mittees to push through legislation that provides a tax loophole for this industry and a subsidy for that agricultural product? When our elected representatives do such contradictory things, we shake our heads. Or we joke about it.

But funny or not, Congress *is* important. It is important constitutionally because it has some very impressive powers granted to it which place it at the center of American national politics. And it is important theoretically because it was in the national legislature that James Madison's hope (his reservations notwithstanding) for a genuinely republican form of government at the national level rested. The Congress is absolutely central to the Republic because it is the institution that comes closest to embodying the principle of representation, at least in theory.

Recall that represention operates at two levels. Chapter 6 dealt with the first: micro, or constituency, representation. From the relationship between individual legislators and their constituencies was to come the second level of representation. Macro, or institutional, representation was to be characterized by conflict among the many factional interests brought into government by virtue of strong ties between constituencies and their representatives. Institutional representation and the way it relates to the many constituency-legislator connections are the concerns of this chapter.

Organizing Conflict Out of Congress

Madison's hope that micro representation would produce conflict in the institution is seriously disappointed in the contemporary Congress. The relationship between the two levels of representation does not play itself out in the manner hoped for by Madison. There is good evidence that the ways MCs maintain support in their constituencies detract from the ability of Congress to provide macro representation. Ultimately, the pattern of constituency representation in today's Congress undermines the institution's power in Washington.

At first blush this situation may appear to be consistent with Madison's idea that self-interest would check the use of power in the institution, but it is not at all consistent with his hopes. The norm of universalism and all that it implies minimizes conflict in Congress and permits power to be exercised by the few for the few. It is an exclusive use of power, rather than the inclusive concept presented in *Federalist* 10. MCs have strong incentives to protect their own personal careers and too few reasons to commit themselves to protecting the institution's power and legitimacy in the larger political system. As a result, Congress has suffered a protracted decline in its influence in national government. This is a development profoundly disturbing to many proponents of popular government. If Congress fails to retain its power as the constitutionally preeminent national institution, that power very likely will find a home elsewhere in the government where republican principles are less likely to prevail.

The Division of Labor in Congress

One of the most important organizational principles in Congress is its division of labor into relatively specialized areas of legislation. Members of Congress cannot possibly master all the issues before the legislature. **Specialization** is no less necessary in Congress than in many other organizations that seek to accomplish something. And make no mistake about it, Congress has a lot of work to do. In the first 100 years of its existence, Congress considered an average of about 3,100 measures per congress (a two-year period). It passed an average of 387 bills into law. But in the twentieth century it has considered an average of almost 20,000 measures, passing well over 1,000 of them into law per congress. In just the past thirty years, Congress has more than doubled the number of committee meetings and the number of hours it is in session.[2]

Specialization is necessary because the policy questions before Congress not only cover a wide range but are extremely complex. Members must spend a great deal of time learning the details of their specialty, much as college professors must devote their lives to mastering a relatively small portion of what is known. Imagine a university, charged with teaching and adding to knowledge, without specialists. It would not have departments. Each of its faculty members would attempt to unravel the mysteries of organic chemistry, medieval history, classical Greek literature, and modern psychology. Faced with such a task, all but the hyperactive (and foolish) would throw up their hands in despair.

Like the modern university, Congress organizes itself into specialties. Like professors, its members develop expertise in relatively few areas of public policy. The Congress's committees and subcommittees are rather like a university's departments. Just as the chemistry department is devoted to learning in the field of chemistry, the agriculture committees in the House and Senate devote their institutional resources to agricultural policy. Just as chemists remain largely indifferent to the hot debates in medieval history, specialists in agricultural policy are unlikely to be well informed about transportation or health issues.

An extremely important implication of specialization, then, whether in the university or in the Congress, is that specialists

---

[2]Roger H. Davidson and Walter J. Oleszek, *Congress and Its Members*, 2nd ed. (Washington, D.C.: Congressional Quarterly Press, 1985), pp. 29–30.

devote their energies to becoming expert in one small area and as a consequence remain relatively uninformed about most others. Some exceptions to this tendency toward specialization in Congress are discussed below, but for now it is a very important generalization to understand. It is a powerful norm or expectation in Congress that its members will not attempt to speak out or affect legislation in all policy areas. Rather, they accumulate expertise in a limited policy area.[3]

Because specialization inevitably results in ignorance as well as knowledge, it is almost always accompanied by some form of **reciprocity.** Reciprocity occurs because of the high cost of information, and because information is closely related to power. Take the university again. Specialists in the various departments tend to leave each other alone with respect to such matters as the curriculum and the hiring of new faculty. They do so on the grounds that specialists know what they are doing better than anyone else in matters related to their specialty. Thus when mathematicians consider a curricular change or a candidate for a faculty position, art historians do not normally become involved because they do not have the information necessary to make an informed decision. Likewise, when art historians make decisions in matters related to their disciplinary expertise, mathematicians *reciprocate* by not becoming involved in their decisions. Reciprocity, then, means that specialists defer to one another's expertise by leaving primary decision making to those with the relevant knowledge.[4]

In Congress, too, specialization is accompanied by reciprocity. Members of Congress divide up the legislative pie and leave each other alone to eat in peace. Because information is costly, no lawmaker can be informed on the full range of policy on the congressional agenda. Without good information about the issues in a policy debate—the possible consequences of proposed alternatives, the data that support competing arguments, who will be helped and who will be hurt—nonspecialists tend to remove themselves from the policy debate. As a result, *policies are normally made in Congress*

---

[3]The norm of specialization is stronger in the House than in the Senate because the Senate is smaller and each member therefore must cover a larger portion of the institution's business. Senators, for example, average almost twice as many committee and subcommittee assignments as Representatives. See Norman J. Ornstein et al., *Vital Statistics on Congress, 1984–1985 Edition* (Washington, D.C.: American Enterprise Institute, 1984), p. 111.

[4]Colleges and universities have ways to overcome some of the dangers associated with specialization and reciprocity. For example, deans review decisions made by specialists in the departments to make sure they are consistent with institutional policy and standards. If they are not, the dean has the authority to intervene and reverse departmental decisions. No one in Congress has authority comparable to that of a university dean.

by a limited number of its members in response to a narrow range of outside interests.

Committees and the Division of Labor

Generalizing about committees in Congress is a humbling exercise, as there are many differences among the sixteen Senate and twenty-two House standing committees.[5] When one includes the well over two-hundred active subcommittees, the complexity is staggering. Despite the richness of variation and detail found in the congressional **committee system,** however, some patterns are discernible which reinforce the implications of the division of labor. Consider the following statements about the congressional committee system:

The committees and subcommittees in Congress are the institutional expressions of specialization and reciprocity. A legislator who wishes to specialize in agricultural policy must be assigned to the agriculture committee in her chamber; a senator with a special interest in tax policy will gravitate toward the Finance Committee; and a House member interested in educational issues seeks an assignment to Education and Labor. These fairly broad policy concerns are more precisely defined by the subcommittees, which deal with narrower policy questions. For example, the Agriculture committee in the House has subcommittees that deal with such specific commodities as grain and tobacco and peanuts.[6] One clear implication, then, is that individual members pursue their substantive legislative interests within the committee and subcommittee framework.

Having said that the committees formalize specialization, we must also acknowledge that some specialize more than others. The most prestigious committees in both chambers, for example, are also those that have the broadest policy mandates. The budget committees, the tax committees (Finance in the Senate and Ways and Means in the House), the appropriations committees, and the Rules committee in the House all deal with broad policy concerns. Merchant Marine and Fisheries, Armed Services, and Judiciary are among the committees with more specialized concerns.

Most of Congress's legislative work gets done in the committees

---

[5]Three excellent sources on the committees in Congress are Richard F. Fenno, Jr., *Congressmen in Committees* (Boston: Little, Brown, 1973); Steven S. Smith and Christopher J. Deering, *Committees in Congress* (Washington, D.C.: Congressional Quarterly Press, 1984); and Glenn R. Parker and Suzanne L. Parker, *Factions in House Committees* (Knoxville: University of Tennessee Press, 1985).

[6]For a complete list of the committees and subcommittees in the House and Senate, see "Leadership, Committees, and Subcommittees of the 100th Congress," *Congressional Quarterly Special Report,* May 2, 1987.

and subcommittees. Almost all legislation that eventually becomes law begins in a committee or subcommittee. Of the thousands of bills introduced, most are winnowed out by committees and sub-committees. They may be combined with other proposals dealing with similar problems; the committee may rewrite the legislation altogether; or it may simply ignore a bill referred to it. Most bills that survive the committee with primary responsibility for them eventually become law. The committees, therefore, are the gatekeepers of Congress. Everything they do is subject to approval by the entire membership, but they exercise great power by virtue of their ability to veto proposals within their domain.

Members' personal goals are realized through their committee assignments.[7] Why specialize in a given area of public policy? One reason certainly is ideological: members gravitate toward policy questions that they believe are important to the nation's well-being. For many years the House Armed Services Committee was dominated by conservatives because of their ideological commitment to defense policy.

Another factor (often closely related to ideology) influencing the choice of specialization is constituency. As David Mayhew argues, the committee system is tailor-made for lawmakers who claim credit for what they do with their legislative careers.[8] It divides national policy into manageable segments that are then disproportionately influenced by a small segment of the total congressional membership (that is, committee members). Of course, MCs want to claim credit for influencing policy of greatest interest to their constituencies. That is an important part of their reelection quest, and we can now see that the committee system helps individual members pursue their own reelection.

Lawmakers' pursuit of their personal policy and reelection goals through the committee system creates some noticeable biases. Assignments to standing committees are under the control of the political parties in each chamber. Members request committee assignments that reflect their goals, and the parties most often accommodate those preferences.[9] Other criteria besides the preferences of senators and representatives also come into play, but because individual preference is the most influential factor, the committees are not at all representative of the overall membership

---

[7]See Fenno, *Congressmen in Committees.*

[8]David Mayhew, *Congress: The Electoral Connection* (New Haven: Yale University Press, 1974), p. 95.

[9]Kenneth A. Shepsle, *The Giant Jigsaw Puzzle* (Chicago: University of Chicago Press, 1978); Smith and Deering, *Committees in Congress,* p. 241.

in the chamber.[10] House members from rural farming areas tend to gravitate toward the Agriculture Committee, those from coastal areas to Merchant Marine and Fisheries, those from the west toward Interior and Insular Affairs, and those from constituencies with concentrations of labor union members to the Education and Labor Committee.

We shall return to the role of the parties in assigning members to committees, but for now it is enough to recognize that the committee system reflects members' need to build support in their constituencies. Particularly in order to satisfy the attentive and organized interests in their constituencies, MCs attempt to build a legislative career around areas of specialty that are of concern to the constituency. A large proportion of the membership of some committees is motivated by constituency interests. In fact, scholars have labeled them "constituency committees."[11] Other committees, typically those more prestigious and general in their authority, attract members concerned with status and influence within Congress. Even these MCs, however, are often strongly motivated by the desire to serve their constituents' interests.[12]

Committees are vitally instrumental in the distribution of power in Congress. The committees' role in the distribution of power follows closely from the role of specialization and reciprocity in the organization of Congress. Members of a committee that considers a legislative proposal have disproportionate influence over the outcome. They usually have more to do with whether the proposal lives or dies than anyone else in Congress. They also have more to do with what is included in and excluded from a bill when it goes to the floor, and they often have great influence over the disposition of the proposal by the entire Congress.

Seniority is another way in which influence is distributed in

---

[10]Roger Davidson, "Representation and Congressional Committees," *Annals of the Academy of Political and Social Sciences*, January 1974, pp. 48–62. For more recent data, on the ideological differences among committees, see Ornstein et al., *Vital Statistics*, pp. 187–197.

[11]Smith and Deering, *Committees in Congress*, chap. 3. Smith and Deering include the following House committees as "constituency committees": Agriculture, Armed Services, Education and Labor (which is also a "policy" committee), Interior, Merchant Marine, Public Works. Most scholars agree that these committees attract MCs interested in promoting constituency concerns through their legislative work.

[12]"Power" or "prestige" committees in the House include Appropriations, Budget, Rules, and Ways and Means. Smith and Deering show that Appropriations members have a high level of constituency motivation (ibid., p. 90). For an interesting account of an Appropriations subcommittee chair using his power for constituency and ideological ends, see Nick Kotz, "Jamie Whitten: Permanent Secretary of Agriculture," in *American Government: Readings and Cases*, ed. Peter Woll, 8th ed. (Boston: Little, Brown, 1984), pp. 438–451.

committees. Although the **seniority system** was modified in 1974, it still has great influence over the way power is distributed in Congress.[13] In its unadulterated form, the seniority system gives the chair of a committee to the lawmaker of the majority party in the chamber who has the longest service on that committee. According to Roger Davidson and Walter Oleszek, "committee chairmen call meetings and establish agendas, hire and fire committee staff, arrange hearings, designate conferees, act as floor managers, control committee funds and rooms, develop legislative strategies, chair hearings and markups, and regulate the internal affairs and organization of the committee."[14] These are hardly absolute powers, and the effectiveness of committee chairs depends as much on their political skills as on the formal prerogatives of the position. Nonetheless, committee chairs (and to a lesser degree subcommittee chairs) wield significant influence over legislative outcomes. Their positions are coveted by other members, and their status accords them the attention of interest groups and the media, as well as the respect of their colleagues.

The committee system encourages responsiveness by Congress to organized interests. Since standing committees exist pretty much unchanged from congress to congress, the jurisdictions are well understood by interested parties in and out of Congress. Interest groups know which committees and subcommittees deal with legislation of greatest concern to them. They know whom to contact in order to make their case, which hearings to attend to monitor congressional action of particular interest to them, and which MCs to help by financial contributions to their campaigns. Many committees therefore attract clusters of organized interests and bureaucrats intensely eager to influence congressional policy. On any given legislative day, dozens of committees and subcommittees meet and weigh legislative proposals. Organized interests have the resources necessary to monitor this complex and fragmented process.

The committee system rewards organized interests also because of the way assignments are made. Members seek to claim credit for helping to make policies that in turn help interests that

---

[13]Leroy N. Rieselbach, *Congressional Reform* (Washington, D.C.: Congressional Quarterly Press, 1986). Senior members must now be approved by the Democratic Caucus before they can assume committee chairs. According to Rieselbach, "there have been a sufficient number of departures from the [seniority] rule [three in 1975 and one in 1985] to restrain the most arbitrary exercise of chairs' authority," (p. 80). These departures have occurred in the House and may also have modified chair behavior in the Senate, where the seniority rule for selecting committee chairs has not been breached since the reforms of 1974.
[14]Davidson and Oleszek, *Congress and Its Members*, p. 222.

can help or hurt their careers. Thus, as we have seen, members gravitate toward committees that make policy of direct concern to their constituencies, and particularly of *direct concern to organized interests in their constituencies.* Recognition of the way the committee system favors organized interests is essential to an understanding of the kind of macro representation Congress offers. In the absence of significant checks on the committees, the policy process in Congress strongly favors organized interests. The unorganized are at a serious disadvantage in a legislature that operates under the principles of specialization and reciprocity.[15]

Committees reduce and manage conflict in Congress. An extremely important implication of congressional reliance on committees from the perspective of the Republic is that Congress experiences less conflict than one would expect to find in the absence of strong committees. The wheels of the legislative process are greased by institutionalized specialization and reciprocity. As slow as Congress can sometimes be, the committee system greatly enhances its ability to act. Seniority as a mechanism for allocating positions of significant influence manages conflict by reducing the likelihood of internal fights or external interference.

Most significant, however, the committee system excludes many more interests from the process than it includes. Intensely concerned, organized interests are included, but many other interests are left out. The information costs are simply too high to permit the average citizen to monitor what committees and subcommittees are doing. The popular media cannot report more than a minuscule fraction of what is going on and hope to retain the interest of the reader or listener. Precisely because the committee system fragments and complicates the process, complex organization is itself necessary to monitor what committees and subcommittees are doing. Complexity of organization helps explain an important characteristic of the congressional policy process: the winners usually know they are winning, but the losers often do not know they are losing. It also reinforces the norm of universalism discussed in Chapter 6. If everyone is to win, the interests that are losing must not oppose congressional actions.

Mechanisms that reduce conflict in Congress must be viewed with great suspicion from the perspective of the Republic. Conflict was to be the means by which tyranny was avoided because self-interest would frustrate self-interest. Yet the committee system isolates decision makers in a complex process. Bargains are struck

---

[15]Michael T. Hayes, "The Semisovereign Pressure Groups: A Critique of Current Theory and an Alternative Typology," *Journal of Politics* 40 (1978): 134–161.

among the most intensely concerned interests, without regard for the interests not included.[16]

Implications of the Committee System for Congressional Representation

This discussion of conflict leads us back to a recurrent theme of this book: neither conflict nor instrumentally self-interested behavior is inevitable in politics. Conflict occurs when competing interests are sufficiently informed, organized, and active to press their claims. This has been a continuing problem in our analysis of Madison's Republic. Interest and participation are not automatically present in politics, especially in the fragmented, complex congressional process. Someone must pay the information costs, someone must pay the organization costs. People willing and able to pay will play, and most often they will win. Pluralists and party theorists have different reactions to this problem as it is found in congressional representation, reactions we will examine in more detail.

Figure 7-1 summarizes the argument thus far about the organization of Congress. The heavy work load of the contemporary Congress produces a division of labor into relatively narrow areas of specialization. MCs cannot know everything. Specialization is accompanied by reciprocity: specialists in one policy area defer to specialists in other areas. Information is costly and closely related to influence. Therefore, influence is not distributed equally. People with information about a policy issue tend to have more influence over the relevant policy than those without information. The committee system formalizes specialization and reciprocity. It creates pockets of decision making where attention is focused on the particular policy concern of the committee or subcommittee.

The third box in Figure 7-1 presents the major conclusion of the analysis thus far. Specialization and reciprocity, as formalized in the committees of Congress, reduce conflict and promote responsiveness to the organized. These tendencies help determine the pattern of macro representation in Congress. Specialization and

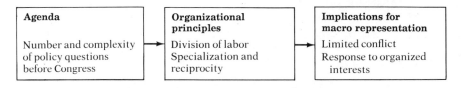

Figure 7-1 Implications of Congressional Organization

---

[16]Theodore Lowi, *The End of Liberalism*, 2nd ed. (New York: Norton, 1979).

reciprocity make expertise a critical resource to the people who try to influence Congress. Organization, whether in the federal bureaucracy (as in the Department of Agriculture) or in the private sector (as in the American Farm Bureau Federation), is the mobilization of expertise. Experts communicate with and respond to other experts because they have the same information, make the same assumptions, and understand the implications of alternatives.

Figure 7-1 provides a hint about the way Congress resolves the tension between micro and macro representation. We have seen that the committee system permits MCs to specialize in policy of interest to their constituents and to others who can help their careers. Under the norm of reciprocity, Congress delegates its power over specific areas of public policy to specialists in committees and subcommittees. Together these experts cover the wide and complex terrain of national public policy in much the same way that the faculty of a university covers the terrain of human knowledge. But in each case, the institution covers the territory by dividing it up. In effect, Congress delegates its institutional authority over each component of policy to a small subset of its members.

We can say, therefore, that micro representation leads to the pattern of macro representation in Congress. Congress is organized in such a way as to protect the interests of the individual legislator. It should be clear, however, that macro representation in today's Congress does not square with the macro representation envisioned by the Republic. The full range of factional interests in society is not normally brought into the debate on a policy question. Indeed, most interests are systematically excluded because they do not have the information necessary to participate. Conflict therefore is much reduced below the levels expected by the Republic. Of course, incorporation of the full range of interests in every aspect of congressional policy making would bring the process to a grinding halt. Congress would effectively be removed from national policy making on most issues so long as the nation's agenda remained as extensive and complex as it is. Yet in accommodating this complexity, Congress departs from the republican principle of response to broad societal interests.

As important as the organizational principles of specialization and reciprocity are to an understanding of Congress, countervailing forces mitigate to some degree the effects we have been discussing. Political parties exist in Congress. They have the potential to organize rather than minimize conflict. And, despite their importance, the committees and subcommittees are only subsets of the entire membership. That membership, gathered on the floor of the House or the Senate, retains full constitutional control over what Congress does. Thus we turn next to the parties and then to the floor in search of forces that may offset the pattern shown in Figure 7-1.

Organizing Conflict into Congress

Political Parties in Congress

Party theory seeks to organize conflict in Congress around the competition between strong parties. In some respects, the parties in Congress are remarkably similar to what party theory hopes for. The majority party in each chamber has formal control over every step of the legislative process. A majority of every committee and subcommittee roughly corresponds to the partisan majority in the chamber. And, of course, the majority party has more votes than the minority on the floor. If the same party controls both House and Senate, then, it has a majority at every step of the legislative process, from the first look given a bill by a subcommittee through a conference committee's reconciliation of House–Senate differences through final passage on the floors of the two houses.

But a formal paper majority does not give the party significant control over its members. Its ability to discipline the membership—to commit itself to a program and then deliver that program through Congress—is distinctly limited. The congressional parties are not irrelevant, but they are not very strong, either. As a consequence, they do not go very far toward correcting what party theorists see as the major flaws in the committee system.

Consider first the power the parties do *not* have as they operate in contemporary congressional politics. They have at best only a very limited role in the recruitment of congressional candidates.[17] A potential candidate with such personal resources as a lot of money or high personal visibility can run in a district or state primary without the approval, to say nothing of the blessing, of anyone in the party. If the candidate wins, he or she appears on the general election ballot under the party's name, whether or not the candidate has any commitment to the party organization and its goals.

Reelection is perhaps an even bigger stumbling block to party theorists' hopes for Congress. As we have seen, incumbents use their perquisites to build *personal* followings in their districts. In their advertising and credit claiming, they often separate themselves from the national party implicitly or explicitly. "Congressman

---

[17]Gary Jacobson shows, however, that the Republican party increased its contributions of funds to congressional campaigns quite dramatically in the early 1980s. For a discussion of this trend toward greater party involvement in recruitment and some of its effects on Congress, see Gary C. Jacobson, "Parties and PACs in Congressional Elections," in *Congress Reconsidered*, ed. Lawrence C. Dodd and Bruce I. Oppenheimer, 3rd ed. (Washington, D.C.: Congressional Quarterly Press, 1985).

Jones works for Indiana" means that Congressman Jones values his independence so he can deliver particularized benefits to his constituency. It does *not* mean that he works for Indiana by being a loyal member of the Republican party. And everyone, from the constituency to the party leaders in Congress, knows it. The very fact that we can talk about a "norm of universalism" in Congress is completely inconsistent with strong party organizations of the sort contemplated by party theory. In contrast to a norm of universalism, by which no member's reelection threatens any other's, party theorists would like to see highly visible conflict between the parties in Congress mirrored by electoral conflict in the districts over the same issues. As a result, voters would be better able to choose candidates (and therefore parties) representative of their views. Under such a system, incumbency would lose its meaning except as it pertains to the party in power. The question for the voter would be simple: "Should the party in power remain in power?"

To describe the alternative is to point up the contrast with the current system of candidate recruitment, election, and reelection. Because the parties do not control access to the institution, they give up most meaningful control over what members do once they get there. Members pursue their legislative careers in relatively autonomous committees and subcommittees. They acquire power through their individual efforts at building a specialty and the personal reputation that goes with their expertise. By getting themselves elected and reelected, they accrue seniority. Normally, they build a power base independent of the party. Their power is not usually subject to meaningful review by the party. So long as they can get reelected, they retain their power. Their responsibility, then, is to forces more or less unique to their constituency, not to the national party.

Despite the fact that the parties do not exercise significant discipline in making committee assignments or in allocating power within the committees, they are not totally bereft of influence. The party leadership, while weaker than party theorists would like, has some meaningful power. For example, the leadership helps select members of the committees, and sometimes uses loyalty to party programs as a criterion.[18] The leadership plays a role in referring some kinds of legislation to committee, scheduling legislation on the floor, and monitoring the debate that takes place on the floor. It can also provide information to party members on legislation with

---

[18]The involvement of party leaders in committee assignments was strengthened by the House Democrats' 1974 reforms. These reforms were explicitly designed to concentrate more power in the hands of the party. Still, as one scholar has observed, "legislators were unwilling to surrender more than a modicum of their freedom to the party leaders, and the movement toward centralization has been halting at best. The parties, on balance, remain weak": Rieselbach, *Congressional Reform*, p. 105.

which they may not be familiar. Leaders give advice on how to vote. Finally, such party leaders as the Speaker of the House and majority leader in the Senate have a degree of national visibility not accorded ordinary members. They can attract media attention, make public pronouncements, and marshal the support of their followers because of their national prominence. The uses to which these sources of power can be put vary with the skills the individual leader brings to the job.

Despite the limited power of party leadership in Congress, the party affiliation of members is a reasonably good guide to the policy preferences they have and the kinds of policies they support. Table 7-1 shows how MCs of the two parties differ in their ideological preferences. In the House a majority of Democrats are liberal, and a much more substantial majority of GOP members are conservative in their overall ideological preferences. The Senate data show less distinction between the parties, but a clear difference nonetheless. This pattern of party difference in the House and Senate has prevailed, with some variation, since World War II. Other research has shown that congressional candidates within the same district differ quite substantially by party in the direction indicated in Table 7-1. Therefore when a Senate or House seat passes from one party to the other, the voters can be reasonably confident that they have elected a candidate who will support policies different from those preferred by his or her predecessor.[19]

These regular differences between members of the two parties *cannot* be attributed to discipline by the congressional party leadership. They result rather from the fact that party activists, including

Table 7-1 Ideological Divisions in House and Senate, 1983, by Party (percent)

	House		Senate	
	Democrats (N = 267)	*Republicans* (N = 167)	*Democrats* (N = 46)	*Republicans* (N = 54)
Liberal	52%	2%	39%	—
Moderate	30	17	39	30%
Conservative	19	81	22	70

SOURCE: Senate data from Norman J. Ornstein et al., "The Senate Through the 1980s: Cycles of Change," in *Congress Reconsidered*, ed. Lawrence C. Dodd and Bruce I. Oppenheimer, 3rd ed. (Washington, D.C.: Congressional Quarterly Press, 1985), p. 15; House data from Lawrence C. Dodd and Bruce I. Oppenheimer, "The House in Transition: Partisanship and Opposition," in ibid., p. 37.

---

[19]John L. Sullivan and Robert E. O'Connor, "Electoral Choice and Popular Control of Public Policy: The Case of the 1966 House Elections," *American Political Science Review* 66 (1972): 1256–1268. For more recent data on the Senate, see Gerald C. Wright, Jr., and Michael B. Berkman, "Candidates and Policy in United States Senate Elections," *American Political Science Review* 80 (1986): 567–588.

congressional candidates, generally have strong ideological preferences and belong to the political party that best represents their views, as we saw in Chapter 4. Much of the impetus for party differences also results from forces lodged in the constituencies. Districts whose residents identify overwhelmingly with the Democratic party tend to elect and reelect Democrats; districts whose residents are predominantly Republican elect Republicans to Congress. Once again, the regularities we observe between the parties are due more to outside forces to which each individual MC must be attentive than to party discipline within Congress.

Party theorists, therefore, are generally disappointed in the congressional parties. The parties are not strong enough to overcome the individualism of MCs. Members depend first on their individual reputations in their constituencies, they get themselves elected and reelected, and they rely on their personal skills to increase their influence in government. The parties can contribute to the individual careers of the membership in marginal ways. They are not irrelevant, but neither do they have the resources to lend much discipline or coherence to the congressional process. As a result, the ability of the congressional parties to organize conflict within the institution along partisan lines is limited.

Floor Voting by Members of Congress

In a very real sense, what Congress does it must do on the floor. We can recognize the importance of committees and subcommittees, of the division of labor, and of positions of particular influence in Congress, but when all is said and done, every piece of legislation must pass a vote of the entire membership if it is to become law. It is possible (though unusual) for legislation to emerge from Congress without the approval of a committee or subcommittee. But it is not possible for a bill to become law without approval by the entire membership, voting as equals, on the floor of the House and Senate.

So what happens on the floor is of paramount theoretical importance. Do all interests participate equally, so that outcomes can be certain to reflect the breadth of interests in society, as Madison hoped? Is the floor a meaningful check on the biases of the committee system? Does the floor, in short, organize conflict into Congress? The answers to these questions are a disappointment to the Republic, at least as they apply to the normal working of Congress. To understand the place of the floor in Congress, we must first appreciate the **decision problem** faced by MCs when they vote on the many issues brought before them.

The MC's Decision Problem

The problem the MC has in deciding whether to vote yea or nay on a proposal brought before the House or Senate is in some ways similar to the problem the citizen has in the voting booth. In both cases, the individuals must decide on a matter that may not be very salient to them and about which they may have little information. But the MC's problem has a twist that adds immeasurably to the difficulty. Whereas the voter can cast an anonymous ballot that will be forever lost in a sea of votes cast by thousands or millions of other citizens, the lawmaker's roll-call vote is often recorded for all time. Thus the MC is publicly accountable for every recorded vote cast.[20] So even though most citizens do not know how their representative is voting in Congress, there is an extensive record of hundreds of roll-call votes on dozens of issues, which political opponents can consult at any time. The use of incumbents' records against them is legitimate politics, and something every MC must worry about whenever a vote is cast.

The sheer number of issues, the complexity of the policy questions involved, and the potential for undesirable political consequences create the MC's problem on the floor. Table 7-2 illustrates the problem simply by listing the issues that came before the U.S. Senate for a recorded vote on one day at the end of a session. Senators and representatives cannot possibly be thoroughly informed on all aspects of such issues. They will have read or thought about some issues about as much as any other well-informed person. On a few votes they will have extraordinary expertise because the issue is part of or close to their area of specialization. On still others they may be uninformed altogether. Indeed, it is possible for an MC to walk on the floor, having been summoned by a quorum call, and cast a vote without the benefit of hearing any debate or understanding any of the subtleties of the question. It is easy to see that the range of complexity just in the issues listed in Table 7-2 is enormous. Can a single person come to grips with the complexities of the government personnel system, foreign policy, and the application of antitrust law to cities? Information is costly to lawmakers too, and sometimes they are simply unable to pay. As one representative frankly put it: "Members don't study things much. They often go in there and vote without knowing anything about the measure."[21]

How Do Members Decide How to Vote?

How can the legislator avoid political trouble and help make policy that is consistent with his goals for society without spending impossible amounts of time and energy to collect information?

---

[20]A representative who was elected to the House in 1972 and served five terms through 1982 would have been called upon to cast 5,979 recorded votes for an average of just under 1,200 votes per term: Ornstein et al., *Vital Statistics*, pp. 143–144.
[21]Quoted in John W. Kingdon, *Congressmen's Voting Decisions*, 2nd ed. (New York: Harper & Row, 1981), p. 231.

Table 7-2 Number of Votes Cast for and Against Substantive Issues on One Day (October 3, 1984) in the U.S. Senate

	Votes	
Issue	*Yea*	*Nay*
Support for the people of Afghanistan	97	0
Limitation of aid to Nicaraguan rebels *(contras)*	45	53
Regulation of sale of armor-piercing ammunition	24	74
Requirement that federal government study its pay and classification system to determine amount of sex discrimination	41	57
Motion to kill amendment permitting Medicaid payments for abortion in cases of rape or incest	54	44
Motion to kill amendment requiring president to certify that funds provided were sufficient to secure U.S. embassies abroad	61	37
Restoration of Federal Trade Commission's authority to apply antitrust law against municipalities	56	42
Motion to kill amendment permitting exceptions to noise standards for foreign airlines at airports in Miami and Bangor, Maine	47	50
Motion to kill amendment barring military aid to Turkey until that nation relinquished control of a town on the island of Cyprus	51	46
Amendment to rescind $9 billion of funding for Synthetic Fuels Corporation	37	60
Authorization of $11 billion in water projects	36	60
Motion to kill amendment prohibiting U.S. participation in Inter-American Investment Corporation	50	49
Amendment to reduce military aid bill by $212 million	46	54
Amendment to bar intelligence agencies from spending funds on action against Nicaraguan government and to provide funds for withdrawal and resettlement of *contras*	42	57

NOTE: The procedural details of the issues, sometimes complex, are explained in *Congressional Weekly Report*, October 6 and 13, 1984. Note that this day came at the end of a session, and therefore the number of bills considered is not typical. The day was chosen to illustrate the range of issues that lawmakers must consider.

I suggest a simple model of the way MCs reach decisions on the floor. It is based most directly on the work of John Kingdon, but other scholars have wrestled with the question and the model incorporates their ideas as well.[22] The model, depicted in Figure 7-2, suggests that MCs go through a three-step process in casting their

[22]Ibid.; Aage R. Clausen, *How Congressmen Decide* (New York: St. Martin's Press, 1973); Donald Matthews and James A. Stimson, *Yeas and Nays: Normal Decision-Making in the U.S. House of Representatives* (New York: Wiley, 1975).

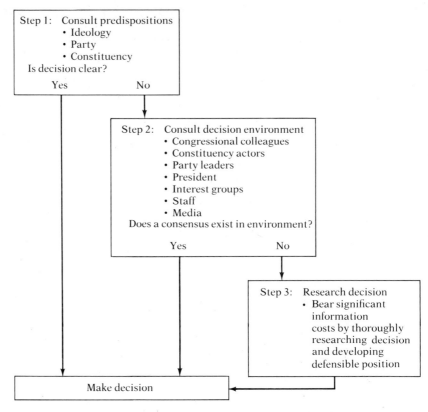

Figure 7-2 Model of Decision Making on the Floor of Congress

votes. The central idea of the model is that MCs make decisions with as little information as possible but in a manner that is generally consistent with what they would do if they had more information.

Step 1: Consult predispositions. There is considerable evidence that MCs make something like standing decisions on clusters of issues. For example, issues related to regulation of the economy might be considered as part of a cluster in the lawmaker's mind and toward which she has a general predisposition. She might, for example, generally oppose regulation of the economy in the absence of a compelling argument for an exception in a particular case. Such moral issues as prayer in school and abortion might be clustered separately with a different standing decision ("The government must act to protect certain moral values"). Such clusters of issues are often related to a coherent ideology that can form the basis for voting decisions (ideology is discussed in Chapter 3).

Party and constituency are part of the lawmaker's **pre-**

dispositions because they form a kind of backdrop closely related to ideology. We have already seen that liberals in Congress gravitate to the Democratic party and conservatives to the Republican party. Constituencies that elect Democrats tend to be more liberal than those that elect Republicans. So the three factors under predispositions are closely related.

Predispositions work quite powerfully on floor voting decisions. In some cases, MCs may simply vote their predispositions directly. If an issue has clear partisan or ideological implications, the MC can translate those factors into a vote without gathering further information. A congressional staff member put it this way:

> "There's a lot less soul-searching and introspection than you might think. Very little midnight oil is burned. Most members come here with well formed predispositions. They're very opinionated and their minds are made up beforehand. There's very little you can do to change their minds."[23]

Likewise, if a prominent constituency interest is plainly at stake (an amendment to protect the tax loophole of a powerful local industry, for example), the voting decision in effect is made by the predisposition. If the MC can reach a decision simply by consulting his predisposition, the model predicts that the decision will be made on that basis. This procedure minimizes costs and permits the legislator to use resources (time, energy) in the most efficient way possible.

Step 2: Consult decision environment. The **decision environment** is made up of actors capable of helping or hurting the MC. They may control resources useful to the lawmaker's career, or they may have important information. In the model, the MC surveys what he knows of the preferences of these actors, and decides how to vote on the basis of this review. If everyone (or almost everyone) in the environment agrees, the legislator can make a decision that reflects this consensus without gathering much information and without incurring much risk.[24] This is a cost-effective decision

---

[23]Quoted in Kingdon, *Congressmen's Voting Decisions*, pp. 269–270.
[24]Risk is minimized first because the actors who are most likely to hurt the MC if he makes a bad decision are canvassed as part of the relevant environment. Risk is also minimized because it is shared. The decisions that produce the greatest consensus, of course, are those that are unanimous. With unanimous decisions, the individual legislator cannot change the outcome, and so, according to Kingdon, simply votes with the "herd" (ibid., p. 243). Such voting does not protect the legislature from a bad decision, even if it minimizes the political risks to the individual. In 1971, for example, the Texas House of Representatives passed a resolution unanimously that commemorated Albert De Salvo's "noted activities and unconventional techniques involving population control and applied psychology" while Mr. De Salvo was serving a life sentence for crimes committed as the infamous Boston Strangler. William J. Keefe and Morris S. Ogul, *The American Legislative Process* (Englewood Cliffs, N.J.: Prentice-Hall, 1977), p. 259.

rule in light of the MC's problem. He cannot be informed on all decisions. If he votes in such a way as to agree with his environment, he has reduced the possibility of hurting himself politically. He can even hope that he is voting in a way that is consistent with the way he would vote if he had more and better information.

Kingdon found some interesting evidence in support of this idea. He selected for study issues that had generated high levels of attention in and out of Congress. On these unusually visible issues, Kingdon found that MCs *always* voted with their environment when they perceived no disagreement. Even when one or two actors were perceived as disagreeing with the rest, the legislator almost always voted with the majority.

An important relationship exists between step 1 and step 2 in Figure 7-2. The predispositions of the MC have powerful effects on the environment surrounding the decision. The party of the representative or senator, for example, determines which party leaders he or she listens to. Likewise, a Democrat may use a Republican president as a negative referent—"Whatever he's for I'm against"— while a Republican colleague follows the president's leadership. The media sources that MCs read, the staff they hire, the colleagues they respect, the interest groups they consult are also powerfully affected by party, ideology, and constituency. Conflict may fill the air surrounding a particular issue in Congress, but individual members may not experience that conflict as a part of their decision environment. Each MC has a unique environment that she or he has constructed in part to reduce conflict. Reducing conflict simplifies the decision and saves such resources as time and effort.

Step 3: Research decision. In the presence of perceived conflict in the decision environment, however, the legislator has an inescapable problem. On these issues, the MC must bear significant information costs by thoroughly researching the decision and developing a position that can be defended before constituents, colleagues, and interest groups. These issues, though unusual among all those that representatives and senators are called upon to decide, attract a great deal of attention in the media and generate unusual amounts of conflict.

Just as MCs have an incentive to proceed immediately from step 1 to a decision, they will avoid step 3 if they can. Members proceed to the next step in the model reluctantly and only when they must. Even among the highly visible issues that Kingdon studied, he found that his model of **consensus decision making** accurately predicted 92 percent of the votes.[25] So long as a fundamental consensus existed in the decision environment, Kingdon found representatives strongly inclined to go along in their voting on the floor without any necessary commitment to gathering additional information. Only in the event of an extremely visible issue that attracts huge amounts of public attention are MCs forced to move to step 3.

When these kinds of issues arise, the Congress is more likely to function as Madison hoped it would. Debate is protracted and heated. Large numbers of interests become involved, and many ordinary citizens become informed about the issue. The conflict is contagious and it stimulates interest and participation. Under these conditions, Congress may have great difficulty acting, especially acting quickly. Typically, these issues are the most "important" in that they are at the center of the media stage. They often involve key parts of the president's program, such as tax reform, civil rights, or an arms-control treaty.

But far and away the largest part of congressional decision making is conducted in the more serene world of specialization and reciprocity, committee and subcommittee deliberations in relative isolation, and floor ratification. As a consequence, the vast majority of votes cast on the floor of Congress can be described by steps 1 and 2 in the model. This is no accident. Interest groups understand that the more conflict surrounding an issue, the greater its visibility. With increased visibility comes more interest and participation. Potential losers become aware of their stake and the congressional process changes dramatically. If such results are pleasing to the theoretical expectations of the Republic, they are not consistent with the goals of the powerful interests that impinge on the contemporary Congress. These interests are usually content to restrict the scope of conflict to the people most intensely concerned, to those involved in legislation at the subcommittee and committee stages. Conflict thus controlled protects the interests of those involved in the more restricted committee setting from the intrusion of the plethora of interests that *might* become involved in a visible fight on the floor. As a result, the floor does not often provide a serious check on the specialization found in committees. The biases there in favor of the intensely interested and the well organized are not normally frustrated by the parent body. That they *sometimes* are subject to intense scrutiny by the membership is very important. Whether the potential, sometimes realized, of a Congress that involves the many factions in its deliberations is close enough to the ideal of the Republic is a question to which we now turn.

---

[25]Kingdon, *Congressmen's Voting Decisions*, p. 255.

Stepping Back: Self-Interest
and Representation in Congress

Reducing Conflict and the Public Interest

One thing is clear: members of Congress have figured out how to reduce conflict. A reduction of conflict is contrary to the public interest as Madison conceived it. Whether it is a desirable feature of the contemporary Congress is open to debate, but there is no doubt that many devices currently in place manage and reduce conflict below the levels the Republic anticipated.

Electoral conflict between two candidates with roughly equal resources is in the public interest. But incumbents reduce conflict by exploiting the perquisites they have granted themselves, by pursuing particularized benefits that do not arouse opposition, and by failing to grant challengers access to public financing. Most challengers are unable to raise the funds necessary to get the attention of the average citizen in the district. Lacking information about the race, citizens tend to think very highly of the incumbent and to vote accordingly.

Conflict is also reduced within Congress, so that the pattern of macro representation posited by the Republic is skewed. The norm of universalism, which permits incumbents to conspire with one another against challengers, certainly reduces conflict. Specialization and reciprocity reinforce the norm of universalism. Formalized in the committee system, specialization and reciprocity reduce conflict by isolating decision making in the hands of specialists. Bargains are struck among the interests most closely associated with the issue, and outsiders are unlikely to know when policy that may affect them is being made. Strong parties in Congress might offset this tendency, but strong parties do not exist. All legislation must pass a floor vote. The floor certainly could be the place in Congress where conflict among competing interests occurs. But we have seen that a consensus model of decision making, not a conflict model, best describes what happens on the floor. On some highly visible issues, conflict occurs. But such issues are unusual. On most questions Congress considers, specialists make policy without much involvement by the many other factional interests that may be affected.

At bottom, the problem with the Republic's theory of representation is a familiar one. If citizen self-interest cannot be taken for granted, neither can representation. And if representation (of the micro variety) is problematic, conflict among the many interests that representation is supposed to bring into government cannot be expected to occur. If many interests are not brought into the policy process, the theory of macro representation found in the Republic is contradicted by the reality of congressional politics. Therefore, the Republic does not offer a very accurate picture of the way Congress works, nor does it provide an adequate normative defense for congressional representation in the twentieth century.

Congressional Power in the American System

In order to assess the damage done to our political system by a political institution (Congress) that the founding theory (the Republic) does not adequately understand, we must consider the power of Congress in the American system of government. This is a question important throughout Part II because Chapter 8 argues that the presidency has gained power in national politics. The presidency has benefited from a decline in congressional power. So what happens to one institution in part explains what happens to the other.

We can think of **congressional power as a collective good** for members of the institution. Certainly it is in the interest of every lawmaker for Congress to have significant power over national policy because each member shares in that power. But, like other collective goods, the power of Congress is in large part indivisible. Each MC, if he is strictly self-interested, pursues a free-rider strategy. That is, the legislator protects his own congressional career by concentrating first on what is necessary to get reelected. He attends primarily to organized interests and constituents who can help or hurt his career. No strictly rational MC will sink too many resources into maintaining the institution, especially if those resources are necessary to protect the individual's ability to stay in Congress. The self-interested MC will not permit the institution to create rules that preserve institutional power at the expense of his control over his own career.[26]

While it is certainly not true that all MCs are strict free riders, they generally worry first about doing what is necessary to protect their private interests. Once their careers are safe, they may turn to protecting the collective good of congressional power. This is the reason Congress's rules have such a strong strain of individualism. The parties do not have much power to discipline members. Individual incumbents have the resources they need to get themselves reelected. They pursue their careers in committees and subcommittees that permit them maximum personal influence over the policy areas of greatest concern to the people who can help or hurt

---

[26]For two analyses of Congress consistent with this interpretation, see Jacobson, *Congressional Elections*, chap. 7; and Lawrence C. Dodd, "Congress and the Quest for Power," in *Congress Reconsidered*, ed. Dodd and Oppenheimer (New York: Praeger, 1977).

their careers. They usually have little incentive to become well informed or to bear the risks associated with expanded conflict in areas outside their specialties.

The theory of collective goods suggests that since individuals have little or no incentive to provide the good, it will not be produced, or it will be produced at a suboptimal level. Such is the case with congressional power. It is provided at a lower level than the Republic expects, because the Republic does not anticipate the problem of collective goods and free riders. The paradox of collective action, therefore, works to reduce congressional power because that power depends on members of the group (members of Congress) contributing significant resources to the maintenance of a collective benefit. Despite the fact that each MC has a very real interest in congressional power, no individual has an interest in helping to pay for it.

The paradox of collective action implies that institutional power will decline but that individual careers will flourish. Lawmakers devote their resources to their own careers (a private benefit) while slighting the interests of the institution (a collective benefit). In accord with this argument is the finding that public evaluations of Congress as an institution are quite negative even as evaluations of individual incumbents are very strongly positive.[27] When Glenn Parker and Roger Davidson analyzed national survey data, they found that Congress as an institution is much more likely than individual lawmakers to be evaluated on policy grounds. Individual members of Congress are evaluated on the basis of their constituency service. Policy evaluations are overwhelmingly negative, but the public tends not to blame individual senators and representatives for policy failures. Rather, Congress takes the heat.[28] But the fact that the public is unhappy with the institution in which incumbents serve has no political force unless MCs suffer the consequences. Parker and Davidson's findings strongly suggest that legislators have successfully insulated their personal careers from the negative consequences of unpopular institutional behavior. Incumbents use their perquisites to bolster their careers and to separate themselves from what the institution does.

A concrete example may help explain how this system works. Better than a decade after Parker and Davidson's survey, the deficit in the federal government's budget was of widespread political

[27]Richard F. Fenno, Jr., "If, as Ralph Nader Says, Congress Is the 'Broken Branch,' How Come We Love our Congressmen So Much?" in *Congress in Change: Evolution and Reform*, ed. Norman J. Ornstein (New York: Praeger, 1975).
[28]Glenn R. Parker and Roger H. Davidson, "Why Do Americans Love Their Congressmen So Much More than Their Congress?" *Legislative Studies Quarterly* 4 (1979): 53–62.

interest. Any incumbent worthy of the name would have no trouble taking a position against all that red ink. He would lament its effects on the national economy, and he would blame either the president (if he was a Democrat) or the Congress (if he was a Republican) for the large and growing national debt. In the same newsletter in which the MC took a position against the deficit, he might also claim credit for keeping that local army base open, or for a tax loophole that protected a major industry in the state.

Imagine that every incumbent took a position against the deficit and claimed credit for spending money on some local interest. What would the effects be? Three major consequences follow as night follows day: (1) popular evaluations of Congress would be negative because the public would get the message that the institution was failing to deal with the deficit; (2) individual MCs would be popular because they were "working for Indiana"; and (3) the national budget deficit would continue to grow.

So long as MCs can insulate their careers from popular evaluations of Congress, the institution's power will be in jeopardy. Those in and out of Congress who would make some hard choices to reduce the deficit have great difficulty doing so because they seek to interfere with members' ability to generate particularized benefits for which they can claim credit. So long as the unpopularity of Congress has no immediate consequences for the typical MC's political career, the ability of Congress to represent national interests is hindered. Individual lawmakers may be responsible to local constituencies, but little in the way of collective responsibility is offered by the institution. In focusing first on their private interests (in power, in a career, in reelection), they fail to invest adequate resources to maintain the power of the institution. A national problem such as a long-term deficit has to be dealt with somewhere. If the problem is not confronted successfully by Congress, then pressure mounts on other institutions, such as the presidency, to handle it. That pressure comes even from the Congress itself. When the chief executive steps in to solve the national problem, the result is a loss of power in the legislative branch. Without adequate power, Congress cannot provide meaningful representation of national interests.

Evaluating Congress

So Congress is in a spot. It is not hard to see why it is in need of "adult supervision." Much of the problem has to do with the tension between the ways individual members of Congress relate to their constituencies (micro representation) and the goal of Congress to make national policy (macro representation).

Individual members of Congress who are self-interested *take positions* on issues of symbolic importance to their constituents; they *claim credit* for producing policy outcomes pleasing to constituents, organized interests, and others with the resources to help their careers; and they *advertise* their names to solidify support in their districts. The institution is organized to promote their individual control over their careers without major interference from a strong party, and without substantial conflict as a "necessary and ordinary" way of doing business on the floor. Ironically, then, as individual members succeed in solidifying their personal popularity, they contribute to the decline of the institution intended to be closest to the people.

Congress has not failed in some absolute sense. Rather, it generally does not measure up to the standards set for it in the Republic. Party theorists, who are most pessimistic about Congress, argue that fundamental changes consistent with their program (spelled out in Chapter 4) must be made. Pluralists are much more optimistic about Congress, arguing that it represents a reasonable adaptation to the realities of contemporary politics. Nonetheless, it should be clear that in contrast to Madison's hope that "the private interest of every individual may be a sentinel over the public rights," self-interest in Congress can seriously undermine the public good as that good is understood by the Republic. In party theory and pluralism we find two very different reactions to the contemporary reality of Congress.

Party Theory and Congress

Party theorists are critical of American governmental institutions, and certainly Congress is no exeption. They view the risks associated with reform as entirely justified. Indeed, they would put it the other way: Given the problems, the risks associated with *not* changing Congress are far greater than those associated with major reform.

One of the attractions of party theory is that it does not take interest, participation, or conflict for granted. It recognizes their importance in politics and seeks to stimulate them. Recall from Chapter 4 that party theorists would like to concentrate governmental power in the hands of the party that wins a national majority. They would do so primarily to fix responsibility for outcomes in the minds of citizens. By thus reducing the costs of information, party theorists hope to stimulate interest and rejuvenate the instrumental model of elections. Concentration of power, to party theorists, necessarily requires party organizations with sufficient resources to discipline their members. Thus the organization could make commitments as part of its national platform and have some hope of keeping them when in control of government. If the party in power has the ability to keep its promises, it can be held responsible for breaking them.

How would the party theorists' program affect the parties in Congress? The parties could effectively determine who ran and who did not run for Congress. Candidates would have to go to the party for its blessing in the form of resources such as money, campaign activists, and endorsement. In return, the party would presumably exercise some disciplinary control. It would not permit the candidacy of any person who stood for policies that differed markedly from those to which the party was committed. It would require its candidates to associate themselves firmly with the national party's goals. Party control over reelection would be its most important source of leverage over the membership. This control, of course, would radically change the nature of representation in Congress. In short, it would cause lawmakers to be at least as responsive to the national parties as they currently are to their individual (and separate) constituencies. According to party theory, it would remove the tension between micro and macro representation by encouraging voters and representatives alike to act in response to the differences between competing national parties.

The list of ills that justifies alteration of Congress in accordance with party theory is by now familiar.[29] The most serious problem is the manner in which individual representatives and senators have managed to insulate themselves from dissatisfaction with the institution. So long as this condition exists, party theorists argue, members will not be politically responsible for what the institution does or fails to do.[30] They will have few reasons to risk their careers in order to produce collective outcomes. As a result, either policies that address national problems will not be produced or they will not be produced by Congress. If they are not produced at all, immobility and incoherence are likely to characterize our national politics. If they are produced by another institution (such as the president), they may be less democratic. Congress, because it incorporates many different interests, should be a prominent partner with the president in national policy making. Note that the ideal is partnership, not the separation and conflict between institutions envi-

---

[29]Morris P. Fiorina, "Decline of Collective Responsibility in American Politics," *Daedalus* 109 (Summer, 1980): 25–45.

[30]An intriguing study comparing the U.S. Congress (in which the parties are weak) with the British Parliament (in which the parties are stronger) found that popular evaluation of legislators is more closely tied to evaluations of the legislature as a whole in Britain than in the United States. See Bruce Cain, John Ferejohn, and Morris Fiorina, *The Personal Vote: Constituency Service and Electoral Independence* (Cambridge: Harvard University Press, 1987), p. 200.

sioned by the Republic. So while the goal is consistent with Madison's in its linking of self-interest to public interest, the means for forging the link (concentration rather than dispersal of power) are radically different.

The Pluralist View of Congress

Pluralists side with Madison on the crucial question of what to do with power (disperse it), even if they see some problems with the argument in the Republic. The concern here is with the major differences of interpretation between pluralists and party theorists as they examine the contemporary Congress.[31] Four normative propositions summarize the pluralists' understanding of the proper place of Congress in American government.

Congress should retain its constitutional status as an independent institution. In other words, pluralists agree with Madison that members of Congress should be elected independently, and that the authority of Congress should remain substantial. They resist reform proposals that would forge strong links between the Congress and the president on the basis of common party loyalty. Here we find a fundamental difference between pluralists and party theorists, for the latter see the independent, individual nature of congressional careers as the heart of the problem. For pluralists, concentration of power would deprive diverse interests of the opportunity they currently have to participate in the bargaining and mutual adjustment that the American system facilitates.

In addition to the independence of Congress, pluralists point to its impressive constitutional authority as an effective means to disperse power. Indeed, in comparison with other legislatures throughout the world, Congress exerts great influence over national policy. Congress played a major role in civil rights reform and it has confronted the presidency directly on the Vietnam war, on presidential impoundment of funds, and on the Watergate scandal. More recently Congress has been at least an equal partner of the chief executive in social security and tax reforms. It is able to challenge the president, to share in the making of national policy, because it has an independent political base, and because it has the constitutional authority to tax, spend, raise an army, and declare

---

[31]There is always room as well for differences over the evidence. For example, some people would argue that I have overstated the degree to which individual MCs can insulate themselves from dissatisfaction with Congress and national policy outcomes. There is indeed some evidence of a marginal effect of such factors on voting in congressional elections, but it is small and numerous questions arise about what it really means. For an excellent summary of the relevant work, see Gary C. Jacobson and Samuel Kernell, *Strategy and Choice in Congressional Elections,* 2nd ed. (New Haven: Yale University Press, 1983), especially chap. 2.

war.[32] Congress's power depends on its ability to divide its work load among specialists. Without the body of expertise available through specialization, Congress would become utterly ineffective in the face of today's complex policy issues. Without the ability to control conflict, Congress would be immobilized in the face of today's extensive policy agenda and the incredible work load burdening the institution.

Congress is an important forum for the expression of diverse views among the public. Pluralists are well aware of the symbolic nature of much of what happens in Congress. They know that MCs may have a stronger incentive to take visible stands on issues than they have to produce public policy. Policy ideas are often "incubated" for years in Congress before they are acted upon. This is not all bad in an open, diverse society.

Aside from Congress's role as a forum for national debate, its symbolism can have substantial consequences for policy. The fact that prominent senators were willing to speak out against the Vietnam war doubtless encouraged protesters and others who mobilized against the war outside of Congress. The ability of members of both houses to make political hay out of the investigation of President Richard Nixon's conduct led to his resignation in the wake of the Watergate scandal. Position taking is not simply an empty or self-serving gesture to satisfy constituents. It can contribute to the momentum for change building elsewhere in society.

A large and complex society has a need for particularism and response to organized interests; Congress helps meet that need. National policy inevitably creates dislocations in individual lives, some of which are unjust and should be rectified. Members of Congress, through their casework and because of their need to claim credit, help to meet those needs.

Moreover, the fact that the highly fragmented, decentralized congressional process favors organized interests over those that are not organized serves an important function. Democracy must have ways to register the interests of the many—the majority, if you will—but it must also have ways to register the interests of the few who have a very intense concern about a policy question. And it is a nice question whether the many who do not care deeply should win over the few who do. Because Madison took this question seriously, he was wary of investing too much power in the hands of the majority. When it is sufficiently aroused (when it cares enough), the

---

[32]Two studies that illustrate the potential of Congress to have a significant independent impact on national policy are Gary Orfield, *Congressional Power: Congress and Social Change* (New York: Harcourt Brace Jovanovich, 1975), and Paul Light, *Artful Work: The Politics of Social Security Reform* (New York: Random House, 1985).

majority is most assuredly heard in Congress. But so also are the well organized who have the resources to monitor what is going on and to help their friends in Congress.

Take the tobacco subsidy. Most Americans, were they aware that the government subsidizes tobacco producers, would oppose the policy. The opposition would probably be overwhelming in numbers but weak in intensity. That is, most citizens of New York or California would respond to an opinion poll in the negative if they were asked about the tobacco subsidy, but they would not go out of their way to write a letter, question their senators at a public meeting, or contribute to the campaign of a candidate who vowed to fight the subsidy.

Tobacco producers in North Carolina, in contrast, care very deeply about the tobacco subsidy. They elect (or defeat) their senators on the basis of the issue. They write letters, they extract promises. They are well organized, and they make sure their representatives pursue their interests in Congress. The cost to them of going unrepresented is their livelihood. The cost to the average citizen in New York or California is much less. Therefore, one can argue, a democratic society should pay more attention to the intense minority than to the majority so long as the majority remains relatively indifferent. Congress is uniquely capable of responding to intense, well-organized minorities and equally capable of gauging when the majority cares enough to be heard and represented.

Evaluation of the Congress must take into consideration the fact that governmental power is centralized in the presidency. Pluralists argue that the weaknesses of the Congress are offset by the strengths of the executive branch, and vice versa. If much of what the Congress does is invisible to the average citizen, the president's every move is scrutinized and reported in the media. If Congress manages conflict by limiting the scope of participation, conflict constantly swirls around the president because of the visibility of his actions. If Congress is sensitive to the organized and to minorities, the president is responsive to the unorganized and the majority. And if Congress tends to shun national problems in its concern for particularized, distributed benefits, the president is held accountable for collective benefits (such as the state of the economy and national security).

In Madisonian fashion, pluralists argue that a healthy balance is struck between the two major national policy-making institutions. One cannot examine only the Congress, for Congress does not make policy alone. Ultimately, one must examine the partnership (or the conflict) between president and Congress to understand and evaluate the national government.

Conclusion

The pluralists have a point. We turn next to the presidency in order to understand it as an institution and to see how it fits into a national government based on the "scheme of representation." In this chapter we have examined one branch of government, the U.S. Congress, from the perspective offered by the Republic. A central proposition of the Republic is that private self-interest can be channeled to produce the public good. The national legislature channels self-interest by distributing the power of the institution among many different interests. Each interest is brought into government via the link between the self-interest of the legislator to the self-interest of his or her constituents. Hence this chapter's preoccupation with the relationship between the micro and macro levels of representation.

My thesis has been that there is a fundamental tension between the Republic's ideal of micro representation and its concept of macro representation. We saw in Chapter 6 that members of Congress are indeed attentive to their constituencies. They worry about reelection and they invest no small effort in building and maintaining support in their districts and states. And, by and large, they are remarkably successful. The results of their efforts, however, are not the widespread involvement of diverse interests and conflict in congressional policy making anticipated by the Republic. Because MCs can get reelected without threatening each other's reelection, conflict is reduced, not exacerbated. Power is normally exercised on behalf of a few interests rather than in response to many. Moreover, the tension between individual and institutional interests results in institutional drift and decline.

What are we to make of the contemporary Congress? Certainly if we adopt the strict standards of the Republic as our guide, we must be disappointed. Such disappointment is registered by party theorists in their reaction to Congress. They seek to "reconnect" private to institutional interest. They explore ways to make the individual in Congress accountable for what the institution does or fails to do. In this way, they believe, the citizen ultimately will have more control over government.

Pluralists are much less critical of Congress. They believe its operational methods can be justified in accordance with Madisonian principles even if the theoretical expectations surrounding self-interest are not supported. Congress helps disperse the power of the national government. It is sensitive to minority as well as majority interests. To be sure, Congress experiences periods—even prolonged periods—of decline in relation to the president. But it retains the constitutional authority and (sometimes) the political will to check the president. Witness the Watergate hearings and the forced resignation of Richard Nixon. On a less grandiose scale, no president gets everything he seeks from Congress. Congress checks the president, and that is a good thing.

Ultimately, one's evaluation of Congress, like one's evaluation of the American party system or the ways in which interest groups participate in our politics, depends on one's values. If one seeks to determine the place where critical issues surrounding day-to-day governance are joined with the fundamental value questions associated with representative government, there is no better place to look than Congress.

Key Concepts

committee system

congressional power as a collective good

consensus decision making

predispositions decision environment

decision problem

reciprocity

seniority system

specialization

Presidential Leadership
Beyond Self-Interest?

How do you balance the budget, cut taxes, and increase defense spending at the same time? It's very simple. You do it with mirrors.

—John B. Anderson,
presidential candidate, 1980

John Anderson's quixotic campaign for the presidency in 1980 went nowhere. But he did make a useful point in his attacks on the eventual winner's campaign promise to balance the budget. Ronald Reagan's program stimulated doubts in the minds of many observers, not least those who realized that balancing the budget, cutting taxes, and increasing defense spending are all activities specifically reserved by the Constitution to the Congress, not the president. That, however, was not Anderson's point. He thought the promises were contradictory, and therefore irresponsible. He believed that Reagan could not possibly carry out this part of his program, and he wanted voters to know it.

Reagan's promises and Anderson's response are interesting from the perspective of the question posed by this chapter's title. Reagan did promise to balance the budget by 1984, despite the fact that the Constitution assigns the "power of the purse" to the Congress. Reagan did not, in fact, deliver on his promise before the 1984 election (perhaps he should have tried mirrors). Nevertheless, he was reelected by a landslide.

Why do presidential candidates make promises beyond the constitutional boundaries of the office to which they aspire? Are presidents held accountable for promises not upheld? Do contemporary presidents provide leadership that somehow transcends self-interest, or are they merely manipulative opportunists preying on citizens' hopes and fears? Presidents, because of their visibility and central place in the government, have the opportunity to achieve

205

more than any other single individual. They have the opportunity to be heroes. Heroic presidents of the past, Americans seem to believe, have provided true leadership and gone well beyond the limits of narrow self-interest—of ambition checked by ambition. At the same time, Madison's warnings that "enlightened statesmen" will not always be at the helm seems fair in light of recent experience. Must we now, two hundred years after Madison wrote, abandon hope for consistent leadership in the one national institution best equipped to provide it?

For Madison, self-interest could produce the public good provided the institutional framework within which it operated was properly constructed. Thus he saw Congress as the centerpiece of the Republic because in that institution representation would help produce the public good. But our analysis of self-interest in Congress does not bear out Madison's hope. Representatives have an interest in reelection, and they pursue it with a vengeance. Yet zeal for reelection does not necessarily produce representation.

One of the most serious problems on the congressional side of national government is the absence of collective responsibility. Citizens may be unhappy with national policy generally and with Congress specifically, but representatives and senators escape political consequences. That being the case, they have few incentives to put their careers on the line in order to attack national policy problems. The absence of collective responsibility in Congress, I have argued, can be attributed to self-interest. Another problem with Madison's theory, as we saw in Chapters 2 and 3, is the failure of citizens to act on their political interests. Inactivity, remember, may actually be in the self-interest of the citizen. Even when citizens vote, they may do so without much information, since bearing information costs may not be rational. It is useful to call to mind these failures in Madison's Republic as we begin our analysis of the presidency, because a case can be made for the proposition that they are rectified in the contemporary operation of that institution. Pluralists are inclined to argue that the presidency provides the kind of collective responsibility that the legislative branch lacks. Likewise, presidential actions are so highly visible to the average citizen that the problem of information costs and free ridership is mitigated. Party theorists, as you might guess, are not so optimistic.

The question for this chapter—Does presidential leadership get us "beyond self-interest?"—is a crucial one not only for our understanding of the American system of government but also for our daily lives as citizens. We tend to look to the president to provide leadership, especially in times of crisis. When the stock market takes a nose dive, when American citizens are held hostage in a foreign city, when a scandal breaks in the administration, when tensions develop in the Middle East or in Eastern Europe, the president is on the spot. President Harry Truman's little sign, THE BUCK STOPS HERE, demonstrates what every modern president knows: political good fortune for the president is closely related to national success; political failure is inseparable from the deterioration of the national interest. If we can equate the political self-interest of the person who occupies the Oval Office with the national good, have we vindicated Madison's hope for the Republic? Perhaps. That is the question this chapter addresses.

The Presidency in the Republic

Pretty clearly, the constitutional place of the executive presents a problem for the Republic. Unhappily for the tidiness of our analysis, Alexander Hamilton, not James Madison, wrote the relevant *Federalist Papers* on the presidency. And it is no secret that Hamilton was an advocate of a strong, vigorous government built around the executive branch. Hamilton's defense of a strong executive prefigures in some important respects the development of the presidency well beyond the boundaries set for it by the Republic.

The essential principles of governance in Madison's Republic were representation and dispersed power. These principles are consistent with a limited government and a fear of tyranny. Yet, as Hamilton points out, the presidency specified in the Constitution serves to infuse the national government with "energy" and vigor. Consider his scornful rejection (in *Federalist* 70) of the argument for a weak chief executive:

> A feeble executive implies a feeble execution of the government. A feeble execution is but another phrase for a bad execution; and a government ill executed, whatever it may be in theory, must be, in practice, a bad government.

Hamilton then goes on to reject the idea of a "dual" or "plural" executive. Such a structure would destroy the energy and enfeeble the "execution of the government." It would also "conceal faults and destroy responsibility." Hamilton's elaboration of this point is worth quoting in full:

> It is evident from these considerations that the plurality of the executive tends to deprive the people of the two greatest securities they can have for the faithful exercise of any delegated power, *first*, the restraints of public opinion, which lose their efficacy, as well on account of the division of the censure attendant on bad measures among a number as on account of the uncertainty on whom it ought to fall; and,

second, the opportunity of discovering with facility and clearness the misconduct of the persons they trust, in order either to their removal from office or to their actual punishment in cases which admit of it.

Incredibly, Hamilton is making exactly the same case against the idea of a plural executive (such as some sort of executive council) which contemporary critics of Congress make against the legislature. *First*, members of the council would have no incentive to respond to public opinion on matters of national policy because, *second*, the public would have difficulty fixing the blame for policy failures on individual officeholders. In short, there would be no collective responsibility.

Hamilton's answer to the problem is the **unitary executive.** With one person as executive, you get the energy the government needs *and* responsibility. You get, according to Alexander Hamilton, leadership.

But what of James Madison? If we hold Madison to his own principles, he has to worry. Energetic, vigorous government carries a significant risk. The presidency, by virtue of its unitary structure, concentrates the power of the institution in the hands of one person. Unlike the Congress, its major rival in the national government, the president is subject to no formal *internal* checks. Congressional power, according to the argument in the Republic, is checked because so many different factions share in the institution's power. Further, power is checked internally by its bicameral structure. Yet the unitary presidency, in capturing the virtues described by Hamilton, has no such restraints. When an institution is embodied in one person, one interest may be represented there. A government in which power is held and exercised by a single person is subject to all of the pitfalls described in Madison's characterization of tyranny.

The solution, of course, is to rely on external checks. The president shares power with the Congress and can do little, according to the Constitution, without congressional approval. The congressional powers enumerated in Article I are both more extensive and more precise than those granted to the chief executive in Article II. The legislature is at the heart of republican government. Indeed, it is possible that the ambiguity of the Constitution's vague "executive power" results from the ambivalence of the founders about granting significant power to an institution that embodies the principle of concentrated power. The mandates to be commander in chief of the armed forces and to negotiate treaties are very sharply bounded by congressional authority in the Constitution. The president may be commander in chief, but the Congress declares war and raises (and pays for) an army. Treaties are subject to the "advice and consent" of an extraordinary two-thirds majority in the Senate.

An Overview of Presidential Leadership

The concept of presidential leadership, as I employ it, has two important components: power and responsiveness.[1] Neither is in itself sufficient; both power and responsiveness are essential. Each of these components is complex and difficult to analyze with confidence.

Power is a necessary component of presidential leadership for the reasons spelled out by Alexander Hamilton. The political system needs "energy" and direction, and much of both must come from the president. To exercise leadership, in this context, is to determine policy priorities (a tax reform, budget cuts or allocations, foreign policy objectives such as a reduction in nuclear weapons or increased cultural exchange with the People's Republic of China). Presumably these policy priorities spring from the party and from the president's own campaign. They do not come without opposition. If the tax code is to be significantly revamped, for example, some interests will win and others will lose. Power is relevant, then, since the president must overcome opposition. **Presidential power** is the ability of the president to get his way.[2] So if the president is successful in persuading members of Congress to go along with a treaty proposal or to follow his recommendations on the budget, he has exercised power.

This concept of power is distinct from notions that emphasize "presidential powers," such as the "power" to veto legislation proposed by Congress. The veto power and other constitutional and official "powers" are better thought of as resources that may be converted into actual power. For example, a president committed to cutting domestic welfare expenditures can threaten to veto spending legislation that does not meet his priorities. In this way, the constitutional *authority* to veto becomes a resource that the president can use in his bargaining with others who share in the making of policy. A powerful president is one who can convert such resources as the veto authority into policy outcomes consistent with his will.

Two kinds of resources are relevant to presidential power. Some, such as the constitutional authority to veto legislation and to be commander in chief of the armed forces, are part of the office no

---

[1] Insightful discussions of presidential leadership can be found in the following works, which I draw on heavily: Richard Neustadt, *Presidential Power*, 2nd ed. (New York: Wiley, 1980); James MacGregor Burns, *Leadership* (New York: Harper & Row, 1978), especially chaps. 1, 14, and 16; Bert Rockman, *The Leadership Question* (New York: Praeger, 1984); and Murray Edelman, *The Symbolic Uses of Politics* (Urbana: University of Illinois Press, 1964), especially chap. 4.

[2] This concept is closely related to Neustadt's in *Presidential Power*, p. 27.

matter which individual happens to occupy it at a given moment. These **formal resources of the president** extend beyond authority specifically mentioned in the constitution (and anticipated in Madison's Republic) to such attributes of the office as an extensive staff, popular expectations surrounding the office, and congressional delegations of authority. These resources are less permanent than those included in the Constitution's description of the office, but they nonetheless reside in the office and are distinct from the individual incumbent.

The second kind of resource is strictly personal. One can imagine that a Ronald Reagan would have acted differently (and more or less successfully) under the conditions that prevailed during the Carter years. Would Carter have gotten into a Watergate-style scandal if he had faced the pressures of the Nixon years? That question cannot be answered, but it highlights the importance of the **personal resources of the president,** which are quite separate from the formal attributes of the office and which also affect the president's power.

Power is not enough. Leadership must also include some degree of responsiveness to the needs and wants of followers. Indeed, power without responsiveness is surely a form of tyranny, whether it is found in a left- or right-wing dictatorship or in the classroom. Responsiveness, like power, can be broken down into two components. A leader's responsiveness may address material demands and interests, or it may be symbolic. Both material and symbolic responses are probably necessary for political leadership, and both can degenerate into something less than ideal leadership.

Figure 8-1 summarizes the concept of presidential leadership and provides a map of the analysis that follows.

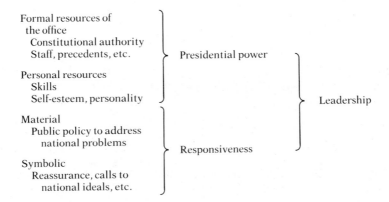

Figure 8-1 A Summary of the Concept of Presidential Leadership

Presidential Power

Formal Sources of Presidential Power

Few political institutions in existence two hundred years ago have changed so dramatically as the American presidency. James Madison feared the power of the legislature and argued that only if it were divided against itself (through bicameralism) could the balance between executive and legislature be maintained. Today the "imperial presidency" seems to dominate national politics, while Congress plays a secondary role. Many nineteenth-century presidents handled their own correspondence and had only limited visibility outside of governmental circles. Presidential candidates then did not campaign publicly on their own behalf, nor did they actively set the policy direction of the national government. Today the nation looks to the president for direction, Congress awaits his program (and adopts most of it), and the public visibility of candidates and incumbents is extremely high. What accounts for this change? What are its implications?

Figure 8-2 suggests how the presidency has grown since the founding period. Briefly, additional authority tended to gravitate to the presidency under certain conditions (especially in times of national crisis). Both the Congress and the Supreme Court participated in this delegation of authority, which, when exercised, set precedents for future presidents to call upon. Power thus exercised generated expectations and roles that presidents must fulfill. Campaign rhetoric also contributed to a set of rising expectations about what presidents could and should do. And once these expectations were firmly in place, it only stands to reason that the "president needs help" to get his job done. Thus a giant administrative apparatus surrounds the contemporary president to help him keep the peace, monitor what other nations are doing, oversee and manage the domestic economy, promote the health and welfare of citizens, maintain justice, promote education, foster good relations with the press, and all the rest. To be sure, this development is part and

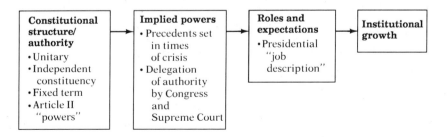

Figure 8-2 Development of the American Presidency

parcel of the growth of "big government," but in many respects the presidency is bigger than big government.[3]

Let us take each step in Figure 8-2 and explore it in a bit more depth.

Constitutional Structure and Authority

The structure of the office described in the Constitution is simple: the presidency is "unitary" (the chief executive is a single person rather than a council or "plural" executive); the president has a fixed term of office, which is terminated only through death or impeachment (or resignation); and the president has an independent constituency. He is chosen directly by the Electoral College, which convenes for that purpose and that purpose only. He is *not* chosen by the legislature, as in parliamentary systems.

Article II of the Constitution lists the authorities granted the president. On the whole, the Constitution is less generous to the executive than to the legislature, a fact consistent with the Republic's argument that the exercise of power must be checked through conflict. No authority granted the executive is without a significant check by Congress. For example, treaties negotiated by the president depend on Senate approval; the commander-in-chief role assigned to the president by the Constitution is presumably subject to Congress's authority to "raise" and fund the military and to declare war. The veto gives the president a firm foothold in the legislative process, but it can be overriden by a two-thirds vote in each chamber.

The constitutional key to the development of the office probably lies more in the structure of the office than in the enumerated "powers." Here Hamilton's analysis is prescient. The presidency is a source of vigor and direction in the government. A president can act more quickly than the Congress, and without unseemly public haggling. If need be, the president can act in secret. When affairs appear to drift, and especially when the nation confronts a crisis, the president has an opportunity to step into the breach and provide direction. President Lincoln during the Civil War, President Wilson during World War I, and President Franklin Roosevelt during the Great Depression and World War II are among the presidents who most clearly served in this way.

Implied and Delegated Powers

Especially in times of crisis, strong-willed presidents have had to go beyond the authority specified in the Constitution and exercise

---

[3]See Theodore Lowi, *The Personal President: Power Invested, Promise Unfulfilled* (Ithaca: Cornell University Press, 1985).

what they have usually termed **implied powers.** That is, they have
justified their actions by claiming that the authority and structure
explicitly described in the Constitution imply the power to do what
they have done. They have argued that no other branch of government is capable of meeting the crisis because none can provide the
energy and vigor that a unitary executive is capable of sustaining.
Consider Abraham Lincoln's justification for the extraordinary (and
clearly unconstitutional) actions he took to deal with the crisis of
the South's secession:[4]

> Are all the laws, but one [the Constitution], to go unexecuted, and the
> government itself to go to pieces, lest that one be violated? Even in
> such a case, would not the official oath be broken, if the government
> should be overthrown, when it was believed that disregarding the
> single law would tend to preserve it?[5]

Franklin Roosevelt, in facing World War II, also argued for
executive "prerogative" beyond the bounds set by the Constitution.[6]
In requesting from Congress a policy that would stabilize the wartime economy, Roosevelt chastised the legislature for its inaction
and issued a threat made more credible by the actions of other
activist presidents in times of crisis, such as Lincoln:

> I ask the Congress to take this action by the first of October. Inaction on
> your part by that date will leave me with an inescapable responsibility
> to the people of this country to see to it that the war effort is no longer
> imperiled by threat of economic chaos.
>
> In the event that the Congress should fail to act, and act adequate-
> ly, I shall accept the responsibility, and I will act.[7]

The Congress acquiesced in the initiatives of both Lincoln and
Roosevelt, and both exercised real power. Both cases, too, set precedents that established presidential prerogative. Congressional leaders, the press, and the public have learned to look to the White
House for decisive action in a crisis. Lincoln and Roosevelt provide
dramatic examples of what has occurred scores of times, from
George Washington's insistence that the president must be free to

---

[4]Among other things, Lincoln mobilized the state militias and proclaimed a blockade
of southern ports without a congressional declaration of war; he increased the size of
the military and spent funds unappropriated by Congress for military construction
and procurement; and by executive order he suspended various civil rights in areas
threatened by insurrectionists.
[5]Abraham Lincoln, "Message to the Special Session of Congress, 1861," in *The Political Thought of Abraham Lincoln*, ed. Richard N. Current (Indianapolis: Bobbs-
Merrill, 1967, pp. 181–182).
[6]See Richard Pious, *The American Presidency* (New York: Basic Books, 1979), chap. 2.
[7]Franklin D. Roosevelt, "Message to Congress on Wartime Stabilization," in *The
Power of the Presidency: Concepts and Controversy*, ed. Robert S. Hirschfield (New
York: Atherton, 1968), p. 107.

conduct diplomacy without interference by Congress to Theodore Roosevelt's "big stick" foreign policy to Ronald Reagan's military actions in the Carribean and the Persian Gulf. Each time the president defines a crisis and acts, a precedent is set and earlier precedents are reinforced. The effect is like that of a ratchet: each such action boosts the formal resources of the office up a notch and makes it more difficult for Congress to check future presidential action.

This is not to say that Congress is helpless in the face of presidential power, or that it never restrains presidents from doing what they would like to do. Indeed, every modern president could point to instances when he was frustrated by restraints that Congress placed on his ability to act. Richard Nixon was driven from office by congressional investigations of his conduct in the Watergate affair and by the Supreme Court's refusal to agree with his interpretation of "executive privilege" as part of the formal authority of his office. Following the Vietnam experience, Congress passed a War Powers Resolution, which is intended to restrict such "presidential wars" and to reassert Congress's constitutional authority in that domain.

But on the whole, the history of the presidency has been one of increasing authority and resources. In particular, the presidency is structurally best capable of dealing with crisis. Precedents are set, Congress often delegates authority directly or ratifies presidential actions, and the result of presidential action is often an expanded set of expectations surrounding the office.

Roles and Expectations

Once Franklin Roosevelt took on direct responsibility for managing the economic crisis of the 1930s, no future president could escape similar responsibilities. Thus Dwight Eisenhower and the Republican party, who were ideologically ill disposed toward interference with the economy, were nonetheless held responsible for economic recession in the 1958 congressional elections. Richard Nixon, in dealing with inflationary pressures during his first term, explicitly rejected the idea of wage and price controls as contrary to his ideals. When Congress in 1970 nonetheless granted him that authority, he exercised it and imposed controls on wages and prices.

More generally, consider the expectations that surround the contemporary presidency. Thomas Cronin characterizes the "presidential job description" as extensive and permeating all aspects of government:

Setter of national agenda. Determines priorities for government and nation, designs programs to solve economic and foreign policy problems. Calls nation to adhere to its fundamental values and ideals. Presidential program will monopolize congressional, media, and popular attention in regard to public affairs.

Crisis manager. Identifies, manages, and resolves crises, whether resulting from oil shortage, strikes by coal workers or traffic controllers, the seizure of U.S. citizens as hostages, or other hostile actions by a foreign power.

Coalition builder. Must build support for proposals and actions. A congressional defeat for a presidential initiative is perceived as a defeat for the president. It is not enough to "take a position." The president must win.

Program implementer. Must assume responsibility for the government's failures as well as its successes. When an embassy is seized, when a toxic-waste fund is mismanaged, when security has been breached, when the defense of a military base fails to stop a terrorist, the president is pressed for an explanation.[8]

This "job description" is much more extensive than the one outlined in the Constitution. Yet the roots of the energy and visibility that so characterize the office today can be found in the original document. Establish a unitary executive and you create a focus of attention in a political system otherwise characterized by dispersed power and divided responsibility. Give the president an independent constituency and he will appeal directly to it for support. That constituency, which, after all, he shares with the Congress, will inevitably look to him for the vigor and energy Hamilton argued he would provide. As presidents expand their role, their successors are pressured to meet the expectations that have been generated. Campaign rhetoric also feeds the expanding job description of the president. When a challenger criticizes the incumbent or outgoing administration for mishandling of a problem or failure to address an issue, he is adding to his own burden once he takes the oath of office.

Thus the expectations surrounding the office can be a trap that limits a president or even contributes to his political demise. But these roles and expectations are fundamental to the expansion of presidential authority. If the president is expected to deal with a crisis or a problem, that expectation makes his voice dominant over others competing to be heard. The fact that the nation today looks to a president to define critical problems is an enormously important resource, since the president's priorities tend to dominate the attention of other centers of authority in the system. And finally, these expectations generate pressures to provide the office with the institutional resources it needs to carry out its responsibilities.

---

[8]I present an abbreviated version of Cronin's "job description." See Thomas E. Cronin, *The State of the Presidency*, 2d ed. (Boston: Little, Brown, 1980), p. 155.

Institutional Extensions of the Presidency

The expanding responsibilities of the presidency have resulted in a huge bureaucratic apparatus that supports the president. The growth of the cabinet and the creation and expansion of the Executive Office of the President have added institutional resources to the presidency. Indeed, it is no accident that the Executive Office was created during Franklin Roosevelt's tenure, with the famous observation that "the president needs help."[9] Since Roosevelt's time, the staff directly under the president as well as the larger federal bureaucracy have grown tremendously.[10]

The logic behind this growth is a direct result of the change in the presidency since the founding. Is the president responsible for a legislative program that determines national priorities? He must have a Bureau of the Budget (now the Office of Management and Budget) to control the executive branch and to enforce and coordinate budgetary priorities. Does the president's authority as commander in chief make him responsible for monitoring intelligence about the intentions and actions of foreign powers? Then he must have a National Security Council and a Central Intelligence Agency to help with these tasks. Is the chief executive responsible for educational policy? A Department of Education can help him coordinate that part of his job description. Is there an energy crisis? A Department of Energy can help the president meet it.

The list of responsibilities matched with institutional developments could go on virtually indefinitely. The bureaucratic resources available to the president in the executive branch are substantial, but, like the expectations surrounding the office, not wholly an unmixed blessing. Indeed, many recent presidents have felt as much victimized by the bureacracy as benefited by it in their efforts to further their own ends. Some have taken extraordinary measures to try to bend it to their will.[11] Several reasons for the difficulties presidents face with the "institutional extensions" of their office in the bureaucracy are worth reviewing.

First, bureaucrats, like other political actors, pursue their own interests, which may or may not be consistent with the president's. Executive control over the bureaucracy can be furthered by the

---

[9]See Pious, *American Presidency*, p. 243. His chap. 7 describes the Executive Office of the President and the problems of executive control over the administrative functions of government.

[10]The average size of the White House staff has grown more than tenfold since Roosevelt's first term. For an extensive accounting of the growth in the institutionalized presidency, see Gary King and Lyn Ragsdale, *The Elusive Executive* (Washington, D.C.: Congressional Quarterly Press, 1988), chap. 4.

[11]Richard P. Nathan, *The Plot That Failed: Nixon and the Administrative Presidency* (New York: Wiley, 1975).

president's ability to appoint and dismiss top-level executives, but that authority does not extend very far into the bureaucracy. As most officials in the executive branch are protected by the civil service system, they are usually hired for their professional expertise and their commitment to their careers. A president committed to cutting back on social services runs squarely up against professionals in the executive branch who are dedicated to carrying out those programs. "Cutting back" may mean reducing the budget, removing some personnel, or reducing the authority of an agency. The agency will often resist.

Interests in the executive branch which run contrary to the president's can usually find allies in Congress. And, despite the fact that much of the executive branch is formally part of a hierarchy under the direction of the chief executive in the White House, Congress retains significant control. Congress can hold investigative hearings on an agency, and it retains ultimate control over the authority, budget, and very existence of most executive agencies. So, understandably, the self-interest of executives often is colored by the interests of patrons on the relevant committees and subcommittees in Congress. Further, just as we saw interest groups exercising significant influence over what Congress does, they often maintain similar kinds of influence over the bureaucracy. In part, this is merely an extension of their power on Capitol Hill. But many agencies in the executive branch cultivate ties with the interest groups they "service" in order to insulate themselves from too much control either by the president or by hostile forces in Congress.[12]

Despite the problems presidents encounter in their efforts to harness the institutional resources at their disposal, these extensions of the office remain important factors in their power. The immense intelligence-gathering apparatus in government, the vast amount of expertise in the employ of the national government, and the powerful political forces with a foothold there can be significant allies. When the president's will coincides with the interests of others in the executive branch, he can be a formidable force. None of this is to say that the larger constitutional framework within which the president must operate is without effect. Congress has substantial influence over the executive bureaucracy because of the "separation of powers" principle. The president's power, after all, depends on his ability to persuade others (in the executive branch, in Congress, and in interest groups) to act in ways consistent with his will. The resources attached to the office are substantial and have expanded dramatically since the founding, but they remain

---

[12]See Randall B. Ripley and Grace A. Franklin, *Congress, the Bureaucracy, and Public Policy* (Chicago: Dorsey, 1980), chap. 4.

largely inert without the personal skills of the individual president in office to activate them.

Personal Sources of Presidential Power

Separating the man from the office is always a difficult analytical task. But several significant attempts have been made to defend the hypothesis that it matters a great deal who the individual president in office is. The more skillful and the more capable the president is, the argument goes, the more successful he will be in harnessing the resources of his office.

The President's Skills

Richard Neustadt's book *Presidential Power,* first published in 1960, called attention to the importance of personal sources of presidential power. Neustadt was acutely aware of the larger institutional framework within which presidents must operate. In fact, he argued that the U.S. Constitution made the personal qualities of the president all-important. Presidents cannot command. They cannot exercise power simply by virtue of their position. Because the American system is based on the principle of "separate institutions sharing power," presidential power is the "power to persuade." In Neustadt's words, "the essence of a President's persuasive task with congressmen and everybody else *is to induce them to believe that what he wants of them is what their own appraisal of their own responsibilities requires them to do in their interest, not his.*"[13] Other political leaders, such as members of Congress, interest-group leaders, and cabinet officers, have different constituencies. Therefore, their interests differ from the president's (which, according to Madison, is a very good thing). Thus a president is in some sense at the mercy of others whose support he needs. What kinds of qualities does a president need to succeed?

Figure 8-3 is a highly simplified version of Neustadt's argument.[14] A president's skill, his tenacity in the face of opposition or obstacles, his ambition, and his ability to maintain the unique perspective that comes with his office are prominent among the personal qualities a successful president must have. A president must understand, for example, that no one else fully shares his perspective or his interests. Cabinet officers and other advisers have their own policy agenda and may be sensitive to particular interests

---

[13]Neustadt, *Presidential Power,* p. 35; emphasis in original.
[14]A much more detailed representation of Neustadt's theory (along with a critical evaluation of the argument) can be found in Peter W. Sperlich, "Bargaining and Overload: An Essay on Presidential Power," in *Perspectives on the Presidency,* ed. Aaron Wildavsky (Boston: Little, Brown, 1975), pp. 406–430.

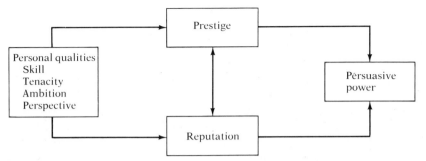

Figure 8-3 Richard Neustadt's Theory of Presidential Power

linked to their own goals. The skillful president understands this, and discounts advice accordingly. The president must learn to bargain effectively with others in order to get what he wants. The skillful president uses the formal resources associated with the presidency to strike favorable bargains.

The effective president, according to Neustadt, is one who converts these kinds of personal qualities into persuasive power. Two of the most important political resources a president can have are his **prestige** and his **reputation.** His prestige amounts to his popularity among ordinary citizens throughout the nation. His reputation is based on his ability to make Washington insiders take him seriously—to consider him effective, tenacious, skillful, and resourceful. Wise presidents concerned about their power nurture their prestige because they can convert it into persuasive power. After all, every senator and member of the House has a popular constituency that is also a part of the president's national constituency. A "photo opportunity" at the White House which yields a picture the senator can display to good effect in campaign materials or a promise of a presidential visit to his state in an upcoming campaign may also help to persuade the senator to support the president, provided the president's prestige is high. Careful analysis of the effects of presidential popularity shows that members of Congress tend to cooperate with popular presidents.[15]

Reputation is linked to prestige, but it is not wholly dependent on popularity. Government insiders work closely enough with the president to form their own opinions of his abilities. They are more attentive than the average citizen, and they are in a much better

---

[15]George C. Edwards, *Presidential Influence in Congress* (San Francisco: W. H. Freeman, 1980).

position to take his measure. Thus even a popular president may not have a strong reputation among members of Congress, journalists, military leaders, bureaucrats, and others closely linked to the government.[16]

Ultimately, Neustadt's analysis is quite consistent with Madison's Republic. His book can be read as a handbook for presidents: "How to Protect your Self-Interest in the White House." The "successful" president is one who maximizes his power. Neustadt encourages presidents to pursue their personal ambitions and power. He warns of competing self-interests in the government and offers advice on how to get others to go along. He applauds presidents who have succeeded at this game; he is critical of presidents who have failed. His analysis is consistent with pluralist theory in that he accepts the Madisonian structure of government. Indeed, his book offers guidance to presidents on how to operate effectively within the pluralist system.

Neustadt goes further. Recall Madison's conclusion that in the Republic the "private interest . . . may be a sentinel over the public rights." In the first edition of his book, Neustadt was quite frank in equating the president's interest in power with the larger public good:

> If skill in maximizing power for himself served purposes no larger than the man's own pride or pleasure, there would be no reason for the rest of us to care whether he were skillful or not. . . . But a President's success serves objectives far beyond his own and far beyond his party's. . . . Policy is kept alive by a sustained transformation of intent into result. Energetic government and viable public policy are at a premium as we begin the seventh decade of the twentieth century. Expertise in presidential power adds to both. A President's constituents, regardless of their party (or their country for that matter), have a great stake in his search for personal influence.[17]

This statement echoes Hamilton's faith in executive power. In fairness to Neustadt, he wrote it before Americans learned some harsh realities about the ways presidential power can be abused through their experience with the Vietnam war and the Watergate scandal. But there is no doubt that Neustadt provided a very strong answer to one of the questions posed at the outset of this chapter: presidential power effectively sought and aggressively exercised can

---

[16]Neustadt discusses the example of Eisenhower, who mismanaged his budgetary request in his second term. Though Ike was still enormously popular among ordinary citizens, his Washington reputation suffered. Neustadt discusses reputation in *Presidential Power*, chap. 4.

[17]Neustadt, *Presidential Power* pp. 134–135.

	Active	Passive
Positive	Theodore Roosevelt Franklin D. Roosevelt Harry S. Truman John F. Kennedy Gerald Ford Jimmy Carter	William H. Taft Warren Harding Ronald Reagan
Negative	Woodrow Wilson Herbert Hoover Lyndon B. Johnson Richard M. Nixon	Calvin Coolidge Dwight D. Eisenhower

Figure 8-4 Twentieth-Century Presidents Classified According to James David Barber's Typology of Presidential Character

overcome the limitations of self-interest. The president, because of his ability to energize the government, can provide the direction and leadership missing in Congress. Because of the visibility of the office, the president may also be the national government's most consistent source of collective responsibility.

The President's Personality
Partly as a result of what they viewed as serious failures of presidential power, close observers of the presidency considered a dimension of presidential performance beyond mere skill at manipulating the resources of the office. Perhaps the leading student of presidential personality, or "character," is James David Barber. Barber is concerned with identifying fundamental predispositions that explain why the president acts as he does. These characteristics are fundamental and may in principle be identified well before the person actually becomes president.

Barber conceives of character as "the way the President orients himself toward life—not for the moment, but enduringly." He identifies two dimensions of presidential personality: how active the president is and "whether or not he gives the impression he enjoys his political life."[18] In combination, these two dimensions yield four character types: "active-positive," "passive-positive," "active-negative," and "passive-negative" (see Figure 8-4).

The active-passive dimension measures the amount of energy

---

[18]James David Barber, *The Presidential Character: Predicting Performance in the White House*, 3rd ed. (Englewood Cliffs, N.J.: Prentice-Hall, 1985), pp. 5, 4.

the individual puts into life (and the presidency). Some people are naturally active both in a physical and a psychological sense. "Active" presidents are those who put a great deal of energy into their presidencies, and attempt to shape their environments rather than simply respond to historical and political forces swirling around them. The "positive-negative" dimension is an affective one; it measures the enjoyment and fulfillment the individual derives from his activity. "Positive" personalities are those who enjoy their political life, "negative" personalities are those who are active politically out of a sense of duty or to compensate for their insecurities. Any satisfaction they derive from the presidency results largely from a sense that they have met their obligations or overcome their inadequacies.

On the basis of these personality types Barber sets out to predict how presidents will behave in office.[19] I will not dwell on the two passive types, as they are relatively uncommon among contemporary presidents.[20] **Active-positive presidents** are, according to Barber, best suited psychologically to be chief executive. They exploit the resources of the office most successfully (in much the manner described by Neustadt), they are flexible, and they have high self-esteem. They do political battle with vigor and good humor but can tolerate their inevitable defeats as part of the game. **Active-negative presidents,** in contrast, are dangerous, according to Barber. Their ambition springs not from the joy of exercising power but from a brooding commitment to duty and a need to compensate for their insecurities. They are likely to be inflexible and defensive, especially in the face of criticism. In Barber's words, the self-image of the active-negative president "is vague and discontinuous. Life is a hard struggle to achieve and hold power, hampered by the condemnations of a perfectionist conscience. Active-negative types pour energy into the political system, but the energy is distorted from within."[21]

Barber's theory is an interesting attempt to understand the distinction between the man and the office. The theory goes beyond Neustadt's too-simple equation of the public good with the president's interest in power. Barber offers appropriate warnings about

---

[19]Ibid., pp. 12–13. Barber's theory has generated extensive comment and a fair amount of criticism. For a relatively friendly critical review of Barber's ideas, see Michael Nelson, "James David Barber and the Psychological Presidency," in *Rethinking the Presidency*, ed. Thomas Cronin (Boston: Little, Brown, 1982), pp. 75–86.
[20]For one thing, the contemporary nomination process is so rigorous and taxing that it is difficult to imagine a truly passive personality making a successful run for the office. However, Barber classifies Ronald Reagan as "passive-positive." Barber discusses Reagan in *Presidential Character*, chap. 16. The only other post–World War II president Barber classified as "passive" is Eisenhower ("passive-negative").
[21]Ibid., pp. 12–13.

the dangers of active-negative presidents, who seek power to satisfy inner needs rather than primarily to achieve policy objectives. Lyndon Johnson in his Vietnam policy and Richard Nixon in the Watergate cover-up were both active-negative presidents who pursued policies that led to their political demise. Both men seemed to withdraw from reality and to be unable to correct a destructive course even when danger signals were plentiful.[22] In neither case could the exercise of presidential power be easily equated with the national interest.

Whether these tendencies are due to the presidents' characters, whether active-positive presidents would have behaved differently in the same circumstances, and whether these failures of presidential leadership are due more to an accumulation of power and responsibility in the office than to the failures of particular incumbents are fair questions. Probably the truth is that pathologies and failures in modern presidencies can be explained by a mix of formal institutional developments and the personal qualities of the men who occupied the Oval Office.

How Responsive Is the President?

Leadership is not merely the successful exercise of power. We must ask: power exercised on behalf of whom? Toward what ends?[23] In this sense, leadership is a concept similar to representation. Clearly the president cannot represent the complexity of society in the same way that a legislature can, but it is certainly fair to think of the presidency as an important part of representative government, and to explore its relationship with the public.

Presidential responsiveness may take two forms. Presidents may respond in a material way to the needs and wants of the public. **Material responsiveness** affects the "who gets what" of politics. Had Ronald Reagan been successful in balancing the federal budget, for example, dramatic consequences for who got what would have followed. Even without balancing the budget, Reagan's program substantially cut spending for domestic welfare while it increased

---

[22]Barber's chap. 14, "Nixon Came True," analyzes Nixon's handling of Watergate in light of the theory. On the eve of Nixon's first inauguration in 1969, Barber had predicted that Nixon would have great difficulty responding in a positive way to charges of corruption, that his "first impulse will be to hush it up, to conceal it, bring down the blinds," and that he would "grasp some line of policy or method of operation and pursue it in spite of its failure" (ibid., p. 460). That prediction, which came true in Nixon's conduct of the Watergate scandal, lent considerable credibility to Barber's theory.

[23]Burns, *Leadership*, makes a strong case for incorporating the leader's goals and their relation to the interests of followers in the concept of leadership.

military expenditures.[24] The civil rights program of Lyndon Johnson and the foreign policy overtures to the East which came to be known as "détente" under Richard Nixon are other examples of presidential policies that materially affected the distribution of resources. In each case questions may be raised about how "responsive" the president was in promoting his program, but in no case were the president's initiatives a surprise. Johnson, Nixon, and Reagan all telegraphed their punches in their campaigns, and all argued that their election was in some sense a mandate for the programs they had promised to put in place. And they all had a point. Indeed, the instrumental model of elections (discussed in Chapter 3) suggests that this sort of responsiveness is to be expected and applauded. Presidents are rewarded (elected, reelected) for responding to the needs and wants of a majority of the voters. Therefore, they have powerful incentives to provide leadership.

Symbolic responsiveness expresses some broadly shared value but need not affect the distribution of material resources. As Murray Edelman puts it, "The clue to what is politically effective is to be found not so much in verifiable good or bad effects flowing from political acts as in whether the incumbent can continue indefinitely to convey an *impression* of knowing what is to be done."[25] Edelman's argument is complex, but its essence relies on qualities of citizens and the political world we have already discussed. Politics, as we saw in Chapter 3, is fundamentally ambiguous and remote from the daily concerns of most citizens. Therefore much of what goes on—claims and counterclaims by candidates, presidents, leaders in Congress—is unverifiable. At the same time, according to Edelman, the ambiguity of politics creates anxiety in citizens. People are aware that such events as wars and depressions can have powerful effects on their lives. So the anxiety felt by citizens generates a need for reassurance, and the successful leader is one who provides that reassurance. Hence the president who exercises symbolic leadership conveys "an impression of knowing what is to be done."[26]

Responsive presidents engage in both material and symbolic leadership, often at the same time. The reassuring phrase uttered by Franklin Roosevelt in the depths of the Great Depression, "The only

---

[24]For a critical analysis of the effects of Reagan's program, see Thomas Byrne Edsall, *The New Politics of Inequality* (New York: Norton, 1984).

[25]Murray Edelman, *The Symbolic Uses of Politics* (Urbana: University of Illinois Press, 1964), p. 76; emphasis added.

[26]Edelman is quite explicit in linking the ambiguity of politics to the need for reassurance in the form of symbolic leadership: "in an ambiguous situation people may, as the result of their own anxieties, perceive a leader's acts to be what they want them to be" (ibid., p. 81).

thing we have to fear is fear itself," is a marvelous expression of symbolic leadership. It says "I'm in charge" even as it acknowledges the fear and anxiety experienced by the citizen. At the same time, Roosevelt put into place a program that greatly expanded the role of the federal government in the regulation of the economy and the provision of benefits to individuals. A strong case can be made for the proposition that Roosevelt was as successful as he was in determining who gets what because he was so effective in conveying the image of being in control, and because he communicated his commitment to fundamental American values.

Because the symbolic and material sides to responsiveness are so intimately connected, we can proceed without sharply discriminating between them. Some examples are clearly pure symbol; others (usually much less visible examples of presidential action) are material without the trappings of symbolism. But because so much of what presidents do is highly visible, the two kinds of response are often related in complex ways.

Do Presidents Keep Their Promises?

Certainly a president who is responsive keeps his promises. Again, think of the instrumental model of elections. Voters are supposed to compare candidates' promises or programs and vote for the one who best approximates their self-interest. The winning candidate receives a mandate to carry out his program. He also has a powerful incentive to keep his promises because he will be held accountable in the next election.

We have many reasons to be skeptical about presidential candidates' promises. We know that voters only imperfectly (at best!) approximate the instrumental ideal in their behavior. We have seen (Chapter 4) that candidates in a two-party system have incentives to muddy their differences. One way of doing so is to make vague or meaningless promises, such as to "restore decency to the government." We have also heard party theorists charge that the Madisonian system of dispersed power inevitably disperses responsibility. Thus we may not be surprised when a President Carter fails to produce the comprehensive energy policy he promised or when a President Reagan falls dramatically short of his promise to balance the budget by the end of his first term.

But a careful analysis of the promises made by presidents since Kennedy is actually quite reassuring. Jeff Fishel found that, on average, about 55 percent of a president's legislative proposals were either fully or partially comparable to promises he made during the campaign. Only 13 percent of presidential proposals to Congress were classified as "token actions" or actually contrary to campaign promises.[27] These findings show that a president's effort as measured by his attempts to push a program through Congress is related to his campaign for office. Put another way, presidential candidates provide a fairly clear picture of what they will try to do if they are elected.

If we require that in addition to making an effort to get their programs through Congress, presidents succeed in getting Congress to go along, presidential performance is lower. Fishel found that about 44 percent of all promises that required congressional action met the dual condition of being at least partially consistent with the president's legislative proposals *and* passed by Congress.[28] Of course, these data do not speak directly to the strictest interpretation of material responsiveness. Without much more extensive study, we cannot know how much legislation passed actually affects the distribution of society's resources. Lyndon Johnson was successful in getting much of his antipoverty program through Congress. But Johnson's program certainly did not end poverty. Is it fair to say, then, that Johnson's "war on poverty" and "Great Society" were primarily symbolic benefits aimed at mobilizing an important part of the Democratic party's coalition rather than material responses to the needs and wants of a significant portion of society? Doubtless Johnson's programs had both material and symbolic dimensions. A comparison of a president's promises and the legislation enacted under his leadership can therefore indicate only very loosely how responsive he actually was.[29]

What Makes Presidents (Un)Popular?

How does the American public evaluate its chief executives? A president's popularity—or his prestige, in Neustadt's terms—is an important resource that can affect his ability to persuade others to go along with him. The sources of a president's popularity can influence the way he uses his power. If he can increase his popularity by symbolic gestures, then we can expect symbolic gestures that have no necessary policy impact. If the president's popularity depends on such factors as the state of the economy, then we can expect him to try to create a healthy economy.

The evidence is fairly consistent that presidents are held

---

[27]Jeff Fishel, *Presidents and Promises* (Washington, D.C.: Congressional Quarterly Press, 1985), p. 39. The percentages are calculated from data provided by Fishel. Gerald Ford is excluded from the analysis because he did not run a campaign before his term in office.

[28]Ibid., p. 42.

[29]Fishel is aware of the limits of his analysis, and discusses in detail its implications for the larger question of presidential responsiveness.

accountable for the state of the nation's economy.[30] Indeed, people are apparently more likely to blame a president for the state of the national economy than they are to hold him accountable for such personal financial problems as the loss of a job. Thus presidents tend to enjoy high popularity in times of low unemployment, low inflation, and economic growth. When these indicators show the economy to be suffering, the president's popularity declines. An incumbent president lucky enough to be running when the economy looks relatively good (such as Ronald Reagan in 1984) will be very difficult to beat. An incumbent president unlucky enough to be up for reelection when the economy is in trouble (such as Jimmy Carter in 1980) will be vulnerable.

These patterns are not lost on sitting presidents. They know that they will be held accountable for the state of the economy for good or ill, and probably whether or not their policies are responsible for the economic health of the nation. Thus they try to manage the economy, and especially to promote economic growth when they face reelection. In his insightful study of the problem, Edward Tufte found that the economy was significantly more likely to be improving in years when an incumbent president was up for reelection than in nonelection years. Tufte uncovers evidence that growth in real disposable income in the pockets of citizens grew at over twice the normal rate when an incumbent president was running for reelection.[31] Such evidence suggests a kind of material responsiveness, although it is not always sound economic policy to stimulate growth at the time the president is campaigning for reelection.

Presidents also seem to be held accountable for the results of their foreign policy, especially when the policy is not working. President Lyndon Johnson declined to run for a second full term in 1968 because of opposition to the Vietnam war within his own party. President Carter suffered defeat in 1980 because of a general feeling that he had failed both to manage the economy and to maintain a coherent foreign policy. President Nixon faced severe domestic pressure because of his Vietnam policy, although he did win reelection overwhelmingly against an opponent (George McGovern) clearly opposed to the war. The contemporary presidential "job description" is so extensive that presidents are put on the spot in a way that other holders of national offices are not.

---

[30]Good summaries of the literature can be found in Samuel Kernell, *Going Public* (Washington, D.C.: Congressional Quarterly Press, 1986), chap. 7; and George C. Edwards III, *The Public Presidency* (New York: St. Martin's Press, 1983), chap. 6.
[31]Edward Tufte, *Political Control of the Economy* (Princeton: Princeton University Press, 1978).

Presidents have reasons to respond not only materially but in purely symbolic ways. Indeed, the frequent characterization of President Reagan as a "Teflon" president suggested that many observers considered his success as a symbolic leader to overshadow his leadership in things material.

George Edwards identifies a "positivity bias" that permits presidents, once they are elected, to garner a tremendous amount of goodwill. After winning a fall campaign, a president usually enjoys a surge in popularity immediately following the inaugural ceremony.[32] Richard Nixon, for example, won the 1968 election with only 43 percent of the popular vote but received the approval of 60 percent of the public in the first postinaugural poll taken. The symbolism of national unity celebrated in the inauguration exercises a powerful pull; the divisiveness of the campaign is forgotten, and the president can expect to experience an extended "honeymoon" period in the first months of his term. Enterprising presidents take advantage of that symbolic goodwill to advance their programs in the Congress and with the public.

Presidents can also benefit from a "rallying" effect. At times of national crisis, as when a U.S. embassy is attacked or when the president acts in a dramatic and visible way, as at a summit meeting, public opinion often shifts in his favor. The president is not merely a partisan leader elected to put into effect a program. He is also the head of state, the personification of the national identity. Some presidents have been charged with manipulating events in order to take advantage of this sort of rallying effect. President Carter (like several of his predecessors) pursued a "Rose Garden strategy" in response to the challenge from Senator Edward Kennedy for the Democratic nomination in 1979 and 1980. Carter claimed that the efforts to free the hostages held by Iranian militants who had seized the U.S. embassy in Tehran demanded his full attention, so that he could not engage Kennedy on the campaign trail. By calling attention to the crisis and to his role in managing it, he avoided the need to face the challenge within his own party.

Presidential Leadership Appraised

What are we to make of the contemporary presidency? From the perspective of Madison's Republic, we have many reasons to be disturbed. The presidency does have much more power today than the Framers contemplated. The formal dimensions of the office—the presidential job description, if you will—has expanded enormously,

---

[32]Edwards, *Public Presidency*, chaps. 2 and 6, especially p. 217.

as have the resources of the office designed to further the president's objectives. Madison would be alarmed by the extraordinary power of the office today.

What problems follow from executive-centered government? For the Republic, the great fear must be of tyranny. Presidents in the twentieth century have pursued policies that, strictly speaking, are the preserve of the legislative branch. Can the president take the nation to war? Korea, Vietnam, and numerous smaller presidential adventures suggest that he can. Yet the Constitution asserts that Congress has the authority to declare war. Instances of congressional delegation of legislative authority have been legion in all areas of public policy, usually in the form of a very broad or vague mandate to the executive to solve some problem. Such actions are highly questionable in light of the principles found in the Republic.[33] Presidential abuses of power—pick your own example from recent history—are inevitable given too great a concentration of power in the hands of a single individual. When a president has too much power, his ambition can too often get the upper hand. Counteracting interests may not have the institutional resources to prevail in a confrontation with an aggressive president.

Pluralism's Assessment of the Presidency

Pluralists emphasize two aspects of the contemporary presidency: (1) it is an adaptation of Madisonian principles to the realities of the late twentieth century; and (2) it nonetheless must continue to operate within a larger institutional framework that checks presidential abuses of power.

The potential for presidential energy was recognized by the Founders, especially by Hamilton in his defense of the unitary executive. With the development of a modern economy, a world leadership role, and contemporary communications and transportation systems, the need for decisive action and active leadership in the national government has grown. The president is uniquely suited to meet this need. More generally, the Madisonian system of "separate institutions sharing power" continues to work well both when presidents succeed and when they fail. Active leadership is more necessary today than it was at the founding. Therefore, the presidency has grown beyond the confines of the institution described in the Constitution. It has more authority, and it has more resources. Increases in both are appropriate and necessary. Institutional development of this sort reveals the flexibility built into the Madisonian system. Because the presidency is built on centralized power

---

[33]Theodore Lowi, *The End of Liberalism*, 2nd ed. (New York: Norton, 1979).

and the Congress is organized around the principle of fragmented, dispersed power, together they can respond to changing needs and demands.

At the same time, presidential abuses of power are inevitable. Madison was certainly aware of the potential for the mischievous use of power both in and out of government. Separation of powers was designed to check such abuses, and the principle still works today. The Vietnam war, while not formally declared by the Congress in the strict manner described by the Constitution, nonetheless required and received the full participation of Congress. The war had to be paid for, the troop levels in Southeast Asia had to be raised, the draft had to be extended. Congress had dozens of opportunities to disapprove the policy. As opposition to the war mounted in society, Congress registered and expressed that discontent. When Congress passed the War Powers Resolution, it sharply curtailed the president's ability to pursue foreign military adventures. The resolution, passed over President Nixon's veto, was a major reassertion of congressional power against an overly aggressive presidency.

The abuses revealed by the Watergate affair provide a clear example of presidential power run amok. For personal political gain, President Nixon supported the illegal activities of his aides, counseled them to obstruct justice, and systematically misled the Congress. For his sins, Congress reacted within its constitutional authority to make certain the investigation proceeded. Nixon escaped impeachment only by resigning from office. Congress met the challenge of tyrannical action in the executive exactly as the Constitution anticipated.

From Lincoln to Reagan, therefore, presidents have expanded their power to meet the conditions of their times. Pluralists certainly do not always agree with a particular president's actions, nor do they contend that the system works perfectly. Presidents sometimes lack the strength they need to deal with a crisis, but their weakness is as often due to personal or other limitations as to institutional constraints. Presidents are sometimes too strong, and engage in "wicked projects." But no system—no political theory—can completely guard against such transgressions. The Madisonian system, based as it is on institutional conflict, strikes a happy balance between too much power and too little, between paralysis in the government and capricious action. So say the pluralists.

Party Theory and the Presidency

Party theorists agree with the pluralists' contention that growth in the presidency is evidence of a need for energy and leadership in the national government. One of party theorists' major points is that the Madisonian system has no center. The Republic is a theory that is antigovernment. When government action is necessary—even

crucial—immense pressure is brought to bear on the president to provide the necessary energy and direction. Congress tends to step aside, especially when a crisis looms, and the president is given tremendous leeway. When Congress does not step aside, the result is often deadlock and inaction even when action is imperative.[34] Rather than producing a coherent program designed to attack national problems, therefore, policy making tends to be halting, inconsistent, and fragmented. When a president does seek to provide leadership, he often is able to escape responsibility because, in the event of failure, he inevitably can (with some justification) point to congressional delay or recalcitrance to account for it.

Party theorists want to concentrate governmental power in the hands of the winning party. Growth in presidential power is not the solution because it encourages emphasis on the *personal* president without ongoing, institutionalized responsibility.[35] It invites citizens to search among the possible presidential candidates for a heroic savior. It stimulates candidates to promise great statesmanship and the quick fix to long-term and difficult problems. Presidents escape responsibility not only by blaming other individuals and institutions in national government but by emphasizing symbol over substance. Even when individual presidents are held accountable by plunging popularity polls or by denial of reelection, the nation does not benefit. Instead, attention is devoted to the wrong question: Who can save us? Citizens and scholars alike seek a leader who has either the necessary skills (with Neustadt) or the appropriate degree of self-esteem and other personality traits (with Barber). The constant search for the heroic leader may sometimes produce truly remarkable presidents, but it will not correct the fundamental flaws deeply embedded in the Madisonian system. Ironically, Madison himself knew that such attempts to center government on individual qualities would founder on the hard rocks of human nature. He was correct in emphasizing institutional solutions to political problems, even if his solutions are no longer viable.

Party theorists, then, recommend that power be concentrated in an institution, not in an individual. The institution is, of course, the winning political party. To be sure, the nation needs someone to provide leadership in the capacity of a chief executive. In a parliamentary system, the leader of the winning party becomes the prime minister. Power is concentrated by the guarantee that the

---

[34]James MacGregor Burns, *The Deadlock of Democracy* (Englewood Cliffs, N.J.: Prentice-Hall, 1963).
[35]Lowi, *Personal President*, discusses some of the relevant problems, with emphasis on the president as a person who has no broad accountability to his party.

party that wins a popular majority in the legislature will also organize the executive branch. In fact, the winning party selects the prime minister and the cabinet officials from among its own members of parliament. The reforms suggested by party theorists in the United States are variations on this idea. At the very least they would guarantee that the Congress and the presidency would be controlled by the same party, and that the president and the congressional majority would share a commitment to the party's program.[36]

Party theorists, we have seen in Chapter 4, emphasize the importance of the party as the source of power and the focus of responsibility in national politics. The party must be able to discipline its members (including the president) in order to keep its commitments. If the party theorists' reforms were instituted, the party would develop its program in the knowledge that if it won an election it would have the opportunity to carry its program out. Thus it would be responsible for its failures and would be justified in claiming credit for its successes. Presidential candidates would be selected from among senior party officials by their peers. They would have a long record in national government, having served in the legislature when their party was in the minority and in the cabinets of past administrations when their party was in the majority. They would be known by other officials and by the public. They would be viewed as part of a team committed to the program offered by their party. Most important, the focus would be on the governing party rather than on any single individual. Parties outlast individuals, and their interests transcend those of any single individual. Thus parties would have powerful incentives to deter their executive leaders from promising more than they could hope to deliver. At the same time, by concentrating power between elections, the system would meet the genuine need for vigorous leadership in a manner consistent with responsibility, electoral democracy, and equality. So say the party theorists.

Conclusion

I have said throughout this book that the question of what to do with political power is among the most basic questions political scientists can ask. Certainly it is at the core of the debate between pluralists/Madison and party theorists. Modern presidents are un-

---

[36]See Charles Hardin, "The Crisis and Its Cure," and Lloyd N. Cutler, "To Form a Government," both in *Reforming American Government*, ed. Donald L. Robinson (Boulder, Colo.: Westview Press, 1985).

deniably powerful. While a strong argument can be made on behalf of presidential power, a problem just as clearly remains. Power, once possessed, can be abused. Power, as Madison knew, could be used to serve narrow, selfish interests rather than the public good. How to harness political power to the public good is the question. Is the presidency the answer?

Certainly there is room for the case made by Neustadt and other pluralists that the president, by pursuing his interest in power, serves the larger national interest. In particular, pluralist theory looks for balance between Congress and president in the exercise of power and in the interests represented. Because of the visible and unitary character of the president, energy will come from that office, and the president is more likely than Congress to be sensitive to national issues. The presidency also is more responsive to unorganized interests. On the other hand, the presidency is less likely than Congress to capture the diversity found in society, and it will be less sensitive to intensely concerned organized minorities. With its attention to "particularized" benefits, with its incentives for responsiveness to demands even from individual citizens, the contemporary Congress provides a kind of representation impossible in a majoritarian, national institution such as the presidency. Congressional representation comes at a price, but many of its limits are offset by today's presidency. The presidency is capable of getting us "beyond self-interest" when national leadership is essential, although no system of government can (or should try) to transcend the limits of self-interest in politics.

Party theorists do not accept this sort of "balance" argument. They contend that the national government will function properly when—and only when—it serves the basic values of responsibility, equality, and democracy. The presidency does correct some of the flaws found in congressional representation, but it nonetheless is forced to operate in a system based on a fundamental misunderstanding of the relationship between the citizen and the state. Therefore, it introduces its own peculiar form of pathology into American politics: overdependence on the individual leader, a lack of institutionalized political responsibility, and rampant symbolism. It fails to activate *political* self-interest in a manner that can lead to the common good. Representative government is fragile and is made more so by the pressures of the late twentieth century. How much longer can we limp along with a system based on a flawed understanding of political behavior? The presidency does not and cannot get us "beyond self-interest." In fact, because of the larger flaws in the Madisonian system, it cannot even get us to the point where interests in society are regularly heard in the councils of government. To achieve truly representative government, we must solve problems more fundamental than those that can be addressed through the adaptive qualities of the executive branch.

Key Concepts

active-negative presidents

active-positive presidents

formal resources of the president

implied powers

material responsiveness

personal resources of the president

presidential power

prestige

reputation

symbolic responsiveness

unitary executive

Republic at Risk

James Madison's theory of the Republic has occupied our attention throughout this book. The Republic is probably history's best example of a political theory put into practice. It represents great confidence in the ability of theory to identify the appropriate levers to pull to achieve a desired end in social and political life. But in the late twentieth century, after Freud, after Stalin and Hitler, and after the Bomb, confidence in political theory is probably not high. Can we identify the levers? Should we pull them?

Like it or not, we have no choice. We cannot avoid pulling the levers, we cannot avoid forming institutions that affect our shared living. We cannot avoid the problems associated with scarcity, with our differences, and with the fact that we must share space. We cannot, that is to say, avoid politics, so we had better strive for better understanding.

The nice thing about Madison's Republic is that it faces the problems head on and proposes some answers. It argues against letting institutions develop out of habit or gradual adaptation, and for thinking systematically about the problems and then acting on that understanding.

The purpose of this book has been to put both the thinking and the acting at risk by critically analyzing the theory and its relation to contemporary American politics. In today's political culture the Constitution justified by Madison's Republic has taken on a symbolism akin to that of a religious artifact. It is revered. It is celebrated and honored. One consequence is that the political institutions that it describes and that govern our daily lives have a degree of popular legitimacy not found in those of most other political systems. That legitimacy may be good, but it does not support clear-headed thinking about these institutions, or about the ideas that can be used to justify them. It promotes acquiescence, not critical analysis. This lack of critical thinking about our fundamental political institutions may be the greatest risk of all.

Conclusion
Self-Interest and
Representative Government

For James Madison, self-interest is the problem. It is the problem because it is an immutable part of human nature and because its consequences in politics are potentially devastating. People act for their own gain without thinking of the interests of others, or of the larger public good. Although everyone benefits in the long run from a stable social order, people may pursue their short-run interests in ways that harm or destroy that order. This consequence of self-interest—social instability and chaos—is relatively easy to manage. The problem is complicated by the fact that the governments created to protect against instability and disorder are themselves subject to self-interest. The problem here is defined as tyranny. The people with power naturally use it to pursue their own interests, again without concern for the interests of others or for the larger public good. Those with power often have a compelling interest in avoiding instability and chaos, but stability is not enough. Great care must be taken to avoid tyranny—by a majority over the minority or by the government over the governed.

For Madison, self-interest is the solution. It must be the solution because it is the basis for political action, and because it is an immutable part of human nature. The very differences that generate instability must be employed to control the power necessary to bring about stability. The solution is a carefully crafted set of institutions with adequate power, but also with the necessary relations among themselves and between them and the people to control that power. The solution connects the self-interest of the governed to the self-interest of those in government to protect against the dangers of self-interest. Madison solves the problem—the "defect of better motives"—"by so contriving the interior structure of the government, as that its several constituent parts may, by their mutual relations, be the means of keeping each other in their proper

237

places." In this way, "the private interest of every individual may be a sentinel over the public rights."[1]

The Critique Summarized

I have argued that Madison's Republic runs into difficulty precisely where it claims its greatest strength: in its theory of self-interest. The theory does not anticipate the nature of self-interest in politics, nor does it comprehend its implications for a theory of representation. It does not expect the self-interested citizen to be indifferent, uninformed, and inactive in the political world. From the citizen's perspective, much of political conflict is over the distribution of collective benefits. Truly self-interested citizens—individuals who rigorously pursue selfish gain without regard for the interests of others—remain free riders in the face of such conflicts, no matter how great their interest in the outcome.

Only the relatively small subset of citizens for whom such conflicts hold the promise of some private benefit act in a genuinely self-interested fashion by becoming involved. This is a crucial distinction. "Elites" are those who participate in order to receive a private good. They may also help produce a collective good, but their incentives are qualitatively different from those of the mass of citizens, for whom collective goods are the primary concern. Candidates for office compete for positions in government with the accompanying power, prestige, and visibility. These private goods help compensate candidates for the immense outlay of resources they must commit to their quest. Leaders of interest groups and others intensely involved in policy debates compete for governmental preferments in the form of subsidies and contracts.

The pursuit of private benefits associated with the elite side of politics cannot explain all of political conflict, by any means. Many people enter the political arena at the elite level out of an intense moral or ideological commitment to political values. Nonetheless, this imbalance between the interest of ordinary citizens in collective goods and the interest of elites in private goods distorts the theory of representative government found in the Republic. The costs of entering the elite level of politics are normally quite high. Extraordinary resources are required for extraordinary forms of participation, and the associated resource bias can be severe. Typical citizens do not participate in atypical ways. Therefore, the kinds of interests represented at the elite level of politics are not at all typical of the much broader range of interests in society at large.

---

[1]The quotations, of course, are from Madison's *Federalist* 51.

A resource bias in participation is not very interesting or important so long as mechanisms to hold elites accountable to broader interests are firmly in place. Elections are designed to achieve this end, since the bias associated with voting is relatively slight and large numbers of citizens can be expected to vote. But the quality of citizen participation in elections is nonetheless colored by self-interest. Because electoral outcomes are collective goods, voters do not invest heavily in promoting results consistent with their political interests. Citizens who participate in elections have little interest in self-interest.

Therefore, the link championed by the Republic between the self-interest of citizens and the self-interest of people in public office is at risk. It is fragile, not robust; tentative, not secure. Self-interest strains the link between the interests of followers and those of leaders at least as much as it ensures it. Elites organize resources in order to compete successfully for private benefits; citizens do not normally organize themselves to realize their potential to influence the distribution of collective benefits.

With the Republic's faith in the ability of self-interest to motivate representative government in doubt, what follows? First, unless some way can be found to "reconnect" the average citizen to politics, the resource bias suggests that those interests with more resources will often win at the expense of those with fewer resources. Representation as a way of including in government the full range of interests in society—"the spirit of party and faction"—will favor those factions richly endowed with such resources as organization, political skill, status, and wealth over those less capable of pressing their claims. The inclusive nature of the Madisonian solution is in danger to the extent that interests are excluded from representation. It is in even greater jeopardy if the explanation of that exclusion lies in self-interest. That is, if some claims are not heard in government because the relevant interests have an interest in not participating (Chapter 2), in not bearing the necessary information costs to invest their participation with instrumental meaning (Chapter 3), or in not organizing to compete with other groups capable of monitoring what government does (Chapter 5), self-interest becomes the explanation for bias rather than the force that produces representative government.

Second, the conflict that is supposed to result from the representation of diverse interests in government is also subject to doubt. Collusion among holders of public office may be based on a common interest that overwhelms the differences that Madison expected to divide them. Their collusion can lead to such means of reducing conflict as actions to bias the electoral process in favor of incumbents and the more general norm of universalism in Congress

(Chapters 6 and 7). The overwhelming agenda of modern government creates additional pressures on officeholders and institutions to manage conflict (Chapters 7 and 8). The result can be such adaptive patterns as an increasing reliance on specialists in Congress and a frenzied search for a great leader. While these adaptations to the demands of contemporary politics are understandable, they are not consistent with the founding theory. The mere fact that they are embedded in the institutional framework described by the Constitution does not mean that they warrant our uncritical acceptance or celebration.

There are, of course, various possible reactions to this critique of Madison's Republic. Because this book has focused on representative government, I have emphasized the means proposed by pluralism and party theory to reconnect the citizen to government. Pluralism generalizes political self-interest to include most social and economic activity, and concludes that the Madisonian solution works rather well in accommodating the diverse character of society. The citizen is reconnected to politics without being overtly political.

Party theory despairs of achieving representative government in the absence of politically motivated action. Party theorists, therefore, seek to reconnect the citizen to government by explicitly political means: strong political parties competing in popular elections.

Pluralism offers a way of accommodating the Republic to contemporary theory and evidence, and is largely satisfied with the way the founding theory plays out in American politics. It accepts the Republic's normative commitment to individualism, diversity, and limited government. It does not support a major program of reform, although many individual pluralists would like to tinker with some component of the system. Party theory rejects this accommodation and posits values that lead to major reform. It tempers the Republic's devotion to individualism and diversity by emphasis on equality and responsibility. Its program of reform is, like the Republic itself, a result of faith in our ability to understand the political world and to change it for the better. Where pluralism is cautiously optimistic about what is, party theory is aggressively sanguine about what can be.

Despite their significant differences, neither pluralism nor party theory directly challenges the most fundamental Madisonian position: self-interest is both problem and solution. The theories differ in the importance they attribute to the Republic's failure to understand the nature of political self-interest, and they differ in their beliefs as to the way self-interest can and should be organized to produce representative government. But they do not challenge self-interest as the foundation of political theory. Both accept the idea that the public good can be a by-product of selfish action.

Some Implications of Starting with Self-Interest

The appeal of Madison's definition of the problem and the solution is its hardheaded analytical power. One need not be concerned with such concepts as statesmanship, wisdom, and virtue. One need not even tarry long over the public good. Rather, the negative consequences of self-interest can be identified (chaos, tyranny) and things constructed so as to avoid them. It is a cautious approach because it takes as given a characteristic of "human nature" which is readily observable in political life. It does not seek to change that characteristic by drawing individuals out of themselves. It does not demand of people's public action more than self-aggrandizing acquisitiveness. Madison thought he had good reason for starting with self-interest. He thought that was an accurate characterization of human nature. He thought that differences in property, religion, and geography would produce different opinions and "passions" in regard to public affairs which would animate much of political life. He argued that human fallibility would hinder agreement and facilitate conflict in politics even when no substantial differences existed.

What are the consequences of building a political theory on self-interest? I argued in Chapter 1 that Madison's Republic, like any political theory, is also an ideology. The ideas contained within the theory have everyday consequences for the way we live our lives. Given the importance of self-interest to the theory, it is fair to ask about some of the implications of self-interest as a starting point. I will briefly suggest three that are closely related to one another (I am sure there are others): the theory emphasizes the divisive rather than the shared dimensions of political life; the theory lacks a fundamental conception of justice external to the political process it defends; and the theory may be a self-fulfilling prophecy.

Emphasis on the divisive character of politics. Self-interest is enshrined in the theory as the basis both for representation and for the conflict necessary to protect against tyranny. Ultimately, self-interest is what is protected as well as what is feared. It is feared because of its potentially negative consequences. It is protected by a theory that builds its government upon it, encourages the "spirit of party and faction" in government, and defines tyranny as that which ignores or tramples self-interest. The ultimate effect of such a theory is to emphasize what divides citizens and groups from one another rather than what unites them. Factions are encouraged to seek representation in order to combat other factions with contrary interests. Governmental institutions are set up to be in conflict with one another. The dangers of social living are emphasized more than the benefits. The risks of governmental power are stressed more than the advantages.

Although pluralism and party theory rest on self-interest, they both can claim to soften the emphasis on divisiveness found in the Republic. Because pluralism conceives of interests as broadly based on social, occupational, and religious affiliations, its idea of "self-interest" carries fewer dangers for the polity. Pluralism is less concerned with breaking the "violence" of faction than with maintaining the diversity found in American society and reflecting that diversity in government. Its conception of groups as the primary units of politics is more positive and less threatening than Madison's conception of factions. Interest is diffused, not focused; intermittent, not impassioned. It is a naturally occurring phenomenon that gives rise to diversity and complexity, and calls less for control than for legitimate channels.

Party theory, by seeking to activate political interests and conflict between the parties, encourages an admittedly divisive quality in politics. However, the theory's focus on collective responsibility promotes conflict around collective issues rather than narrowly selfish concerns. Parties are necessarily divisive in that they represent a part of the whole, but they also aggregate and unite interests. They seek what is shared as well as promote division.

All three theories, by working from self-interest, accept conflict as a necessary component of politics. Madison and the pluralists argue that interests generate conflict among factions and groups. That conflict, in turn, is an important way to check the impulse of any single interest to dominate others. Party theorists contend that political interest must be stimulated in the public before government can be expected to respond. Thus an important function of conflict in the form of electoral competition between the parties is to stimulate politically motivated action in the public. But in their focus on self-interest, all three theories suggest that larger, common interests can be realized only through the divisive process of politics.

Implications for the conception of justice. A second charge against Madison's Republic is that it lacks a firmly rooted conception of justice independent of the process it describes. In creating an arena where self-interest competes with self-interest, the process celebrates self-interest rather than more fundamental values. How does one assess the results of political conflict so long as the fundamental rules are obeyed? If injustices (by some other standard) prevail, what recourse is there beyond mobilization, coalition building, persuasion, and more political conflict? The experience of blacks, women, gays, and others suggests that moral rights may be reduced

to a matter of interests, and any gains they make must be the result
of their successes in the political field. Standards of justice such as
equality, fairness, and due process may themselves be subjected to
political conflict in which interests clash and win or lose. That
process may be haphazard or dangerous.

The absence of an overarching conception of justice beyond the
creation of an arena where the clash of interests takes place puts the
resources necessary in the competition of interests at a premium.
Winning is everything. We have grappled with the implications of
the resource bias throughout this book, and a theory based on
self-interest will always face the problem of how to limit the consequences of bias. Pluralists suggest that political resources are
multifaceted and noncumulative. The implication is that players
will always find some way to representation. Party theorists contend that forcing the competition into the electoral arena creates
equality because every citizen has one and only one vote. In both
cases, however, there are good reasons to believe that the resource
bias is not so easily mitigated. Many interests in the pluralist world
are not well organized. Some resources, such as organization,
credibility, status, and wealth, may be worth much more than
others in political competition. Party theorists rest their case on a
more active electorate, but surely there must be some method for
reconciling intraparty differences. It is likely that the interests with
more resources would be more successful in setting the direction of
their party and defining the nature of partisan conflict. In so doing,
they would wield disportionate influence.

To some extent, the charge against the Republic is unfair, because the Constitution includes ten amendments that explicitly
define such rights as freedom of expression and of assembly. The
Bill of Rights appeals to such underlying concepts of justice as equal
opportunity for access to the political process. The courts have a
tradition (though not a completely unblemished record) of enforcing those rights, even when other institutions are not responsive to
them as political claims. Nonetheless, because of the concern with
self-interest, much of political life is characterized by the clash of
interests and of the institutions designed to encompass it.

The self-fulfilling prophecy. Madison begins with a conception of
human nature which he assumes to be God-given and immutable.
But what if he's wrong? What if human nature is less the result of
fixed qualities common to us all and more the product of the social
environment? If self-interest is what you expect, self-interest may be
what (and all) you get. Individuals and factions may reasonably
react to the Republic by saying, "If we don't look out for our interests, who will?" If interest is to check interest, if ambition is to

counteract ambition, where is cooperation to be found? What if it is possible to call forth something more from the people and the institutions of government? Would not a focus on avoidance of the dangers of self-interest preclude the possibility of finding anything other than self-interest?

David Schuman points out that it is no accident that Madison Avenue is the symbol of grasping, acquisitive, self-interested behavior in American society. "We are encouraged to be a private, materialistic people. We are essentially an uncommunitarian, anti-political people who may act differently in spite of—certainly not at the urging of—the state."[2] What you want is what you get. If self-interest is the solution, how could we live without it?

Consider John Stuart Mill's conception of the good state:

> . . . the most important point of excellence which any form of government can possess is to promote the virtue and intelligence of the people themselves. The first question in respect to any political institutions is how far they tend to foster in the members of the community the various desirable qualities, . . . moral, intellectual, and active.[3]

Madison's Republic would not stand up well to Mill's test because it is asking the wrong question. The question should not be how to control self-interest, or even how to create the public good out of self-interest. The question is how "to promote the virtue and intelligence of the people." Madison's conception of human nature prevents him from asking Mill's question.

For James Madison, there could be no more dangerous question than that posed by Mill. Who is to judge what "virtue and intelligence" are and when they have been promoted? In a government of "angels over men," such a question might have an answer, but in a society governed by fallible men and women, prone to self-love and subject to passion, such standards become the means whereby "wicked projects" and tyranny infect the polity.

The difference between Madison's and Mill's questions reveals the stakes involved in political theory. For Madison, to ask the questions raised by Schuman and Mill is to open the door for the worst form of tyranny—a cure worse than the disease. For Schuman and Mill, to ask Madison's question is to doom the polity to the worst in human nature, so that its citizens will have little chance to transcend selfish and "anti-political" perspectives and achieve fulfillment.

---

[2]David Schuman, *A Preface to Politics*, 2nd ed. (Lexington, Mass.: D. C. Heath, 1977), pp. 17–18.
[3]John Stuart Mill, *Considerations on Representative Government*, quoted in Jack L. Walker, "A Critique of the Elitist Theory of Democracy," *American Political Science Review*, June 1966, p. 288.

Conclusion

An answer to the sort of debate raised by Schuman and Mill is beyond my purpose. Nor is it my purpose to challenge self-interest as an appropriate starting point for a theory of politics. Indeed, I think the assumption of self-interest lends considerable analytical power to a theory even though it does not explain everything. Important and nonobvious conclusions are available to theories that start with the axiom of self-interest. At the same time, there can be no higher purpose than looking for ways to achieve Madison's goal of protecting the "public rights," of pushing past the limitations of selfish motives in the political world, even if the mechanism for doing so ends up being some form of self-interest.

The central (and more limited) task of my analysis has been to examine the Republic's theory of representative government as it plays itself out in contemporary American politics. Much of that analysis has been critical. But the criticism in no way denies the tremendous impact the theory has on the American republic as it goes about determining who gets what, when, and how. In the republic of everyday life, citizens are regularly consulted in the conduct of public affairs, and in that way are connected to government. The strength and meaning of the connection is subject to debate, but there can be no doubt that the government is in some genuine sense "popular." The "scheme of representation" is the cornerstone of the system, although analysts profoundly disagree about who gets represented, who gets left out, and why. The dispersal and fragmentation of power among competing governmental institutions has extensive implications for our politics.

Inevitably, the reality departs from the theory. In the slippage between theory and practice we find productive controversy about competing theories and potential reform. It is essential to subject the American republic to this sort of review, for the consequences of its actions and inaction are profoundly important. It is a republic under immense pressure to respond to the needs of a diverse population. It is a republic that regularly claims positions of moral and material leadership in the world. It is a republic that, as often as not, falls short of its own ideals and aspirations. It is, in short, a republic at risk.

Appendix

Federalist No. 10

Among the numerous advantages promised by a well constructed Union, none deserves to be more accurately developed than its tendency to break and control the violence of faction. The friend of popular governments, never finds himself so much alarmed for their character and fate, as when he contemplates their propensity to this dangerous vice. He will not fail therefore to set a due value on any plan which, without violating the principles to which he is attached, provides a proper cure for it. The instability, injustice and confusion introduced into the public councils, have in truth been the mortal diseases under which popular governments have every where perished; as they continue to be the favorite and fruitful topics from which the adversaries to liberty derive their most specious declamations. The valuable improvements made by the American Constitutions on the popular models, both ancient and modern, cannot certainly be too much admired; but it would be an unwarrantable partiality, to contend that they have as effectually obviated the danger on this side as was wished and expected. Complaints are every where heard from our most considerate and virtuous citizens, equally the friends of public and private faith, and of public and personal liberty; that our governments are too unstable; that the public good is disregarded in the conflicts of rival parties; and that measures are too often decided, not according to the rules of justice, and the rights of the minor party; but by the superior force of an interested and over-bearing majority. However anxiously we may wish that these complaints had no foundation, the evidence of known facts will not permit us to deny that they are in some degree true. It will be found indeed, on a candid review of our situation, that some of the distresses under which we labor, have been erroneously charged on the operation of our governments; but it will be found, at the same time, that other causes will not alone account for many of our heaviest misfortunes; and particularly, for that prevailing and increasing distrust of public engagements, and alarm for private rights, which are echoed from one end of the continent to the other. These must be chiefly, if not wholly, effects of the unsteadiness and injustice, with which a factious spirit has tainted our public administrations.

By a faction I understand a number of citizens, whether amounting to a majority or minority of the whole, who are united and actuated by some common impulse of passion, or of interest, adverse to the rights of other citizens, or to the permanent and aggregate interests of the community.

There are two methods of curing the mischiefs of faction: the one, by removing its causes; the other, by controlling its effects.

There are again two methods of removing the causes of faction: the one by destroying the liberty which is essential to its existence; the other, by giving to every citizen the same opinions, the same passions, and the same interests.

It could never be more truly said than of the first remedy, that it is worse than the disease. Liberty is to faction, what air is to fire, an aliment without which it instantly expires. But it could not be a less folly to abolish liberty, which is essential to political life, because it nourishes faction, than it would be to wish the annihilation of air, which is essential to animal life, because it imparts to fire its destructive agency.

The second expedient is as impracticable, as the first would be unwise. As long as the reason of man continues fallible, and he is at liberty to exercise it, different opinions will be formed. As long as the connection subsists between his reason and his self-love, his opinions and his passions will have a reciprocal influence on each other; and the former will be objects to which the latter will attach themselves. The diversity in the faculties of men from which the rights of property originate, is not less an insuperable obstacle to a uniformity of interests. The protection of these faculties is the first object of Government. From the protection of different and unequal faculties of acquiring property, the possession of different degrees and kinds of property immediately results: and from the influence of these on the sentiments and views of the respective proprietors, ensues a division of the society into different interests and parties.

The latent causes of faction are thus sown in the nature of man; and we see them every where brought into different degrees of activity, according to the different circumstances of civil society. A zeal for different opinions concerning religion, concerning Government and many other points, as well of speculation as of practice; an attachment to different leaders ambitiously contending for pre-eminence and power; or to persons of other descriptions whose

fortunes have been interesting to the human passions, have in turn
divided mankind into parties, inflamed them with mutual animos-
ity, and rendered them much more disposed to vex and oppress each
other, than to co-operate for their common good. So strong is this
propensity of mankind to fall into mutual animosities, that where
no substantial occasion presents itself, the most frivolous and fanci-
ful distinctions have been sufficient to kindle their unfriendly passions, and excite their most violent conflicts. But the most common
and durable source of factions, has been the various and unequal
distribution of property. Those who hold, and those who are without property, have ever formed distinct interests in society. Those
who are creditors, and those who are debtors, fall under a like
discrimination. A landed interest, a manufacturing interest, a mer-
cantile interest, a monied interest, with many lesser interests, grow
up of necessity in civilized nations, and divide them into different
classes, actuated by different sentiments and views. The regulation
of these various and interfering interests forms the principal task of
modern Legislation, and involves the spirit of party and faction in
the necessary and ordinary operations of Government.

No man is allowed to be a judge in his own cause; because his
interest would certainly bias his judgment, and, not improbably,
corrupt his integrity. With equal, nay with greater reason, a body of
men, are unfit to be both judges and parties, at the same time; yet,
what are many of the most important acts of legislation, but so
many judicial determinations, not indeed concerning the rights of
single persons, but concerning the rights of large bodies of citizens;
and what are the different classes of legislators, but advocates and
parties to the causes which they determine? Is a law proposed
concerning private debts? It is a question to which the creditors are
parties on one side, and the debtors on the other. Justice ought to
hold the balance between them. Yet the parties are and must be
themselves the judges; and the most numerous party, or, in other
words, the most powerful faction must be expected to prevail. Shall
domestic manufactures be encouraged, and in what degree, by restrictions on foreign manufactures? are questions which would be
differently decided by the landed and the manufacturing classes;
and probably by neither, with a sole regard to justice and the public
good. The apportionment of taxes on the various descriptions of
property, is an act which seems to require the most exact im-
partiality; yet, there is perhaps no legislative act in which greater
opportunity and temptation are given to a predominant party, to
trample on the rules of justice. Every shilling with which they
over-burden the inferior number, is a shilling saved to their own
pockets.

It is in vain to say, that enlightened statesmen will be able to adjust these clashing interests, and render them all subservient to the public good. Enlightened statesmen will not always be at the helm: Nor, in many cases, can such an adjustment be made at all, without taking into view indirect and remote considerations, which will rarely prevail over the immediate interest which one party may find in disregarding the rights of another, or the good of the whole.

The inference to which we are brought, is, that the *causes* of faction cannot be removed; and that relief is only to be sought in the means of controlling its *effects*.

If a faction consists of less than a majority, relief is supplied by the republican principle, which enables the majority to defeat its sinister views by regular vote: It may clog the administration, it may convulse the society; but it will be unable to execute and mask its violence under the forms of the Constitution. When a majority is included in a faction, the form of popular government on the other hand enables it to sacrifice to its ruling passion or interest, both the public good and the rights of other citizens. To secure the public good, and private rights, against the danger of such a faction, and at the same time to preserve the spirit and the form of popular government, is then the great object to which our enquiries are directed: Let me add that it is the great desideratum, by which alone this form of government can be rescued from the opprobrium under which it has so long labored, and be recommended to the esteem and adoption of mankind.

By what means is this object attainable? Evidently by one of two only. Either the existence of the same passion or interest in a majority at the same time, must be prevented; or the majority, having such co-existent passion or interest, must be rendered, by their number and local situation, unable to concert and carry into effect schemes of oppression. If the impulse and the opportunity be suffered to coincide, we well know that neither moral nor religious motives can be relied on as an adequate control. They are not found to be such on the injustice and violence of individuals, and lose their efficacy in proportion to the number combined together; that is, in proportion as their efficacy becomes needful.

From this view of the subject, it may be concluded, that a pure Democracy, by which I mean, a Society, consisting of a small number of citizens, who assemble and administer the Government in person, can admit of no cure for the mischiefs of faction. A common passion or interest will, in almost every case, be felt by a majority of the whole; a communication and concert results from the form of Government itself; and there is nothing to check the inducements to sacrifice the weaker party, or an obnoxious individual. Hence it is, that such Democracies have ever been spectacles of turbulence and contention; have ever been found incompatible with personal security, or the rights of property; and have in general been as short in their lives, as they have been violent in their deaths. Theoretic politicians, who have patronized this species of Government, have erroneously supposed, that by reducing mankind to a perfect equality in their political rights, they would, at the same time, be perfectly equalized and assimilated in their possessions, their opinions, and their passions.

A republic, by which I mean a government in which the scheme of representation takes place, opens a different prospect, and promises the cure for which we are seeking. Let us examine the points in which it varies from pure democracy, and we shall comprehend both the nature of the cure and the efficacy which it must derive from the union.

The two great points of difference, between a democracy and a republic, are, first, the delegation of the government, in the latter, to a small number of citizens, elected by the rest; secondly, the greater number of citizens, and greater sphere of country, over which the latter may be extended.

The effect of the first difference is, on the one hand, to refine and enlarge the public views, by passing them through the medium of a chosen body of citizens, whose wisdom may best discern the true interest of their country, and whose patriotism and love of justice, will be least likely to sacrifice it to temporary or partial considerations. Under such a regulation, it may well happen, that the public voice, pronounced by the representatives of the people, will be more consonant to the public good, than if pronounced by the people themselves, convened for the purpose. On the other hand the effect may be inverted. Men of factious tempers, of local prejudices, or of sinister designs, may by intrigue, by corruption, or by other means, first obtain the suffrages, and then betray the interest of the people. The question resulting is, whether small or extensive republics are most favorable to the election of proper guardians of the public weal; and it is clearly decided in favor of the latter by two obvious considerations.

In the first place, it is to be remarked that, however small the republic may be, the representatives must be raised to a certain number, in order to guard against the cabals of a few; and that however large it may be, they must be limited to a certain number, in order to guard against the confusion of a multitude. Hence, the number of representatives in the two cases not being in proportion to that of the constituents, and being proportionally greatest in the small republic, it follows, that if the proportion of fit characters be not less in the large than in the small republic, the former will present a greater option, and consequently a greater probability of a fit choice.

In the next place, as each Representative will be chosen by a greater number of citizens in the large than in the small Republic, it will be more difficult for unworthy candidates to practise with success the vicious arts, by which elections are too often carried; and the suffrages of the people being more free, will be more likely to center on men who possess the most attractive merit, and the most diffusive and established characters.

It must be confessed, that in this, as in most other cases, there is a mean, on both sides of which inconveniences will be found to lie. By enlarging too much the number of electors, you render the representative too little acquainted with all their local circumstances and lesser interests; as by reducing it too much, you render him unduly attached to these, and too little fit to comprehend and pursue great and national objects. The Federal Constitution forms a happy combination in this respect; the great and aggregate interests being referred to the national, the local and particular, to the state legislatures.

The other point of difference is, the greater number of citizens and extent of territory which may be brought within the compass of Republican, than of Democratic Government; and it is this circumstance principally which renders factious combinations less to be dreaded in the former, than in the latter. The smaller the society, the fewer probably will be the distinct parties and interests composing it; the fewer the distinct parties and interests, the more frequently will a majority be found of the same party; and the smaller the number of individuals composing a majority, and the smaller the compass within which they are placed, the more easily will they concert and execute their plans of oppression. Extend the sphere, and you take in a greater variety of parties and interests; you make it less probable that a majority of the whole will have a common motive to invade the rights of other citizens; or if such a common motive exists, it will be more difficult for all who feel it to discover their own strength, and to act in unison with each other. Besides other impediments, it may be remarked, that where there is a consciousness of unjust or dishonorable purposes, communication is always checked by distrust, in proportion to the number whose concurrence is necessary.

Hence it clearly appears, that the same advantage, which a Republic has over a Democracy, in controlling the effects of faction, is enjoyed by a large over a small Republic—is enjoyed by the Union over the States composing it. Does this advantage consist in the substitution of Representatives, whose enlightened views and virtuous sentiments render them superior to local prejudices, and to schemes of injustice? It will not be denied, that the Representation of the Union will be most likely to possess these requisite endow-

ments. Does it consist in the greater security afforded by a greater
variety of parties, against the event of any one party being able to outnumber and oppress the rest? In an equal degree does the increased variety of parties, comprised within the Union, increase this security. Does it, in fine, consist in the greater obstacles opposed to the concert and accomplishment of the secret wishes of an unjust and interested majority? Here, again, the extent of the Union gives it the most palpable advantage.

The influence of factious leaders may kindle a flame within their particular States, but will be unable to spread a general conflagration through the other States: a religious sect, may degenerate into a political faction in a part of the Confederacy but the variety of sects dispersed over the entire face of it, must secure the national Councils against any danger from that source: a rage for paper money, for an abolition of debts, for an equal division of property, or for any other improper or wicked project, will be less apt to pervade the whole body of the Union, than a particular member of it; in the same proportion as such a malady is more likely to taint a particular county or district, than an entire State.

In the extent and proper structure of the Union, therefore, we behold a Republican remedy for the diseases most incident to Republican Government. And according to the degree of pleasure and pride, we feel in being Republicans, ought to be our zeal in cherishing the spirit, and supporting the character of Federalists.

PUBLIUS

Federalist No. 51

To what expedient then shall we finally resort for maintaining in practice the necessary partition of power among the several departments, as laid down in the Constitution? The only answer that can be given is, that as all these exterior provisions are found to be inadequate, the defect must be supplied, by so contriving the interior structure of the government, as that its several constituent parts may, by their mutual relations, be the means of keeping each other in their proper places. Without presuming to undertake a full development of this important idea, I will hazard a few general observations, which may perhaps place it in a clearer light, and enable us to form a more correct judgment of the principles and structure of the government planned by the convention.

In order to lay a due foundation for that separate and distinct exercise of the different powers of government, which to a certain extent, is admitted on all hands to be essential to the preservation of liberty, it is evident that each department should have a will of its own; and consequently should be so constituted, that the members of each should have as little agency as possible in the appointment of the members of the others. Were this principle rigorously adhered to, it would require that all the appointments for the supreme executive, legislative, and judiciary magistracies, should be drawn from the same fountain of authority, the people, through channels, having no communication whatever with one another. Perhaps such a plan of constructing the several departments would be less difficult in practice than it may in contemplation appear. Some difficulties however, and some additional expense, would attend the execution of it. Some deviations therefore from the principle must be admitted. In the constitution of the judiciary department in particular, it might be inexpedient to insist rigorously on the principle; first, because peculiar qualifications being essential in the members, the primary consideration ought to be to select that mode of choice, which best secures these qualifications; secondly, because the permanent tenure by which the appointments are held in that department, must soon destroy all sense of dependence on the authority conferring them.

It is equally evident that the members of each department should be as little dependent as possible on those of the others, for the emoluments annexed to their offices. Were the executive magistrate, or the judges, not independent of the legislature in this particular, their independence in every other would be merely nominal.

But the great security against a gradual concentration of the several powers in the same department, consists in giving to those who administer each department, the necessary constitutional means, and personal motives, to resist encroachments of the others. The provision for defense must in this, as in all other cases, be made commensurate to the danger of attack. Ambition must be made to counteract ambition. The interest of the man must be connected with the constitutional rights of the place. It may be a reflection on human nature, that such devices should be necessary to control the abuses of government. But what is government itself but the greatest of all reflections on human nature? If men were angels, no government would be necessary. If angels were to govern men, neither external nor internal controls on government would be necessary. In framing a government which is to be administered by men over men, the great difficulty lies in this: You must first enable the government to control the governed; and in the next place, oblige it to control itself. A dependence on the people is no doubt the primary control on the government; but experience has taught mankind the necessity of auxiliary precautions.

This policy of supplying by opposite and rival interests, the defect of better motives, might be traced through the whole system of human affairs, private as well as public. We see it particularly displayed in all the subordinate distributions of power; where the constant aim is to divide and arrange the several offices in such a manner as that each may be a check on the other; that the private interest of every individual, may be a sentinel over the public rights. These inventions of prudence cannot be less requisite in the distribution of the supreme powers of the state.

But it is not possible to give to each department an equal power of self defense. In republican government the legislative authority, necessarily, predominates. The remedy for this inconveniency is, to divide the legislature into different branches; and to render them by different modes of election, and different principles of action, as little connected with each other, as the nature of their common functions, and their common dependence on the society, will admit.

It may even be necessary to guard against dangerous encroachments by still further precautions. As the weight of the legislative
authority requires that it should be thus divided, the weakness of
the executive may require, on the other hand, that it should be
fortified. An absolute negative, on the legislature, appears at first
view to be the natural defense with which the executive magistrate
should be armed. But perhaps it would be neither altogether safe,
nor alone sufficient. On ordinary occasions, it might not be exerted
with the requisite firmness; and on extraordinary occasions, it
might be perfidiously abused. May not this defect of an absolute
negative be supplied, by some qualified connection between this
weaker department, and the weaker branch of the stronger department, by which the latter may be led to support the constitutional
rights of the former, without being too much detached from the
rights of its own department?

If the principles on which these observations are founded be
just, as I persuade myself they are, and they be applied as a criterion, to the several state constitutions, and to the Federal Constitution, it will be found, that if the latter does not perfectly correspond
with them, the former are infinitely less able to bear such a test.

There are moreover two considerations particularly applicable
to the federal system of America, which place that system in a very
interesting point of view.

First. In a single republic, all the power surrendered by the
people, is submitted to the administration of a single government;
and usurpations are guarded against by a division of the government into distinct and separate departments. In the compound
republic of America, the power surrendered by the people, is first
divided between two distinct governments, and then the portion
allotted to each, subdivided among distinct and separate departments. Hence a double security arises to the rights of the people. The different governments will control each other; at the same
time that each will be controlled by itself.

Second. It is of great importance in a republic, not only to guard
the society against the oppression of its rulers; but to guard one part
of the society against the injustice of the other part. Different interests necessarily exist in different classes of citizens. If a majority
be united by a common interest, the rights of the minority will be
insecure. There are but two methods of providing against this evil:
The one by creating a will in the community independent of the
majority, that is, of the society itself; the other by comprehending in
the society so many separate descriptions of citizens, as will render
an unjust combination of a majority of the whole, very improbable,
if not impracticable. The first method prevails in all governments
possessing an hereditary or self appointed authority. This at best is

but a precarious security; because a power independent of the society may as well espouse the unjust views of the major, as the rightful interests, of the minor party, and may possibly be turned against both parties. The second method will be exemplified in the federal republic of the United States. While all authority in it will be derived from and dependent on the society, the society itself will be broken into so many parts, interests and classes of citizens, that the rights of individuals or of the minority, will be in little danger from interested combinations of the majority. In a free government, the security for civil rights must be the same as for religious rights. It consists in the one case in the multiplicity of interests, and in the other, in the multiplicity of sects. The degree of security in both cases will depend on the number of interests and sects; and this may be presumed to depend on the extent of country and number of people comprehended under the same government. This view of the subject must particularly recommend a proper federal system to all the sincere and considerate friends of republican government: Since it shows that in exact proportion as the territory of the union may be formed into more circumscribed confederacies or states, oppressive combinations of a majority will be facilitated, the best security under the republican form, for the rights of every class of citizens, will be diminished; and consequently, the stability and independence of some member of the government, the only other security, must be proportionally increased. Justice is the end of government. It is the end of civil society. It ever has been, and ever will be pursued, until it be obtained, or until liberty be lost in the pursuit. In a society under the forms of which the stronger faction can readily unite and oppress the weaker, anarchy may as truly be said to reign, as in a state of nature where the weaker individual is not secured against the violence of the stronger: And as in the latter state even the stronger individuals are prompted by the uncertainty of their condition, to submit to a government which may protect the weak as well as themselves: So in the former state, will the more powerful factions or parties be gradually induced by a like motive, to wish for a government which will protect all parties, the weaker as well as the more powerful. It can be little doubted, that if the state of Rhode Island was separated from the confederacy, and left to itself, the insecurity of rights under the popular form of government within such narrow limits, would be displayed by such reiterated oppressions of factious majorities, that some power altogether independent of the people would soon be called for by the voice of the very factions whose misrule had proved the necessity of it. In the extended republic of the United States, and among the great variety of interests, parties and sects which it embraces, a coalition of a majority of the whole society could seldom take place on any other principles than those of justice and the general good; and there being thus less danger to a minor from the will of the major party, there must be less pretext also, to provide for the security of the former, by introducing into the government a will not dependent on the latter; or in other words, a will independent of the society itself. It is no less certain than it is important, notwithstanding the contrary opinions which have been entertained, that the larger the society, provided it lie within a practicable sphere, the more duly capable it will be of self government. And happily for the *republican cause*, the practicable sphere may be carried to a very great extent, by a judicious modification and mixture of the *federal principle*.

PUBLIUS

Index